THE ARDEN SHAKESPEARE

General Editor, C. H. HERFORD, Litt.D., *University of Manchester*

KING LEAR

EDITED BY

D. NICHOL SMITH, M.A.

EDINBURGH

REVISED BY

ERNEST BERNBAUM

PROFESSOR OF ENGLISH IN THE
UNIVERSITY OF ILLINOIS

D. C. HEATH AND COMPANY

BOSTON   NEW YORK   CHICAGO
ATLANTA   SAN FRANCISCO   DALLAS
LONDON

GENERAL PREFACE

In this edition of SHAKESPEARE an attempt is made to present the greater plays of the dramatist in their literary aspect, and not merely as material for the study of philology or grammar. Criticism purely verbal and textual has only been included to such an extent as may serve to help the student in the appreciation of the essential poetry. Questions of date and literary history have been fully dealt with in the Introductions, but the larger space has been devoted to the interpretative rather than the matter-of-fact order of scholarship. Æsthetic judgments are never final, but the Editors have attempted to suggest points of view from which the analysis of dramatic motive and dramatic character may be profitably undertaken. In the Notes likewise, while it is hoped that all unfamiliar expressions and allusions have been adequately explained, yet it has been thought even more important to consider the dramatic value of each scene, and the part which it plays in relation to the whole. These general principles are common to the whole series; in detail each Editor is alone responsible for the play or plays that have been intrusted to him.

Every volume of the series has been provided with a Glossary, an Essay upon Metre, and an Index; and Appendices have been added upon points of special interest which could not conveniently be treated in the Introduction or the Notes. The text is based by the several Editors on that of the *Globe* edition.

1948

CONTENTS

INTRODUCTION

1. LITERARY HISTORY OF THE PLAY

Two quarto editions of *King Lear* bear the date 1608. Their relationship and order of publication were long doubtful, but it is now certain that the earlier is that which bears the following title-page:

M. William Shak-speare: | His | True Chronicle Historie of the life and | death of King Lear and his three | Daughters. | *With the vnfortunate life of* Edgar, *sonne* | and heire to the Earle of Gloster, and his | sullen and assumed humor of | Tom of Bedlam: | *As it was played before the Kings Maiestie at Whitehall vpon* | S. Stephans *night in Christmas Hollidayes.* | By his Maiesties seruants playing vsually at the Gloabe | on the Bancke-side, | London. | Printed for *Nathaniel Butter*, and are to be sold at his shop in *Pauls* | Church-yard at the signe of the Pide Bull neere | Sᵗ. *Austins* Gate. 1608.

This edition was, as usual, authorized neither by Shakespeare nor by the theatrical company for which he wrote. Probably it was based upon a surreptitious stenographic report of a performance; and it is to be regarded as a carelessly printed issue of *King Lear* in approximately the form in which the play was at first acted.

The Second Quarto has the same title, except that it omits the words from "and are to be sold" to "St. *Austins* Gate." The date 1608 is fraudulent, for this edition was not issued until 1619. It was based upon the First Quarto, many of the faults of which it reproduced and aggravated; and it is useless in determining the true text of *King Lear*.[1]

The next edition of the play was that in the Folio of 1623. It is the most valuable, for it appears to have been taken from an acting copy preserved at the theatre. The independent origin of

---

[1] The relationship of the Quartos was first established by the Cambridge editors, though the editor of *King Lear* . . . *collated with the old and modern editions*, published in 1770, had already concluded that the so-called Pide Bull edition was the first. See also Mr. P. A. Daniel's introduction to the facsimile reprints of the two Quartos (1885). Mr. A. W. Pollard and Mr. W. W. Greg have shown that the Second Quarto was issued in 1619. Another Quarto, a careless reprint of the second, was "printed by Jane Bell" in 1655.

the Folio and Quarto texts gives rise to marked divergences. Apart from verbal variations, there is considerable difference in the length of the versions. The Quartos contain about three hundred lines that are not given in the Folio, and on the other hand about a hundred and ten lines in the Folio are omitted in the Quartos.[1] These omissions cannot definitely be explained; but it is probable that the divergences are due to the actors and printers. The First Quarto may follow a slightly condensed copy used in the performance at court in 1606, while the Folio gives the more abridged acting copy of the theatre. The bibliographical difficulties are further complicated by the fact that, though the two editions are based on different texts, the Folio reproduces some of the errors of the Quartos. The explanation of this would seem to be that the printer of the Folio did not work directly on the acting copy, but employed an edition of the First Quarto that had been corrected roughly in accordance with the manuscript. The modern text is considerably longer than that of the original editions by the inclusion of all the passages that occur only in one or the other of them. On the assumption that Shakespeare took no further care of the play after he had given it to the actors, the *King Lear* which we now have is a nearer approach to what it was when it left his hands.

King Lear is one of the Shakespearean plays which were mangled at the Restoration. It appears to have been acted "as Shakespeare wrote it" between 1662 and 1665, and again in 1671 or 1672,[2] but it was more popular in the adapted version of Nahum Tate, which was produced and published in 1681.[3] Tate considered the play "a heap of jewels, unstrung and unpolished," and he set himself to give it what Restoration taste demanded. "'Twas my good fortune," he says, "to light on one expedient to rectify what was wanting in the regularity and probability of the tale, which was to run through the whole a Love betwixt Edgar and Cordelia, that never changed word with each other in the original. This renders Cordelia's indifference and her father's passion in the first scene prob-

---

[1] The chief passages omitted in the Quartos are: i. 1. 41–46; i. 2. 118–124, 181–187; i. 4. 345–356; ii. 4. 46–55, 142–147; iii. 1. 22–29; iii. 2. 80–95; iii. 6. 13–15; iv. 1. 6–9; iv. 6. 169–174. The chief passages omitted in the Folios are: i. 2. 156–163; i. 3. 16–20; i. 4. 154–169; ii. 2. 148–152; iii. 1. 7–15, 30–42; iii. 6. 18–58, 103–122; iii. 7. 99–107; iv. 2. 31–50, 53–59, 62–69; iv. 3. (the whole scene); iv. 7. 85–97; v. 3. 204–221. It is sometimes stated erroneously that only about fifty lines are omitted in the Quartos, and about two hundred and twenty in the Folios.

[2] See Downes, *Roscius Anglicanus* (ed. Davies, 1789), pp. 36 and 43.

[3] *The History of King Lear. Acted at the Duke's Theatre. Reviv'd with Alterations. By N. Tate. London, 1681.* Reprinted 1771.

able. It likewise gives countenance to Edgar's disguise, making that a generous design that was before a poor shift to save his life. The distress of the story is evidently heightened by it; and it particularly gave occasion of a new scene or two, of more success (perhaps) than merit. This method necessarily threw me on making the tale conclude in a success to the innocent distrest Persons. . . . Yet I was wracked with no small fears for so bold a change, till I found it well received by my audience."

The love-making and betrothal of Edgar and Cordelia, the restoration of Lear to his kingdom, the enforced moral that "truth and virtue shall at last succeed," the interpolated scenes, and the entire omission of the Fool, make this version a perfect botch of the original. But it held the stage unchallenged till the time of Garrick, and its tinkerings were not totally discarded until well on in the nineteenth century. Garrick's version, which was produced in 1756, was generally accepted for about fifty years.[1] With all his enthusiasm for Shakespeare, Garrick showed little regard for the plays as Shakespeare left them, and of none did he represent a more garbled version than of *King Lear*. It may not unfitly be described as an adaptation of Tate's. He restored certain passages and omitted many of Tate's additions, but he retained the love scenes and the happy ending, and after serious consideration decided that he could not include the Fool. The version that Colman produced in 1768 was a decided improvement. He endeavored in it, he says, "to purge the tragedy of *Lear* of the alloy of Tate, which has so long been suffered to debase it." He had the taste to recognize that the love scenes between Edgar and Cordelia were entirely out of place, and that, far from heightening the distress of the story, as Tate had asserted, they diffused a languor over all the scenes from which Lear is absent. But he did not condemn Tate entirely. "To reconcile," he says, "the catastrophe of Tate to the original story was the first grand object which I proposed to myself in this alteration." He thus expelled Tate from the first four acts, but retained him in the fifth; but, like Tate and Garrick, he would have none of the Fool, being "convinced that such a character in a tragedy would not be endured on the modern stage." Colman's version, however, was not popular because of the absence of the love scenes, and Garrick's or Tate's kept possession of the stage.[2]

[1] The version of 1756 was not printed, but it is presumably the same as that published by Bell in 1772 or 1773.

[2] See Genest, *English Stage*, iv. 475; v. 191–203; viii. 131. Another version was produced by Kemble in 1809, but it was worse than Garrick's, for Kemble restored passages from Tate that Garrick had omitted.

Throughout the eighteenth century the happy ending, though invariably adopted by the actors, was a moot point of the critics. Addison condemned it and the "ridiculous doctrine" of poetical justice urged in its defense. "*King Lear* is an admirable tragedy," he says, "as Shakespeare wrote it; but as it is reformed according to the chimerical notion of poetical justice, in my humble opinion it has lost half its beauty." [1] Johnson was of the opposite opinion, and represents the prevailing taste of the time when he states with evident satisfaction that "Cordelia, from the time of Tate, has always retired with victory and felicity."

The new school of Shakespearean critics at the beginning of the nineteenth century, and particularly Lamb and Hazlitt, induced Kean to abandon the inartistic conclusion that had been in vogue for over a hundred and forty years. In 1820 he had followed Tate's version, but he had declared that "the London audience have no notion what I can do until they see me over the dead body of Cordelia," and in 1823, in obedience to his dramatic instincts and "the suggestion of men of literary eminence from the time of Addison," he gave the last act as originally written by Shakespeare. But even Kean did not restore the true version in the rest of the play, for Tate's love scenes were retained and the Fool was still excluded. Not till Macready's performance of the play in 1838 was the Fool again permitted to appear. But even in making this restoration Macready had considerable misgivings. "My opinion of the introduction of the Fool," he wrote in his diary, "is that, like many such terrible contrasts in poetry and painting, in acting-representation it will fail in effect; it will either weary, or annoy, or distract the spectator. I have no hope of it, and think that at the last we shall be obliged to dispense with it." Though he doubted the propriety of this part, he has the credit of restoring to the stage the true *King Lear*.

2. THE DATE OF THE PLAY

The date of *King Lear* is not definitely known; but it is certain that the play was written between 1603 and 1606. The later limit is fixed by external evidence. The First Quarto was entered in the Stationers' Registers under the date November 26, 1607, as "A Booke called Master William Shakespeare his 'historye of Kinge Lear' as yt was played before the kinges maiestie at Whitehall vppon Sainct Stephens night at Christmas Last." The performance at

[1] *Spectator*, No. 40.

court must therefore have taken place on St. Stephen's night (December 26), 1606. This is the only piece of external evidence that bears on the date of the play.

But there is internal evidence to show that *King Lear* was not written before 1603. As the notes point out, there are several passages that prove Shakespeare's knowledge of Harsnet's *Declaration of Egregious Popishe Impostures.* The names of the devils mentioned by Edgar when feigning madness are undoubtedly borrowed from this book,[1] while certain other remarks made by him in his rôle of Tom of Bedlam point to a like indebtedness.[2] Harsnet's book was entered in the Stationers' Registers on March 16, 1603, and appeared later in the same year.

Unfortunately this is the only evidence that is at all definite. It is highly probable that the play was written in 1606, though the arguments urged in support of a date nearer the end than the beginning of the period from 1603 to Christmas, 1606, are not conclusive. Some students would assign *King Lear* to 1605 because they surmise that the publication in that year of an old play on the same subject (*The True Chronicle History of King Leir*) was caused by the successful appearance of Shakespeare's version on the stage. Malone notes that in iii. 4. 189 Edgar says "I smell the blood of a *British* man," and he argues therefrom that this must have been written after James's proclamation as King of Great Britain on October 24, 1604. But it has been pointed out that as early as 1603, even before James's arrival in London, the poet Daniel addressed to him a *Panegyrike Congratulatory*, which has the lines:

> "Shake hands with union, O thou mightie state,
>   Now thou art all Great Britain, and no more,
>   No Scot, no English now, nor no debate."

His argument, therefore, has little value.

More weight attaches to the plea put forward by Mr. Aldis Wright, for, though it does not force acceptance, it strengthens the supposition of a late date. In the second scene of the first act there are references to "these late eclipses in the sun and moon." In October, 1605, there was a great eclipse of the sun following an eclipse of the moon in the previous month, and Mr. Wright argues that "it can scarcely be doubted that Shakespeare had in his mind the great eclipse, and that *Lear* was written while the recollection of it was still fresh, and while the ephemeral literature of the day

---

[1] See iii. 4. 120 ; iii. 6. 7, 31 ; and iv. 1. 62.
[2] See ii. 3. 20 ; iii. 4. 51 ; and iv. 1. 54.

abounded with pamphlets foreboding the consequences that were to follow." [1] Similarly, he hazards the further plausible suggestion that the reference in the same scene to "machinations, hollowness, treachery, and all ruinous disorders" may have been prompted by the Gunpowder Plot of November 5, 1605. All this, however, is mere supposition. There were eclipses of the sun and moon in 1598 and again in 1601,[2] and it is not impossible that Shakespeare's words were suggested by a recollection of them. None the less, the trend of the arguments, though inconclusive in themselves, is to support the date 1606; and as *King Lear* was acted before James at Christmas, 1606, and as the plays represented at court were usually new plays, that date may be accepted.[3]

3. THE SOURCES OF THE PLOT

The story of King Lear was familiar in various forms to the Elizabethans. From the twelfth to the sixteenth century it had been told again and again in chronicles and romances, both French and English.[4] It is first found in the *Historia Britonum* of Geoffrey of Monmouth, written in Latin about 1135. Geoffrey attached an immemorially old folk tale about a father and three daughters to a mythical British king, to whom he gave the name of a Celtic sea-god, Leir. From Geoffrey the story passed into Wace's French poem, *Brut* (c. 1155), and thence into Layamon's *Brut* (c. 1200), where the story is first given in English. Thereafter it is told in the metrical chronicles of Robert of Gloucester (c. 1300), Robert Manning (c. 1338), and John Harding (c. 1450), and in the more detailed prose chronicles of Robert Fabyan (1516), John Rastell (*The Pasttime of the People*, 1530), Richard Grafton (1568), and Raphael Holinshed (1577), while a similar story is given in Camden's *Remains* (1605). Two versions of it occur in translations of the *Gesta Romanorum*, the great mediæval storehouse of legendary tales. And it found a poetical setting in Elizabethan literature in John Higgins's contribution to *The Mirror for Magistrates* (1574), in Warner's *Albion's England* (1586, ch. 14), and in Spenser's *Faërie*

---

[1] Preface to the *Clarendon Press* edition, p. xvi.

[2] See *King Lear*, ed. W. J. Craig (1901), p. xxiii.

[3] The metrical evidence affords little or no assistance. For a statement of the metrical characteristics, see Fleay's *Shakespeare Manual*, p. 136, and Prof. Ingram's paper on "Light and Weak Endings" in the *Transactions of the New Shakspere Society*, 1874, pt. ii. Cf. Table I in chapter iv of W. A. Neilson and A. H. Thorndike's *The Facts about Shakespeare* (1913).

[4] See Wilfred Perrett, *The Story of King Lear*, Berlin, 1904.

Queene (1590, Book ii, canto x). Including the early play entitled *The True Chronicle History of King Leir*, which appeared in 1605,[1] there are extant at least eight Elizabethan versions of earlier date than the drama by which it has been immortalized.

Of the contemporary versions Shakespeare may have known those in Holinshed's *Chronicle*, *The Mirror for Magistrates*, and the *Faërie Queene*,[2] as well as the early play.

Holinshed's *Chronicle* was the great source of Shakespeare's histories. Certain passages in some of them, *e.g.* *Henry V* and *Henry VIII*, are little more than versified renderings of Holinshed's prose. But the fact that it provided so much material for Shakespeare's other plays has led to overstatement of its influence on *King Lear*. In Holinshed's account Leir loves Cordeilla far above her two elder sisters, and intends her to succeed to his kingdom; but, being displeased with her answer at the love-test, he determines that his land shall be divided after his death between Gonorilla and Regan (who so far were unmarried), and that a half thereof shall immediately be assigned them, while to Cordeilla he reserves nothing. But in time the two dukes whom the two eldest daughters had married rise against Leir and deprive him of the government, assigning him a portion on which to live. The daughters, however, seem to think that whatever the father has is too much, and gradually curtail his retinue. Leir is constrained to flee the country and seek comfort of Cordeilla, who has married a prince of Gallia. In Gallia he is honored as if he were king of the whole country. Cordeilla and her husband then raise a mighty army, cross over to Britain with Leir, and defeat the forces of Gonorilla and Regan. Leir is restored and rules for two years, and is succeeded by Cordeilla. It will be seen that Holinshed's story, meager as it is, differs in many points from Shakespeare's. It was certainly not used as the basis of *King Lear*. Indeed there is absolutely nothing to prove

---

[1] There is entered in the Registers of the Stationers' Company, under the date May 14, 1594, *The moste famous Chronicle historye of Leire kinge of England and his Three Daughters*. No copy of this is known, but it is probably the same as *The Tragecall historie of kinge Leir and his Three Daughters*, which was entered on May 8, 1605, and appeared in the same year with the following title, *The True Chronicle History of King Leir and his three Daughters, Gonorill, Ragan, and Cordella. As it hath bene diuers and sundry times lately acted.* This is reprinted in George Steevens' *Six Old Plays* (1779), vol. ii; in W. C. Hazlitt's *Shakespeare's Library* (1875), pt. ii, vol. ii; by W. W. Greg for the Malone Society (1907); and by Sidney Lee in the *Shakespeare Classics* (1909). An abstract is given in Furness's *Variorum Shakespeare*. See R. A. Law's "The Date of King Lear" in the *Publications of the Modern Language Association of America*, vol. xxi.

[2] These three versions are reprinted in Appendix A.

that Shakespeare consulted it, though the probability is, considering his use of other parts of the *Chronicle*, that he had read Holinshed's version.

The story in *The Mirror for Magistrates* has more points of similarity. According to it, Leire intended "to guerdon most where favour most he found" (cf. i. 1. 53–54); and Cordell in her reply refers to the chance of bearing another more good-will, meaning a future husband (cf. i. 1. 103–104). Leire does not resign the government at once, but is deprived of his crown and right by the husbands of Gonerell and Ragan, who promise him a guard of sixty knights. This number Gonerell reduces by half, whereupon Leire goes to Cornwall to stay with Ragan, who after a time takes away all his retinue but ten, then allows him but five, and finally but one. Another indignity he has to suffer is that "the meaner upstart courtiers think themselves his mates." And his daughters call him a "doting fool." As in Holinshed, Leire flees to France, returns with Cordell and an army which proves victorious, and is restored to his kingdom. But, generally, this account bears a much closer resemblance than Holinshed's to the story of *King Lear*. Some of the details of *The Mirror for Magistrates* are paralleled in Shakespeare's play.[1] This, however, is a circumstance on which too great stress is apt to be laid, for similarity or even identity of idea does not prove indebtedness. The most striking point is Cordell's allusion in the love-test to her future husband. But it happens that in Camden's *Remains* a similar story of the love-test is told of Ina, king of the West Saxons, and there the youngest daughter replies to her father "flatly, without flattery, that albeit she did love, honour, and reverence him, and so would whilst she lived, as much as nature and daughterly duty at the uttermost could expect, yet she did think that one day it would come to pass that she should affect another more fervently, meaning her husband, when she were married." Malone, who drew attention to this passage, thinks that Shakespeare had it in his thoughts rather than the lines in *The Mirror for Magistrates*, as Camden's book had recently been published, and as a portion near at hand "furnished him with a hint in *Coriolanus*." No definite opinion can be advanced; but the effect is only to render Shakespeare's debt to *The Mirror for Magistrates* more doubtful.

In one striking point Shakespeare is indebted to Spenser. In

---

[1] Perhaps the parallelisms are due to the intermediary of the early play, which resembles in several points the story in *The Mirror for Magistrates*. There would be less difficulty in showing the early dramatist's acquaintance with it than there is in showing Shakespeare's.

Holinshed's *Chronicle* the heroine's name is Cordeilla, in *The Mirror for Magistrates* it is Cordell, and in the early play it is Cordella; in *King Lear* the name has the beautiful form first adopted in the *Faërie Queene*.[1] The two great Elizabethans are alike also in their division of Lear's kingdom, for neither makes Lear reserve to himself any share in the government, while in Holinshed and in *The Mirror for Magistrates* the two elder daughters are not given at once their full share, and wrest the supreme power by force of arms. Shakespeare is sometimes said to be indebted to the simile [2] in Spenser's account; but this is a point that cannot be pressed.

We are on surer ground in dealing with the early play, the anonymous *True Chronicle History of King Leir*. The main incidents of this drama, and in particular some of its deviations from the usual story, have their counterpart in *King Lear*. In one of his snatches of song, Shakespeare's fool speaks of "That lord that counsell'd thee to give away thy land" (i. 4. 154–155). There is nothing in the rest of the play to explain the allusion; but we find that in the old play the love-test is proposed by a courtier, Skalliger by name, and that Lear at once resigns his whole kingdom to Gonorill and Ragan. Another courtier, Perillus, who is entirely the early dramatist's own invention, is the prototype of Kent. He pleads for Cordella, but in vain, and afterwards, with Kent's fidelity, attends in disguise on the old king. A messenger, and the miscarriage of letters, play an important part in the development of the plot. Again, in the pathetic scene in which Leir comes to recognize Cordella, he kneels to her (cf. iv. 7. 59). These are some of the most striking points of similarity in the development of the two plays. But indebtedness may be traced even in minor matters. We seem to catch an echo now and then of some of the statements and phrases of the old play. Thus:

> "I am as kind as is the pellican,
> That kils it selfe to save her young ones lives"

reminds us of Lear's reference to his "pelican daughters" (iii. 4. 77). The allusion to Gonorill's "young bones" —

> "poore soule, she breeds yong bones,
> And that is it makes her so tutchy sure" —

suggests ii. 4. 165, while the sentiment is the same as that expressed in ii. 4. 107–113. It is probable, too, that Perillus's description of

[1] Spenser once has the form "Cordeill," apparently shortened from Holinshed's "Cordeilla." It would appear that the exigencies of metre suggested "Cordelia." Spenser was undoubtedly indebted to Holinshed for the story.
[2] See i. 4. 237.

his master as "the mirror of mild patience" had some bearing on the finer phrase which Shakespeare puts in the mouth of Lear himself, "the pattern of all patience" (iii. 2. 37). There can be no doubt that Shakespeare knew this early play. In itself it is of little account; and yet there are not wanting qualities which show that the story only awaited the master hand to touch it to finer issues.

It is also certain that Sidney's *Arcadia*[1] is the source of the Gloucester story — the underplot that is interwoven with marvellous skill and is so striking a foil to the main theme. The prototypes of Gloucester and Edgar are the "Paphlagonian unkind king and his kind son," whose "pitiful state" is recounted in the second book of Sidney's pastoral romance. Though the story is reproduced in all its essentials, it has furnished Shakespeare with nothing but the bare facts of his underplot.[2]

But when all Shakespeare's borrowings are put together — even though account be taken of those matters in which his debt is very doubtful — how small a part do they form of *King Lear!* The intermingling of the Gloucester episode has entailed new incidents and changed the working out of the catastrophe. The presence of Edmund enhances the villainy of Goneril and Regan, and their adulterous love leads to their deaths. In the older versions their part was ended with the victory of Lear. Shakespeare alone has given a sad ending to the play; and although, as we have seen, he incurred thereby the censure of eighteenth century critics and actors, it is the only ending that is artistically possible. That Lear should be restored and reign happily is fitting enough in the meager stories of Holinshed or the early dramatist, but the tragic intensity which Shakespeare could give the more easily by the addition of the Gloucester episode makes any other ending than his lame and inept. There is no borrowing in the feigned madness of Edgar, nor in the real madness of Lear — the central circumstance, the very essence of the play; and the character of the Fool is Shakespeare's creation. In these points, as in all that gives the play its value, the only "source" is Shakespeare himself. In addition there is the whole setting, and in particular the storm which symbolizes the "great

[1] The passage from which Shakespeare borrowed is reprinted in Appendix A.

[2] Some of the older critics, *e.g.* Johnson and Hazlitt, thought that the play was "founded upon an old ballad," *A Lamentable Song of the Death of King Leare and his Three Daughters.* But this is apparently of later date than Shakespeare's play. It was published, probably for the first time, in Richard Johnson's *Golden Garlands of Princely Pleasures and Delicate Delights* (1620), and has been reprinted in Wilfrid Perrett's *The Story of King Lear* (1904), pp. 125–142.

commotion in the moral world"; and there is the characterization, by which the shadows and puppets of the early stories are turned into flesh and blood.

4. CRITICAL APPRECIATION

The play of *King Lear* presents certain peculiarities in point of structure. It diverges considerably from the form of the Shakespearean dramas with which it is generally associated — *Hamlet, Othello*, and *Macbeth* — and it is even more irregular than the first of these. It is unique in the importance of the opening scene. There is no introductory passage to explain or throw light on the story that is to be unfolded, or, as in *Macbeth*, to symbolize it. We are introduced straightway to the action on which the whole play depends. The first scene on this account has been stigmatized by Goethe as irrational; but the structure of the play emphasizes the fact that the deeds which call the play into being are in themselves of little importance. *King Lear* recounts the consequences following inevitably on a rash and foolish act. Another arrangement of the opening scenes would have tended to give more prominence than the theme of the drama allowed to an act which is important only in so far as it is the occasion of others.

The importance of the underplot is the most notable point in the structure of *King Lear*. Its bearing on the whole play seems almost to mark it out as a survival of the discarded parallelisms of the earlier comedies. But it has a purely artistic value, for it is added not in order to complicate the story, but to enforce its motive. It is in fact a triumphant vindication of the underplot, a characteristic of the romantic drama on which the formal classical critics looked askance. The Gloucester story has had its full share of condemnation by those who are prejudiced by recognized dramatic rules. Joseph Warton, for instance, singled out, as one of the "considerable imperfections" with which the play is chargeable, "the plot of Edmund against his brother, which distracts the attention and destroys the unity of the fable." [1] His other observations on *King Lear* contain passages of wholehearted and eloquent praise, but on this point he was so blinded by the prevailing classicism of the eighteenth century as to fail to recognize that the underplot, far from distracting the attention, really adds to the intensity. Such objections have been answered once and for all in a memorable

[1] *The Adventurer*, No. 122, January 5, 1754, Warton's third and concluding paper of "Observations on *King Lear*."

passage by Schlegel. "The incorporation of the two stories has
been censured as destructive of the unity of action. But whatever
contributes to the intrigue of the *dénouement* must always possess
unity. And with what ingenuity and skill are the two main parts
of the composition dovetailed into one another! The pity felt
by Gloucester for the fate of Lear becomes the means which enables
his son Edmund to effect his complete destruction, and affords the
outcast Edgar an opportunity of being the saviour of his father.
On the other hand, Edmund is active in the cause of Regan and
Goneril, and the criminal passion which they both entertain for
him induces them to execute justice on each other and on themselves.
The laws of the drama have therefore been sufficiently complied
with; but that is the least. It is the very combination which con-
stitutes the sublime beauty of the work. The two cases resemble
each other in the main: an infatuated father is blind towards his
well-disposed child, and the unnatural children, whom he prefers,
requite him by the ruin of all his happiness. But all the circumstances are so different that these stories, while they each make a
correspondent impression on the heart, form a complete contrast for
the imagination. Were Lear alone to suffer from his daughters,
the impression would be limited to the powerful compassion felt
by us for his private misfortune. But two such unheard-of examples
taking place at the same time have the appearance of a great commotion in the moral world." [1] The story of the victim of his own
misdeeds is so skillfully interwoven with the story of the victim
of his indiscretions, and is brought into so suggestive opposition,
that the effect of each is more impressive. The Gloucester story in
itself does not offer any striking chance of successful dramatic treatment, and in respect to the feigned madness of Edgar it rather
lends itself to comedy, but attains a tragic power by its association
with the story of Lear. On the other hand, the main theme is
raised by this conjunction above a purely personal matter, and we
are the more readily brought to think of Lear, not as the man, but
as the victim of filial ingratitude.

Despite these apparently discordant elements, *King Lear* has
complete unity of spirit. But in achieving this unity the art of
Shakespeare has nowhere triumphed more completely than in the
case of the Fool. In less skillful hands his presence would have
been inimical to the pity and terror of the tragedy. We have seen
how actors, for a period of over a hundred and fifty years, from the

---

[1] A. W. Schlegel, *Lectures on Dramatic Art and Literature* (English trans-
lation, 1879, p. 412).

days of Tate to Macready, banished the Fool from the stage because of their failure to recognize the importance of his part. Even in restoring him Macready did not do him justice, for he regarded him as a mere youth, and accordingly intrusted the part to an actress. The Fool's remarks are those of a man of full and rich experience of life. He is not a clown like Othello's servant, introduced merely for the sake of variety. He bears a much closer resemblance to the Fools of the later comedies, to Touchstone in *As You Like It* and Feste in *Twelfth Night*. Like Touchstone, "he uses his folly like a stalking-horse, and under the presentation of that he shoots his wit." At first there is a sharpness in his taunts, for he hopes thereby, with the frankness that is the privilege of his position, to awaken the king to a knowledge of what he has done. Afterward, when the worst has come to the worst, his wit has the gentler aim of relieving Lear's anguish. He no longer "teaches" Lear, but "labours to outjest his heart-struck injuries." He seems to give expression to the thought lurking deep in Lear's mind, as is shown by the readiness with which Lear catches at everything he says, or to voice the counsels of discretion. And he finally disappears from the play when Lear is mad. The Fool is, in fact, Lear's familiar spirit. He is Lear's only companion in the fateful step of going out into the night and braving the storm. Even then, as if in astonishment that his sorrows had not destroyed all his regard for others, Lear says, "I have one part in my heart that's sorry yet for thee." How, then, may it be asked, can the Fool possibly be omitted from *King Lear*?

Apart from this consideration, the Fool has an important function in the drama. The eighteenth century actors unconsciously testified to this, for when they banished the Fool as "a character not to be endured on the modern stage," they with one exception — and success did not attend this effort — made good the want by mawkish love scenes. These they preferred to a rôle that was regarded only as burlesque. But the artful prattle of the Fool does more than give variety and relax the strain on one's feelings. It makes Lear's lot endurable to us, but at the same time it gives us a keener sense of its sadness. The persistent reminders of Lear's folly, the recurring presentment of ideas in a new and stronger light, the caustic wit hidden in a seemingly casual remark, all bring home more forcibly the pity of Lear's plight. In a word, the Fool intensifies the pathos by relieving it.[1]

---

[1] In this connection it is well to record the opinion of Shelley, expressed in his *Defence of Poetry*: "The modern practice of blending comedy with tragedy,

The character of Lear is distinct from those of most of Shakespeare's heroes in that it is not revealed gradually. He is described fully in the very first scene. He has had a successful reign, but he is not a strong man. He is headstrong and rash, and old age has brought "unruly waywardness" and vanity. The play as a whole deals with the effects produced upon this passionate character by a foolish act for which he alone is responsible. The story is strictly that of a British king who began to rule "in the year of the world 3105, at what time Joas reigned in Juda." But Shakespeare has converted it into a tale of universal interest. He makes it but a basis for what Keats has called "the fierce dispute betwixt Hell torment and impassioned clay." [1] All the details of the story are of little importance in themselves, and the art of Shakespeare makes us forget them in thinking of the total effect to which they contribute. The real subject of the play is not so much Lear as the outraged passion of filial affection. "Nobody from reading Shakespeare," says Hazlitt, "would know (except from the *Dramatis Personæ*) that Lear was an English king. He is merely a king and a father. The ground is common: but what a well of tears has he dug out of it! There are no data in history to go upon; no advantage is taken of costume, no acquaintance with geography or architecture or dialect is necessary; but there is an old tradition, human nature, — an old temple, the human mind, — and Shakespeare walks into it and looks about him with a lordly eye, and seizes on the sacred spoils as his own. The story is a thousand or two years old, and yet the tragedy has no smack of antiquarianism in it." [2]

It is this universal quality which allows such anachronisms as that one character should personate a madman of the seventeenth century and speak a southwestern dialect, or that another should refer to the rules of chivalry. The very greatness of *King Lear*, the subordination and even abrogation of all detail, abundant though it is, made Charles Lamb declare the play essentially impossible to be represented on a stage. "The greatness of Lear," he says, "is not in corporal dimension, but in intellectual: the explo-

though liable to great abuse in point of practice, is undoubtedly an extension of the dramatic circle; but the comedy should be, as in *King Lear*, universal, ideal, sublime. It is perhaps the intervention of this principle which determines the balance in favour of *King Lear* against *Œdipus Tyrannus* or the *Agamemnon*. . . . *King Lear*, if it can sustain this comparison, may be judged to be the most perfect specimen of the dramatic art existing in the world, in spite of the narrow conditions to which the poet was subjected by the ignorance of the philosophy of the drama which has prevailed in modern Europe.'

[1] *Sonnet written before re-reading "King Lear."*

[2] Hazlitt, "Scott, Racine, and Shakespeare," in *The Plain-Speaker.*

sions of his passion are terrible as a volcano: they are storms turning up and disclosing to the bottom that sea, his mind, with all its vast riches.   It is his mind which is laid bare.   This case of flesh and blood seems too insignificant to be thought on; even as he himself neglects it.   On the stage we see nothing but corporal infirmities and weakness, the impotence of rage; while we read it, we see not Lear, but we are Lear." [1] His sufferings bring out good qualities that have been stunted in fortune.   When we first know him he is so self-centred as to be absolutely regardless of others.   But he comes to suspect his own "jealous curiosity" (i. 4. 75), tries to find an excuse for his enemies (ii. 4. 106–113), and is finally moved to contrition for his former indifference to the lot of even his meanest subjects (iii. 4. 28–36).   He knows he must be patient.   "You heavens, give me that patience, patience I need" (ii. 4. 274).   He asserts that he will be "the pattern of all patience" (iii. 2. 37).   But the blow has come too late.   His fond old heart cannot endure the outrage of "the offices of nature, bond of childhood, effects of courtesy, dues of gratitude."   He is too old to learn resignation. His remarks only increase in intensity.   When he meets Regan after his rebuff by Goneril, he can greet her only by saying that if she is not glad to see him, her mother must have been an adulteress (ii. 4. 132–134).   At last he becomes almost inarticulate with passion (ii. 4. 281–289).   The strain is too great, and the bonds of reason snap.   Of this the premonitions have been so skillfully given that his madness seems inevitable. [2]   Yet he could never more truly say that he was "every inch a king" than when he threw aside the lendings of royalty and stood against the deep dread-bolted thunder, and defied the villainy of his unnatural daughters.   If he baffles our sympathy or regard in the height of his fortune, he wins our reverence now; and the imagination fondly lingers over his recognition of Cordelia and his contentment with prison if only she is with him, and finds his early folly nobly expiated in his conduct at her death and his inability to live without her. [3]

Yet this ending, as beautiful as it is inevitable, has been con-

---

[1] Lamb, *On the Tragedies of Shakespeare.*

[2] Several accounts of the course of Lear's madness have been given by medical men. See, for example, Bucknill's *Mad Folk of Shakespeare*, pp.160–235.

[3] The *Œdipus Coloneus* of Sophocles offers a remarkable comparison with *King Lear*. Œdipus, too, is a man more sinned against than sinning (see note, iii. 2. 60), but he has learned patience and self control and has a strength of character wanting in the aged Lear.   His curse on Polynices is even more terrible than Lear's on Goneril, because it is deliberate, and does not spring from a passionate desire for revenge.   And Antigone is his Cordelia.

demned on the score of what is called "poetical justice." As Lear
is a man more sinned against than sinning, some would have him
restored to his kingdom. But crime is not the chief tragic motive
in the Shakespearean drama any more than in that of Greece.
Lear is guilty of an error, and through it he meets his fate. The
play of *Macbeth* is an exception to the general rule, in that the
tragedy is founded upon crime; on the other hand, Hamlet and
Othello, for instance, resemble Lear in being the victims of their
own character and the circumstances in which they are placed.
Cordelia can well say, "we are not the first, Who with best meaning
have incurred the worst." That she and Lear, after all that has
happened, should not incur the worst would be contrary to the
Shakespearean method, if only for the reason that it would be
glaringly inartistic. Much as we regret Lear's fate, it alone can
satisfy our sense of the fitness of things. As Charles Lamb has put
it with admirable force: "A happy ending! — as if the living
martyrdom that Lear had gone through, the flaying of his feelings
alive, did not make a fair dismissal from the stage of life the only
decorous thing for him. If he is to live and be happy after, if he
could sustain this world's burden after, why all this pudder and
preparation, why torment us with all this unnecessary sympathy?
As if the childish pleasure of getting his gilt robes and sceptre again
could tempt him to act over again his misused station, — as if at his
years, and with his experience, anything was left but to die." But,
it may be asked, does this ending, which is in accordance with
artistic necessity, entirely fail to satisfy the claims of poetical
justice? Lear is not troubled by the loss of his kingdom. Why,
then, should his kingdom be restored to him, the more especially
as he had in his sane mind given it away? What he feels is not the
actual diminution of his train by his daughters and their other
unkindnesses so much as the brutality which prompted these acts.
Justice can be done him, not by restoration to his kingdom, but by
restoration to filial respect, and it is satisfied by the love of Cordelia.
This alone "does redeem all sorrows that ever I have felt."

King Lear. ... Oedipus ... is a man more sinned against than sinning (As note,

KING LEAR

DRAMATIS PERSONÆ

LEAR . . . . King of Britain

KING OF FRANCE

DUKE OF BURGUNDY

DUKE OF CORNWALL

DUKE OF ALBANY

EARL OF KENT

EARL OF GLOUCESTER

EDGAR . . . . Son to Gloucester

EDMUND . . . . . . Bastard Son to Gloucester

CURAN . . . . A courtier

Old Man . . . . Tenant to Gloucester

Doctor

Fool

OSWALD . . . . Steward to Goneril

A Captain employed by Edmund

Gentleman attendant on Cordelia

A Herald

Servants to Cornwall

GONERIL
REGAN } . . . . Daughters to Lear
CORDELIA

Knights of Lear's train, Captains, Messengers,
Soldiers, and Attendants

SCENE — BRITAIN

KING LEAR

ACT I

Enter Kent, Gloucester, *and* Edmund

Kent. I thought the king had more affected the Duke of Albany than Cornwall.

Glou. It did always seem so to us: but now, in the division of the kingdom, it appears not which of the dukes he values most; for equalities are so weighed, that curiosity in neither can make choice of either's moiety.

Kent. Is not this your son, my lord?

Glou. His breeding, sir, hath been at my charge: I have so often blushed to acknowledge him, that 10 now I am brazed to it.

Kent. I cannot conceive you.

Glou. Sir, this young fellow's mother could: whereupon she grew round-wombed, and had, indeed, sir, a son for her cradle ere she had a husband for her bed. Do you smell a fault?

Kent. I cannot wish the fault undone, the issue of it being so proper.

Glou. But I have, sir, a son by order of law, some year elder than this, who yet is no dearer 20 in my account: though this knave came something saucily into the world before he was sent

1

for, yet was his mother fair; there was good sport at his making, and the whoreson must be acknowledged. Do you know this noble gentleman, Edmund?

Edm. No, my lord.

Glou. My lord of Kent: remember him hereafter as my honourable friend.

Edm. My services to your lordship.

Kent. I must love you, and sue to know you 30 better.

Edm. Sir, I shall study deserving.

Glou. He hath been out nine years, and away he shall again. The king is coming.

Sennet. Enter KING LEAR, CORNWALL, ALBANY, GONERIL, REGAN, CORDELIA, *and* Attendants

Lear. Attend the lords of France and Burgundy, Gloucester.

Glou. I shall, my liege.

[*Exeunt Gloucester and Edmund.*

Lear. Meantime we shall express our darker purpose.

Give me the map there. Know that we have divided

In three our kingdom: and 't is our fast intent

To shake all cares and business from our age; 40

Conferring them on younger strengths, while we

Unburthen'd crawl toward death. Our son of Cornwall,

And you, our no less loving son of Albany,

We have this hour a constant will to publish

Our daughters' several dowers, that future strife

May be prevented now. The princes, France and
        Burgundy,
Great rivals in our youngest daughter's love,
Long in our court have made their amorous sojourn,
And here are to be answer'd. Tell me, my
        daughters, —
Since now we will divest us, both of rule,   50
Interest of territory, cares of state, —
Which of you shall we say doth love us most?
That we our largest bounty may extend
Where nature doth with merit challenge. Goneril,
Our eldest-born, speak first.

    Gon. Sir, I love you more than words can wield
        the matter;
Dearer than eye-sight, space, and liberty;
Beyond what can be valued, rich or rare;
No less than life, with grace, health, beauty,
        honour;
As much as child e'er loved, or father found;   60
A love that makes breath poor, and speech unable;
Beyond all manner of so much I love you.

    Cor. [*Aside*] What shall Cordelia do? Love,
        and be silent.

    Lear. Of all these bounds, even from this line
        to this,
With shadowy forests and with champains rich'd,
With plenteous rivers and wide-skirted meads,
We make thee lady: to thine and Albany's issue
Be this perpetual. What says our second daughter,
Our dearest Regan, wife to Cornwall? Speak.

    Reg. Sir, I am made   70
Of the self-same metal that my sister is,

And prize me at her worth.   In my true heart
I find she names my very deed of love;
Only she comes too short: that I profess
Myself an enemy to all other joys,
Which the most precious square of sense possesses;
And find I am alone felicitate
In your dear highness' love.

   Cor.   [*Aside*] Then poor Cordelia!
And yet not so; since, I am sure, my love's
More ponderous than my tongue.   80

   Lear.   To thee and thine hereditary ever
Remain this ample third of our fair kingdom;
No less in space, validity, and pleasure,
Than that conferr'd on Goneril.   Now, our joy,
Although the last, not least; to whose young love
The vines of France and milk of Burgundy
Strive to be interess'd, what can you say to draw
A third more opulent than your sisters?   Speak.

   Cor.   Nothing, my lord.

   Lear.   Nothing!   90

   Cor.   Nothing.

   Lear.   Nothing will come of nothing: speak
        again.

   Cor.   Unhappy that I am, I cannot heave
My heart into my mouth: I love your majesty
According to my bond; nor more nor less.

   Lear.   How, how, Cordelia! mend your speech a
        little,
Lest it may mar your fortunes.

   Cor.   Good my lord,
You have begot me, bred me, loved me: I
Return those duties back as are right fit,

Obey you, love you, and most honour you. 100
Why have my sisters husbands, if they say
They love you all? Haply, when I shall wed,
That lord whose hand must take my plight shall
        carry
Half my love with him, half my care and duty:
Sure, I shall never marry like my sisters,
To love my father all.
   Lear. But goes thy heart with this?
   Cor.   Ay, good my lord.
   Lear. So young, and so untender?
   Cor. So young, my lord, and true.
   Lear. Let it be so; thy truth, then, be thy
        dower: 110
For, by the sacred radiance of the sun,
The mysteries of Hecate, and the night;
By all the operation of the orbs
From whom we do exist and cease to be;
Here I disclaim all my paternal care,
Propinquity and property of blood,
And as a stranger to my heart and me
Hold thee, from this, for ever. The barbarous
        Scythian,
Or he that makes his generation messes
To gorge his appetite, shall to my bosom 120
Be as well neighbour'd, pitied, and relieved,
As thou my sometime daughter.
   Kent.   Good my liege, —
   Lear. Peace, Kent!
Come not between the dragon and his wrath.
I loved her most, and thought to set my rest
On her kind nursery. Hence, and avoid my sight!

So be my grave my peace, as here I give
Her father's heart from her! Call France; who
      stirs?
Call Burgundy. Cornwall and Albany,
With my two daughters' dowers digest this third: 130
Let pride, which she calls plainness, marry her.
I do invest you jointly with my power,
Pre-eminence, and all the large effects
That troop with majesty. Ourself, by monthly
      course,
With reservation of an hundred knights,
By you to be sustain'd, shall our abode
Make with you by due turns. Only we still retain
The name, and all the additions to a king;
The sway, revenue, execution of the rest,
Beloved sons, be yours: which to confirm,   140
This coronet part betwixt you.   *[Giving the crown.*
   Kent.   Royal Lear,
Whom I have ever honour'd as my king,
Loved as my father, as my master follow'd,
As my great patron thought on in my prayers, —
   Lear. The bow is bent and drawn, make from
      the shaft.
   Kent. Let it fall rather, though the fork invade
The region of my heart: be Kent unmannerly,
When Lear is mad. What wilt thou do, old
      man?
Think'st thou that duty shall have dread to speak,
When power to flattery bows? To plainness
      honour's bound,   150
When majesty stoops to folly. Reverse thy doom,
And, in thy best consideration, check

This hideous rashness: answer my life my judge-
　　　　ment,
Thy youngest daughter does not love thee least;
Nor are those empty-hearted whose low sound
Reverbs no hollowness.

　　Lear. 　　　　　　Kent, on thy life, no more.

　　Kent. 　My life I never held but as a pawn
To wage against thy enemies; nor fear to lose it,
Thy safety being the motive.

　　Lear. 　　　　　　Out of my sight!

　　Kent. 　See better, Lear; and let me still remain 160
The true blank of thine eye.

　　Lear. 　Now, by Apollo, —

　　Kent. 　　　　　　Now, by Apollo, king,
Thou swear'st thy gods in vain.

　　Lear. 　　　　　　O, vassal! miscreant!
　　　　　　　　　[*Laying his hand on his sword.*

　　Alb. }
　　Corn. } Dear sir, forbear.

　　Kent. 　Do;
Kill thy physician, and the fee bestow
Upon thy foul disease.　Revoke thy doom;
Or, whilst I can vent clamour from my throat,
I'll tell thee thou dost evil.

　　Lear. 　　　　　　Hear me, recreant!
On thine allegiance, hear me! 　　　　　170
Since thou hast sought to make us break our vow,
Which we durst never yet, and with strain'd pride
To come between our sentence and our power,
Which nor our nature nor our place can bear,
Our potency made good, take thy reward.
Five days we do allot thee, for provision

To shield thee from diseases of the world;
And on the sixth to turn thy hated back
Upon our kingdom: if, on the tenth day following,
Thy banish'd trunk be found in our dominions,   180
The moment is thy death. Away! by Jupiter,
This shall not be revoked.

    Kent.   Fare thee well, king: sith thus thou wilt
        appear,
Freedom lives hence, and banishment is here.
[*To Cordelia*] The gods to their dear shelter take
        thee, maid,
That justly think'st, and hast most rightly said!
[*To Regan and Goneril*] And your large speeches may
        your deeds approve,
That good effects may spring from words of love.
Thus Kent, O princes, bids you all adieu;
He 'll shape his old course in a country new. [*Exit.* 190

    Flourish. Re-enter GLOUCESTER, *with* FRANCE,
        BURGUNDY, *and* Attendants

    Glou.   Here 's France and Burgundy, my noble
        lord.
    Lear.   My lord of Burgundy,
We first address towards you, who with this king
Hath rivall'd for our daughter: what, in the least,
Will you require in present dower with her,
Or cease your quest of love?
    Bur.   Most royal majesty,
I crave no more than what your highness offer'd,
Nor will you tender less.
    Lear.   Right noble Burgundy,
When she was dear to us, we did hold her so;

But now her price is fall'n. Sir, there she stands: 200
If aught within that little seeming substance,
Or all of it, with our displeasure pieced,
And nothing more, may fitly like your grace,
She 's there and she is yours.

  Bur.   I know no answer.

  Lear. Will you, with those infirmities she owes,
Unfriended, new-adopted to our hate,
Dower'd with our curse, and stranger'd with our
    oath,
Take her, or leave her?

  Bur.   Pardon me, royal sir;
Election makes not up on such conditions.

  Lear. Then leave her, sir; for, by the power
    that made me,   210
I tell you all her wealth. [*To France*] For you, great
    king,
I would not from your love make such a stray,
To match you where I hate; therefore beseech you
To avert your liking a more worthier way
Than on a wretch whom nature is ashamed
Almost to acknowledge hers.

  France.   This is most strange,
That she, that even but now was your best object,
The argument of your praise, balm of your age,
Most best, most dearest, should in this trice of
    time
Commit a thing so monstrous, to dismantle 220
So many folds of favour. Sure, her offence
Must be of such unnatural degree,
That monsters it, or your fore-vouch'd affection
Fall'n into taint: which to believe of her,

Must be a faith that reason without miracle
Could never plant in me.

Cor.   I yet beseech your majesty, —
If for I want that glib and oily art,
To speak and purpose not, — since what I well
          intend,
I 'll do 't before I speak, — that you make known
It is no vicious blot, murder, or foulness,   230
No unchaste action, or dishonour'd step,
That hath deprived me of your grace and favour;
But even for want of that for which I am richer,
A still-soliciting eye, and such a tongue
As I am glad I have not, though not to have it
Hath lost me in your liking.

Lear.   Better thou
Hadst not been born than not to have pleased me
          better.

France. Is it but this, — a tardiness in nature
Which often leaves the history unspoke
That it intends to do?   My lord of Burgundy,   240
What say you to the lady?   Love 's not love
When it is mingled with regards that stand
Aloof from the entire point.   Will you have her?
She is herself a dowry.

Bur.   Royal Lear,
Give but that portion which yourself proposed,
And here I take Cordelia by the hand,
Duchess of Burgundy.

Lear. Nothing; I have sworn; I am firm.

Bur. I am sorry, then, you have so lost a father
That you must lose a husband.

Cor.   Peace be with Burgundy! 250

Since that respects of fortune are his love,
I shall not be his wife.

    France. Fairest Cordelia, that art most rich,
          being poor;
Most choice, forsaken; and most loved, despised!
Thee and thy virtues here I seize upon:
Be it lawful I take up what 's cast away.
Gods, gods! 't is strange that from their cold'st
          neglect
My love should kindle to inflamed respect.
Thy dowerless daughter, king, thrown to my
          chance,
Is queen of us, of ours, and our fair France: 260
Not all the dukes of waterish Burgundy
Can buy this unprized precious maid of me.
Bid them farewell, Cordelia, though unkind:
Thou losest here, a better where to find.

    Lear. Thou hast her, France: let her be thine;
        for we
Have no such daughter, nor shall ever see
That face of hers again. Therefore be gone
Without our grace, our love, our benison.
Come, noble Burgundy.

                [*Flourish. Exeunt all but France,*
                  Goneril, Regan, and Cordelia.

    France. Bid farewell to your sisters.   270

    Cor. The jewels of our father, with wash'd eyes
Cordelia leaves you: I know you what you are;
And like a sister am most loath to call
Your faults as they are named. Use well our
        father:
To your professed bosoms I commit him:

But yet, alas, stood I within his grace,
I would prefer him to a better place.
So, farewell to you both.

   Reg.   Prescribe not us our duties.

   Gon.   Let your study
Be to content your lord, who hath received you   280
At fortune's alms. You have obedience scanted,
And well are worth the want that you have wanted.

   Cor.   Time shall unfold what plaited cunning
           hides :
Who cover faults, at last shame them derides.
Well may you prosper !

   France.   Come, my fair Cordelia.
                 [*Exeunt France and Cordelia.*

   Gon.   Sister, it is not a little I have to say of what
most nearly appertains to us both. I think our
father will hence to-night.

   Reg.   That 's most certain, and with you; next
month with us.   290

   Gon.   You see how full of changes his age is ; the
observation we have made of it hath not been little :
he always loved our sister most ; and with what poor
judgement he hath now cast her off appears too
grossly.

   Reg.   'T is the infirmity of his age : yet he hath
ever but slenderly known himself.

   Gon.   The best and soundest of his time hath
been but rash ; then must we look to receive
from his age, not alone the imperfections of long- 300
engraffed condition, but therewithal the unruly
waywardness that infirm and choleric years bring
with them.

Reg. Such unconstant starts are we like to have
from him as this of Kent's banishment.

Gon. There is further compliment of leave-
taking between France and him. Pray you, let's
hit together : if our father carry authority with such
dispositions as he bears, this last surrender of his   •
will but offend us.   310

Reg. We shall further think on 't.

Gon. We must do something, and i' the heat.

                                     [*Exeunt.*

Scene II — *The Earl of Gloucester's castle*

Enter EDMUND, *with a letter*

Edm. Thou, nature, art my goddess ; to thy law
My services are bound. Wherefore should I
Stand in the plague of custom, and permit
The curiosity of nations to deprive me,
For that I am some twelve or fourteen moon-
        shines
Lag of a brother ? Why bastard ? wherefore base ?
When my dimensions are as well compact,
My mind as generous, and my shape as true,
As honest madam's issue ? Why brand they us
With base ? with baseness ? bastardy ? base, base ? 10
Who, in the lusty stealth of nature, take
More composition and fierce quality
Than doth, within a dull, stale, tired bed,
Go to the creating a whole tribe of fops,
Got 'tween asleep and wake ? Well, then,
Legitimate Edgar, I must have your land :
Our father's love is to the bastard Edmund
As to the legitimate : fine word, — legitimate !

Well, my legitimate, if this letter speed,
And my invention thrive, Edmund the base   2t
Shall top the legitimate. I grow; I prosper:
Now, gods, stand up for bastards!

Enter GLOUCESTER

    Glou.   Kent banish'd thus! and France in choler
           parted!
And the king gone to-night! subscribed his power!
Confined to exhibition! All this done
Upon the gad! Edmund, how now! what news?
    Edm.   So please your lordship, none.
                         [Putting up the letter.
    Glou.   Why so earnestly seek you to put up that
           letter?
    Edm.   I know no news, my lord.
    Glou.   What paper were you reading?   30
    Edm.   Nothing, my lord.
    Glou.   No? What needed, then, that terrible
dispatch of it into your pocket? the quality of
nothing hath not such need to hide itself. Let's
see: come, if it be nothing, I shall not need
spectacles.
    Edm.   I beseech you, sir, pardon me: it is a
letter from my brother, that I have not all o'er-read;
and for so much as I have perused, I find it not fit
for your o'er-looking.   40
    Glou.   Give me the letter, sir.
    Edm.   I shall offend, either to detain or give
it. The contents, as in part I understand them,
are to blame.
    Glou.   Let's see, let's see.

Edm. I hope, for my brother's justification, he wrote this but as an essay or taste of my virtue.

Glou. [*Reads*] "This policy and reverence of age makes the world bitter to the best of our 50 times; keeps our fortunes from us till our oldness cannot relish them. I begin to find an idle and fond bondage in the oppression of aged tyranny; who sways, not as it hath power, but as it is suffered. Come to me, that of this I may speak more. If our father would sleep till I waked him, you should enjoy half his revenue for ever, and live the beloved of your brother, Edgar."

Hum — conspiracy! — "Sleep till I waked him, — you should enjoy half his revenue," — My son Edgar! Had he a hand to write this? a heart and 60 brain to breed it in? — When came this to you? who brought it?

Edm. It was not brought me, my lord; there 's the cunning of it; I found it thrown in at the casement of my closet.

Glou. You know the character to be your brother's?

Edm. If the matter were good, my lord, I durst swear it were his; but, in respect of that, I would fain think it were not.   70

Glou. It is his.

Edm. It is his hand, my lord; but I hope his heart is not in the contents.

Glou. Hath he never heretofore sounded you in this business?

Edm. Never, my lord: but I have heard him oft maintain it to be fit, that, sons at perfect age, and fathers declining, the father should be as ward to the son, and the son manage his revenue.

Glou. O villain, villain! His very opinion in 80 the letter! Abhorred villain! Unnatural, detested, brutish villain! worse than brutish! Go, sirrah, seek him; I'll apprehend him: abominable villain! Where is he?

Edm. I do not well know, my lord. If it shall please you to suspend your indignation against my brother till you can derive from him better testimony of his intent, you shall run a certain course; where, if you violently proceed against him, mistaking his purpose, it would make a great gap in 90 your own honour, and shake in pieces the heart of his obedience. I dare pawn down my life for him, that he hath wrote this to feel my affection to your honour, and to no further pretence of danger.

Glou. Think you so?

Edm. If your honour judge it meet, I will place you where you shall hear us confer of this, and by an auricular assurance have your satisfaction; and that without any further delay than this very 100 evening.

Glou. He cannot be such a monster —

Edm. Nor is not, sure.

Glou. To his father, that so tenderly and entirely loves him. Heaven and earth! Edmund, seek him out; wind me into him, I pray you: frame the business after your own wisdom. I would unstate myself, to be in a due resolution.

Edm. I will seek him, sir, presently; convey the business as I shall find means, and acquaint you 110 withal.

Glou. These late eclipses in the sun and moon portend no good to us: though the wisdom of nature can reason it thus and thus, yet nature finds itself scourged by the sequent effects: love cools, friendship falls off, brothers divide: in cities, mutinies; in countries, discord; in palaces, treason; and the bond cracked 'twixt son and father. This villain of mine comes under the prediction; there 's son against father: the king falls from 120 bias of nature; there 's father against child. We have seen the best of our time: machinations, hollowness, treachery, and all ruinous disorders, follow us disquietly to our graves. Find out this villain, Edmund; it shall lose thee nothing; do it carefully. And the noble and true-hearted Kent banished! his offence, honesty! 'T is strange.

[Exit.

Edm. This is the excellent foppery of the world, that, when we are sick in fortune, — often the surfeit of our own behaviour, — we make guilty of our 130 disasters the sun, the moon, and the stars: as if we were villains by necessity; fools by heavenly compulsion; knaves, thieves, and treachers, by spherical predominance; drunkards, liars, and adulterers, by an enforced obedience of planetary influence; and all that we are evil in, by a divine thrusting on: an admirable evasion of whore-master man, to lay his goatish disposition to the charge of a star! My father compounded with my mother under the

dragon's tail; and my nativity was under Ursa 140
major; so that it follows, I am rough and lecher-
ous. Tut, I should have been that I am, had the
maidenliest star in the firmament twinkled on my
bastardizing. Edgar —

Enter EDGAR

and pat he comes like the catastrophe of the old
comedy: my cue is villanous melancholy, with a
sigh like Tom o' Bedlam. O, these eclipses do
portend these divisions! fa, sol, la, mi.

Edg. How now, brother Edmund! what serious 150
contemplation are you in?

Edm. I am thinking, brother, of a prediction I
read this other day, what should follow these
eclipses.

Edg. Do you busy yourself about that?

Edm. I promise you, the effects he writes of
succeed unhappily; as of unnaturalness between
the child and the parent; death, dearth, dissolu-
tions of ancient amities; divisions in state, men-
aces and maledictions against king and nobles; 160
needless diffidences, banishment of friends, dissipation of cohorts, nuptial breaches, and I know
not what.

Edg. How long have you been a sectary astronomical?

Edm. Come, come; when saw you my father
last?

Edg. Why, the night gone by.

Edm. Spake you with him?

Edg. Ay, two hours together.   170

Edm. Parted you in good terms? Found you no displeasure in him by word or countenance?

Edg. None at all.

Edm. Bethink yourself wherein you may have offended him: and at my entreaty forbear his presence till some little time hath qualified the heat of his displeasure; which at this instant so rageth in him, that with the mischief of your person it would scarcely allay.

Edg. Some villain hath done me wrong. 180

Edm. That's my fear. I pray you, have a continent forbearance till the speed of his rage goes slower; and, as I say, retire with me to my lodging, from whence I will fitly bring you to hear my lord speak: pray ye, go; there's my key: if you do stir abroad, go armed.

Edg. Armed, brother!

Edm. Brother, I advise you to the best; go armed: I am no honest man if there be any good meaning towards you: I have told you what I have 190 seen and heard; but faintly, nothing like the image and horror of it: pray you, away.

Edg. Shall I hear from you anon?

Edm. I do serve you in this business.

[*Exit Edgar.*

A credulous father! and a brother noble,
Whose nature is so far from doing harms,
That he suspects none; on whose foolish honesty
My practices ride easy! I see the business.
Let me, if not by birth, have lands by wit:
All with me's meet that I can fashion fit. [*Exit.* 200

SCENE III — *The Duke of Albany's palace*

Enter GONERIL, *and* OSWALD, *her steward*

Gon.   Did my father strike my gentleman for chiding of his fool?

Osw.   Yes, madam.

Gon.   By day and night he wrongs me; every hour
He flashes into one gross crime or other,
That sets us all at odds: I 'll not endure it:
His knights grow riotous, and himself upbraids us
On every trifle.   When he returns from hunting,
I will not speak with him; say I am sick:
If you come slack of former services,
You shall do well; the fault of it I 'll answer.   10

Osw.   He 's coming, madam; I hear him.

                        [*Horns within.*

Gon.   Put on what weary negligence you please,
You and your fellows; I 'ld have it come to question:
If he dislike it, let him to our sister,
Whose mind and mine, I know, in that are one,
Not to be over-ruled.   Idle old man,
That still would manage those authorities
That he hath given away!   Now, by my life,
Old fools are babes again; and must be used
With checks as flatteries, — when they are seen abused.   20
Remember what I tell you.

Osw.   Well, madam.

Gon.   And let his knights have colder looks among you;
What grows of it, no matter; advise your fellows so:

I would breed from hence occasions, and I shall,
That I may speak: I 'll write straight to my sister,
To hold my very course.   Prepare for dinner.

[*Exeunt.*

Scene IV — *A hall in the same*
Enter Kent, *disguised*

Kent.   If but as well I other accents borrow,
That can my speech defuse, my good intent
May carry through itself to that full issue
For which I razed my likeness.   Now, banish'd
          Kent,
If thou canst serve where thou dost stand con-
          demn'd,
So may it come, thy master, whom thou lovest,
Shall find thee full of labours.

Horns within.   Enter Lear, *Knights,*
and Attendants

Lear.   Let me not stay a jot for dinner; go get
it ready.   [*Exit an Attendant.*]   How now! what
art thou?   10

Kent.   A man, sir.

Lear.   What dost thou profess? what wouldst
thou with us?

Kent.   I do profess to be no less than I seem; to
serve him truly that will put me in trust: to love
him that is honest; to converse with him that is
wise, and says little; to fear judgement; to fight
when I cannot choose; and to eat no fish.

Lear.   What art thou?

Kent.   A very honest-hearted fellow, and as 20
poor as the king.

Lear. If thou be as poor for a subject as he is for a king, thou art poor enough. What wouldst thou?

Kent. Service.

Lear. Who wouldst thou serve?

Kent. You.

Lear. Dost thou know me, fellow?

Kent. No, sir; but you have that in your countenance which I would fain call master. 30

Lear. What's that?

Kent. Authority.

Lear. What services canst thou do?

Kent. I can keep honest counsel, ride, run, mar a curious tale in telling it, and deliver a plain message bluntly: that which ordinary men are fit for, I am qualified in; and the best of me is diligence.

Lear. How old art thou?

Kent. Not so young, sir, to love a woman for 40 singing, nor so old to dote on her for anything: I have years on my back forty-eight.

Lear. Follow me; thou shalt serve me: if I like thee no worse after dinner, I will not part from thee yet. Dinner, ho, dinner! Where's my knave? my fool? Go you, and call my fool hither.   [*Exit an Attendant.*

Enter OSWALD

You, you, sirrah, where's my daughter?

Osw. So please you, —   [*Exit.*

Lear. What says the fellow there? Call the 50 clotpoll back. [*Exit a Knight.*] Where's my fool, ho? I think the world's asleep.

Re-enter Knight

How now! where 's that mongrel?

Knight. He says, my lord, your daughter is not well.

Lear. Why came not the slave back to me when I called him?

Knight. Sir, he answered me in the roundest manner, he would not.

Lear. He would not! 60

Knight. My lord, I know not what the matter is; but, to my judgement, your highness is not entertained with that ceremonious affection as you were wont; there 's a great abatement of kindness appears as well in the general dependants as in the duke himself also and your daughter.

Lear. Ha! sayest thou so?

Knight. I beseech you, pardon me, my lord, if I be mistaken; for my duty cannot be silent when 70 I think your highness wronged.

Lear. Thou but rememberest me of mine own conception: I have perceived a most faint neglect of late; which I have rather blamed as mine own jealous curiosity than as a very pretence and purpose of unkindness: I will look further into 't. But where 's my fool? I have not seen him this two days.

Knight. Since my young lady's going into France, sir, the fool hath much pined away. 80

Lear. No more of that; I have noted it well. Go you, and tell my daughter I would speak with

her. [*Exit an Attendant.*]   Go you, call hither my
fool.   [*Exit an Attendant.*

Re-enter OSWALD

O, you sir, you, come you hither, sir: who
am I, sir?

Osw.   My lady's father.

Lear.   "My lady's father"! my lord's knave:
you whoreson dog! you slave! you cur!

Osw.   I am none of these, my lord; I beseech 90
your pardon.

Lear.   Do you bandy looks with me, you
rascal?   [*Striking him.*

Osw.   I 'll not be struck, my lord.

Kent.   Nor tripped neither, you base foot-ball
player.   [*Tripping up his heels.*

Lear.   I thank thee, fellow; thou servest me, and
I 'll love thee.

Kent.   Come, sir, arise, away! I 'll teach you
differences: away, away! If you will measure 100
your lubber's length again, tarry: but away! go
to; have you wisdom? so.   [*Pushes Oswald out.*

Lear.   Now, my friendly knave, I thank thee:
there 's earnest of thy service. [*Giving Kent money.*

Enter Fool

Fool.   Let me hire him too: here's my coxcomb.   [*Offering Kent his cap.*

Lear.   How now, my pretty knave! how dost
thou?

Fool.   Sirrah, you were best take my coxcomb.

Kent.   Why, fool?   110

Fool. Why, for taking one's part that 's out of favour : nay, an thou canst not smile as the wind sits, thou 'lt catch cold shortly : there, take my coxcomb : why, this fellow has banished two on 's daughters, and did the third a blessing against his will : if thou follow him, thou must needs wear my coxcomb. How now, nuncle ! Would I had two coxcombs and two daughters !

Lear. Why, my boy ?

Fool. If I gave them all my living, I 'ld keep my coxcombs myself. There 's mine ; beg another of thy daughters. 120

Lear. Take heed, sirrah ; the whip.

Fool. Truth 's a dog must to kennel ; he must be whipped out, when Lady the brach may stand by the fire and stink.

Lear. A pestilent gall to me !

Fool. Sirrah, I 'll teach thee a speech.

Lear. Do.

Fool. Mark it, nuncle : 130

> Have more than thou showest,
> Speak less than thou knowest,
> Lend less than thou owest,
> Ride more than thou goest,
> Learn more than thou trowest,
> Set less than thou throwest ;
> Leave thy drink and thy whore,
> And keep in-a-door,
> And thou shalt have more
> Than two tens to a score. 140

Kent. This is nothing, fool.

Fool. Then 't is like the breath of an unfee'd

lawyer; you gave me nothing for 't. Can you
make no use of nothing, nuncle?

Lear.   Why, no, boy; nothing can be made out
of nothing.

Fool.   [*To Kent*] Prithee, tell him, so much
the rent of his land comes to: he will not believe
a fool.

Lear.   A bitter fool!   150

Fool.   Dost thou know the difference, my boy,
between a bitter fool and a sweet fool?

Lear.   No, lad; teach me.

Fool.   That lord that counsell'd thee
                 To give away thy land,
                 Come place him here by me,
                 Do thou for him stand:
                 The sweet and bitter fool
                 Will presently appear;
                 The one in motley here,   160
                 The other found out there.

Lear.   Dost thou call me fool, boy?

Fool.   All thy other titles thou hast given away;
that thou wast born with.

Kent.   This is not altogether fool, my lord.

Fool.   No, faith, lords and great men will not
let me; if I had a monopoly out, they would have
part on 't: and ladies too, they will not let me
have all fool to myself; they 'll be snatching.
Give me an egg, nuncle, and I 'll give thee two   170
crowns.

Lear.   What two crowns shall they be?

Fool.   Why, after I have cut the egg i' the middle,
and eat up the meat, the two crowns of the egg.

When thou clovest thy crown i' the middle, and
gavest away both parts, thou borest thy ass on thy
back o'er the dirt: thou hadst little wit in thy bald
crown, when thou gavest thy golden one away. If
I speak like myself in this, let him be whipped that
first finds it so.   180

[*Singing*] Fools had ne'er less wit in a year;

   For wise men are grown foppish,

   They know not how their wits to wear,

   Their manners are so apish.

Lear. When were you wont to be so full of songs,
sirrah?

Fool. I have used it, nuncle, ever since thou
madest thy daughters thy mother: for when thou
gavest them the rod, and put'st down thine own
breeches,   190

[*Singing*] Then they for sudden joy did weep,

   And I for sorrow sung,

   That such a king should play bo-peep,

   And go the fools among.

Prithee, nuncle, keep a schoolmaster that can teach
thy fool to lie: I would fain learn to lie.

Lear. An you lie, sirrah, we'll have you
whipped.

Fool. I marvel what kin thou and thy daughters
are: they'll have me whipped for speaking true, 200
thou 'lt have me whipped for lying; and sometimes
I am whipped for holding my peace. I had rather
be any kind o' thing than a fool: and yet I would
not be thee, nuncle; thou hast pared thy wit o'
both sides, and left nothing i' the middle: here
comes one o' the parings.

Enter GONERIL

Lear. How now, daughter! what makes that
frontlet on? Methinks you are too much of late i'
the frown.

Fool. Thou wast a pretty fellow when thou hadst 210
no need to care for her frowning; now thou art an
O without a figure: I am better than thou art now;
I am a fool, thou art nothing. [*To Gon.*] Yes,
forsooth, I will hold my tongue; so your face bids
me, though you say nothing. Mum, mum,

　　　He that keeps nor crust nor crum,
　　　Weary of all, shall want some.
[*Pointing to Lear*] That's a shealed peascod.

Gon. Not only, sir, this your all-licensed fool, 220
But other of your insolent retinue
Do hourly carp and quarrel; breaking forth
In rank and not-to-be-endured riots. Sir,
I had thought, by making this well known unto you,
To have found a safe redress; but now grow fearful,
By what yourself too late have spoke and done,
That you protect this course, and put it on
By your allowance; which if you should, the fault
Would not 'scape censure, nor the redresses sleep,
Which, in the tender of a wholesome weal, 230
Might in their working do you that offence,
Which else were shame, that then necessity
Will call discreet proceeding.

Fool. For, you know, nuncle,

　　　The hedge-sparrow fed the cuckoo so long,
　　　That it had it head bit off by it young.
So, out went the candle, and we were left darkling.

    Lear.   Are you our daughter?

    Gon.   Come, sir.

I would you would make use of that good wisdom, 240
Whereof I know you are fraught; and put away
These dispositions, that of late transform you
From what you rightly are.

    Fool.   May not an ass know when the cart draws
the horse? Whoop, Jug! I love thee.

    Lear.   Doth any here know me? This is not
        Lear:

Doth Lear walk thus? speak thus? Where are his
        eyes?

Either his notion weakens, his discernings
Are lethargied — Ha! waking? 't is not so.
Who is it that can tell me who I am?   250

    Fool.   Lear's shadow.

    Lear.   I would learn that; for, by the marks of
sovereignty, knowledge, and reason, I should be
false persuaded I had daughters.

    Fool.   Which they will make an obedient father.

    Lear.   Your name, fair gentlewoman?

    Gon.   This admiration, sir, is much o' the savour
Of other your new pranks. I do beseech you
To understand my purposes aright: 260
As you are old and reverend, you should be wise.
Here do you keep a hundred knights and squires;
Men so disorder'd, so debosh'd and bold,
That this our court, infected with their manners,
Shows like a riotous inn: epicurism and lust
Make it more like a tavern or a brothel
Than a graced palace. The shame itself doth speak
For instant remedy: be then desired

By her, that else will take the thing she begs,
A little to disquantity your train;   270
And the remainder that shall still depend,
To be such men as may besort your age,
And know themselves and you.

    Lear.   Darkness and devils!
Saddle my horses; call my train together.
Degenerate bastard! I 'll not trouble thee:
Yet have I left a daughter.

    Gon.   You strike my people, and your disorder'd
        rabble
Make servants of their betters.

Enter ALBANY

    Lear.   Woe, that too late repents, — [*To Alb.*]
        O, sir, are you come?
Is it your will? Speak, sir. Prepare my horses. 280
Ingratitude, thou marble-hearted fiend,
More hideous when thou show'st thee in a child
Than the sea-monster!

    Alb.   Pray, sir, be patient.

    Lear. [*To Gon.*] Detested kite! thou liest:
My train are men of choice and rarest parts,
That all particulars of duty know,
And in the most exact regard support
The worships of their name. O most small fault,
How ugly didst thou in Cordelia show!
That, like an engine, wrench'd my frame of nature 290
From the fix'd place; drew from my heart all love,
And added to the gall. O Lear, Lear, Lear!
Beat at this gate, that let thy folly in,
                        [*Striking his head.*

And thy dear judgement out! Go, go, my
       people.
  Alb.   My lord, I am guiltless, as I am ignorant
Of what hath moved you.
  Lear.   It may be so, my lord.
Hear, nature, hear; dear goddess, hear!
Suspend thy purpose, if thou didst intend
To make this creature fruitful!
Into her womb convey sterility!   **300**
Dry up in her the organs of increase;
And from her derogate body never spring
A babe to honour her! If she must teem,
Create her child of spleen; that it may live
And be a thwart disnatured torment to her!
Let it stamp wrinkles in her brow of youth;
With cadent tears fret channels in her cheeks;
Turn all her mother's pains and benefits
To laughter and contempt; that she may feel
How sharper than a serpent's tooth it is   **310**
To have a thankless child! Away, away!   [*Exit.*
  Alb.   Now, gods that we adore, whereof comes
       this?
  Gon.   Never afflict yourself to know the cause;
But let his disposition have that scope
That dotage gives it.

Re-enter Lear

  Lear.   What, fifty of my followers at a clap!
Within a fortnight!
  Alb.   What 's the matter, sir?
  Lear.   I 'll tell thee: [*To Gon.*] Life and death!
       I am ashamed

That thou hast power to shake my manhood thus;
That these hot tears, which break from me perforce, 320
Should make thee worth them.　Blasts and fogs
　　　　upon thee!
The untented woundings of a father's curse
Pierce every sense about thee!　Old fond eyes,
Beweep this cause again, I 'll pluck ye out,
And cast you, with the waters that you lose,
To temper clay.　Yea, is it come to this?
Let it be so: yet have I left a daughter,
Who, I am sure, is kind and comfortable:
When she shall hear this of thee, with her nails
She 'll flay thy wolvish visage.　Thou shalt find　330
That I 'll resume the shape which thou dost think
I have cast off for ever: thou shalt, I warrant thee.
　　　　　[Exeunt Lear, Kent, and Attendants.
　　Gon.　Do you mark that, my lord?
　　Alb.　I cannot be so partial, Goneril,
To the great love I bear you, —
　　Gon.　Pray you, content.　What, Oswald, ho!
[*To the Fool*]　You sir, more knave than fool, after
　　　　your master.
　　Fool.　Nuncle Lear, nuncle Lear, tarry and take
the fool with thee.

　　　　　　A fox, when one has caught her,　340
　　　　　　And such a daughter,
　　　　　　Should sure to the slaughter,
　　　　　　If my cap would buy a halter:
　　　　　　So the fool follows after.　　[*Exit.*
　　Gon.　This man hath had good counsel: — a
　　　　hundred knights!
'T is politic and safe to let him keep

At point a hundred knights: yes, that on every
       dream,
Each buzz, each fancy, each complaint, dislike,
He may enguard his dotage with their powers,
And hold our lives in mercy. Oswald, I say!   350
    Alb. Well, you may fear too far.
    Gon.   Safer than trust too far:
Let me still take away the harms I fear,
Not fear still to be taken: I know his heart.
What he hath utter'd I have writ my sister:
If she sustain him and his hundred knights,
When I have show'd the unfitness, —

              Re-enter Oswald

                  How now, Oswald!
What, have you writ that letter to my sister?
    Osw. Yes, madam.
    Gon. Take you some company, and away to
       horse:
Inform her full of my particular fear;   360
And thereto add such reasons of your own
As may compact it more. Get you gone;
And hasten your return. [*Exit Oswald.*] No, no,
       my lord,
This milky gentleness and course of yours
Though I condemn not, yet, under pardon,
You are much more attask'd for want of wisdom
Than praised for harmful mildness.
    Alb. How far your eyes may pierce I cannot tell:
Striving to better, oft we mar what 's well.
    Gon. Nay, then —   370
    Alb. Well, well; the event.   [*Exeunt.*

SCENE V — *Court before the same*

Enter LEAR, KENT, *and* Fool

Lear. Go you before to Gloucester with these letters. Acquaint my daughter no further with any thing you know than comes from her demand out of the letter. If your diligence be not speedy, I shall be there afore you.

Kent. I will not sleep, my lord, till I have delivered your letter.   [*Exit.*

Fool. If a man's brains were in 's heels, were 't not in danger of kibes?

Lear. Ay, boy.   10

Fool. Then, I prithee, be merry; thy wit shall ne'er go slip-shod.

Lear. Ha, ha, ha!

Fool. Shalt see thy other daughter will use thee kindly; for though she 's as like this as a crab 's like an apple, yet I can tell what I can tell.

Lear. Why, what canst thou tell, my boy?

Fool. She will taste as like this as a crab does to a crab. Thou canst tell why one's nose stands i' the middle on 's face?   20

Lear. No.

Fool. Why, to keep one's eyes of either side 's nose; that what a man cannot smell out, he may spy into.

Lear. I did her wrong —

Fool. Canst tell how an oyster makes his shell?

Lear. No.

Fool. Nor I neither; but I can tell why a snail has a house.   30

Lear.   Why?

Fool.   Why, to put his head in; not to give it away to his daughters, and leave his horns without a case.

Lear.   I will forget my nature.   So kind a father! Be my horses ready?

Fool.   Thy asses are gone about 'em.   The reason why the seven stars are no more than seven is a pretty reason.

Lear.   Because they are not eight?   40

Fool.   Yes, indeed: thou wouldst make a good fool.

Lear.   To take 't again perforce!   Monster ingratitude!

Fool.   If thou wert my fool, nuncle, I 'ld have thee beaten for being old before thy time.

Lear.   How 's that?

Fool.   Thou shouldst not have been old till thou hadst been wise.

Lear.   O, let me not be mad, not mad, sweet
                  heaven!   50
Keep me in temper: I would not be mad!

Enter GENTLEMAN

How now! are the horses ready?

Gent.   Ready, my lord.

Lear.   Come, boy.   [*Exeunt.*

Fool.   She that's a maid now, and laughs at my
                  departure,
Shall not be a maid long, unless things be cut
                  shorter.

ACT II

SCENE I — *The Earl of Gloucester's castle*

Enter EDMUND *and* CURAN *meets him*

Edm. Save thee, Curan.

Cur. And you, sir. I have been with your father, and given him notice that the Duke of Cornwall and Regan his duchess will be here with him this night.

Edm. How comes that?

Cur. Nay, I know not. You have heard of the news abroad; I mean the whispered ones, for they are yet but ear-kissing arguments?

Edm. Not I: pray you, what are they?   10

Cur. Have you heard of no likely wars toward, 'twixt the Dukes of Cornwall and Albany?

Edm. Not a word.

Cur. You may do, then, in time. Fare you well, sir.   [*Exit.*

Edm. The duke be here to-night? The better! best!
This weaves itself perforce into my business.
My father hath set guard to take my brother;
And I have one thing, of a queasy question,
Which I must act: briefness and fortune, work!   20
Brother, a word; descend: brother, I say!

Enter EDGAR

My father watches: O sir, fly this place;
Intelligence is given where you are hid;
You have now the good advantage of the night:

Have you not spoken 'gainst the Duke of Cornwall?
He 's coming hither; now, i' the night, i' the haste,
And Regan with him: have you nothing said
Upon his party 'gainst the Duke of Albany?
Advise yourself.

Edg. I am sure on 't, not a word.

Edm. I hear my father coming: pardon me; 30
In cunning I must draw my sword upon you:
Draw; seem to defend yourself; now quit you well.
Yield: come before my father. Light, ho, here!
Fly, brother. Torches, torches! So, farewell.

[*Exit Edgar.*

Some blood drawn on me would beget opinion

[*Wounds his arm.*

Of my more fierce endeavour: I have seen drunk-
ards
Do more than this in sport. Father, father!
Stop, stop! No help?

Enter GLOUCESTER, *and* Servants *with torches*

Glou. Now, Edmund, where 's the villain?

Edm. Here stood he in the dark, his sharp sword
out, 40
Mumbling of wicked charms, conjuring the moon
To stand auspicious mistress, —

Glou. But where is he?

Edm. Look, sir, I bleed.

Glou. Where is the villain, Edmund?

Edm. Fled this way, sir. When by no means
he could —

Glou. Pursue him, ho! Go after. [*Exeunt some
servants.*] By no means what?

Edm.   Persuade me to the murder of your lord-
            ship;
But that I told him, the revenging gods
'Gainst parricides did all their thunders bend;
Spoke, with how manifold and strong a bond
The child was bound to the father; sir, in fine,   50
Seeing how loathly opposite I stood
To his unnatural purpose, in fell motion,
With his prepared sword, he charges home
My unprovided body, lanced mine arm:
But when he saw my best alarum'd spirits,
Bold in the quarrel's right, roused to the encounter,
Or whether gasted by the noise I made,
Full suddenly he fled.
    Glou.   Let him fly far:
Not in this land shall he remain uncaught;
And   found — dispatch.   The   noble   duke   my
            master,   60
My worthy arch and patron, comes to-night:
By his authority I will proclaim it,
That he which finds him shall deserve our thanks,
Bringing the murderous coward to the stake;
He that conceals him, death.
    Edm.   When I dissuaded him from his intent,
And found him pight to do it, with curst speech
I threaten'd to discover him: he replied,
"Thou unpossessing bastard! dost thou think,
If I would stand against thee, would the reposal   70
Of any trust, virtue, or worth in thee
Make thy words faith'd?   No: what I should
            deny, —
As this I would; ay, though thou didst produce

My very character, — I 'ld turn it all
To thy suggestion, plot, and damn'd practice :
And thou must make a dullard of the world,
If they not thought the profits of my death
Were very pregnant and potential spurs
To make thee seek it."
 Glou.   Strong and fasten'd villain !
Would he deny his letter ?   I never got him. 80
         [Tucket within.
Hark, the duke's trumpets !   I know not why he
  comes.
All ports I 'll bar ; the villain shall not 'scape ;
The duke must grant me that : besides, his picture
I will send far and near, that all the kingdom
May have due note of him ; and of my land,
Loyal and natural boy, I 'll work the means
To make thee capable.

   Enter CORNWALL, REGAN, *and* Attendants

 Corn.   How now, my noble friend ! since I came
  hither,
Which I can call but now, I have heard strange
  news.
 Reg.   If it be true, all vengeance comes too short 90
Which can pursue the offender.   How dost, my
  lord ?
 Glou.   O, madam, my old heart is crack'd, is
  crack'd !
 Reg.   What, did my father's godson seek your
  life ?
He whom my friend named ? your Edgar ?
 Glou.   O, lady, lady, shame would have it hid !

Reg.   Was he not companion with the riotous
        knights
That tend upon my father?
    Glou.   I know not, madam: 't is too bad,
        too bad.
    Edm.   Yes, madam, he was of that consort.
    Reg.   No marvel, then, though he were ill
        affected: 100
'T is they have put him on the old man's death,
To have the expense and waste of his revenues.
I have this present evening from my sister
Been well inform'd of them; and with such cau-
        tions,
That if they come to sojourn at my house,
I 'll not be there.
    Corn.   Nor I, assure thee, Regan.
Edmund, I hear that you have shown your father
A child-like office.
    Edm.   'T was my duty, sir.
    Glou.   He did bewray his practice; and received
This hurt you see, striving to apprehend him.   110
    Corn.   Is he pursued?
    Glou.   Ay, my good lord.
    Corn.   If he be taken, he shall never more
Be fear'd of doing harm: make your own purpose,
How in my strength you please.   For you, Edmund,
Whose virtue and obedience doth this instant
So much commend itself, you shall be ours:
Natures of such deep trust we shall much need;
You we first seize on.
    Edm.   I shall serve you, sir,
Truly, however else.

Glou.   For him I thank your grace.

Corn. You know not why we came to visit
you, —   120

Reg. Thus out of season, threading dark-eyed
night:

Occasions, noble Gloucester, of some poise,
Wherein we must have use of your advice:
Our father he hath writ, so hath our sister,
Of differences, which I least thought it fit
To answer from our home; the several messengers
From hence attend dispatch.   Our good old friend,
Lay comforts to your bosom; and bestow
Your needful counsel to our business,
Which craves the instant use.

Glou.   I serve you, madam: 130
Your graces are right welcome.   [*Exeunt.*

Scene II — *Before Gloucester's castle*

Enter Kent *and* Oswald, *severally*

Osw. Good dawning to thee, friend: art of this
house?

Kent. Ay.

Osw. Where may we set our horses?

Kent. I' the mire.

Osw. Prithee, if thou lovest me, tell me.

Kent. I love thee not.

Osw. Why, then, I care not for thee.

Kent. If I had thee in Lipsbury pinfold, I would
make thee care for me.   10

Osw. Why dost thou use me thus?   I know thee
not.

Kent. Fellow, I know thee.

Osw. What dost thou know me for?

Kent. A knave; a rascal; an eater of broken meats; a base, proud, shallow, beggarly, three-suited, hundred-pound, filthy, worsted-stocking knave; a lily-livered, action-taking knave; a whoreson, glass-gazing, superserviceable, finical rogue; one-trunk-inheriting slave; one that wouldst be a bawd in way of good service, and art nothing but the composition of a knave, beggar, coward, pandar, and the son and heir of a mongrel bitch: one whom I will beat into clamorous whining, if thou deniest the least syllable of thy addition. 20

Osw. Why, what a monstrous fellow art thou, thus to rail on one that is neither known of thee nor knows thee!

Kent. What a brazen-faced varlet art thou, to deny thou knowest me! Is it two days ago since I tripped up thy heels, and beat thee before the king? Draw, you rogue: for, though it be night, yet the moon shines; I 'll make a sop o' the moon-shine of you: draw, you whoreson cullionly barber-monger, draw.   [*Drawing his sword.* 30

Osw. Away! I have nothing to do with thee.

Kent. Draw, you rascal: you come with letters against the king; and take vanity the puppet's part against the royalty of her father: draw, you rogue, or I 'll so carbonado your shanks: draw, you rascal; come your ways. 40

Osw. Help, ho! murder! help!

Kent. Strike, you slave; stand, rogue, stand; you neat slave, strike.   [*Beating him.*

Osw. Help, ho! murder! murder!

Enter Edmund *with his rapier drawn,* Cornwall, Regan, Gloucester, *and* Servants

Edm.   How now !   What 's the matter ?

Kent.   With you, goodman boy, an you please : come, I 'll flesh ye ; come on, young master.

Glou.   Weapons !   arms !   What 's the matter 50 here ?

Corn.   Keep peace, upon your lives : He dies that strikes again.   What is the matter ?

Reg.   The messengers from our sisters and the king.

Corn.   What is your difference ? speak.

Osw.   I am scarce in breath, my lord.

Kent.   No marvel, you have so bestirred your valour.   You cowardly rascal, nature disclaims in thee : a tailor made thee.   6c

Corn.   Thou art a strange fellow : a tailor make a man ?

Kent.   Ay, a tailor, sir : a stone-cutter or a painter could not have made him so ill, though he had been but two hours at the trade.

Corn.   Speak yet, how grew your quarrel ?

Osw.   This ancient ruffian, sir, whose life I have spared at suit of his gray beard, —

Kent.   Thou whoreson zed ! thou unnecessary letter !   My lord, if you will give me leave, I will 70 tread this unbolted villain into mortar, and daub the walls of a jakes with him.   Spare my gray beard, you wagtail ?

Corn.   Peace, sirrah !

You beastly knave, know you no reverence ?

Kent. Yes, sir; but anger hath a privilege.

Corn. Why art thou angry?

Kent. That such a slave as this should wear a
sword,

Who wears no honesty. Such smiling rogues as
these,

Like rats, oft bite the holy cords a-twain   80

Which are too intrinse t' unloose; smooth every
passion

That in the natures of their lords rebel;

Bring oil to fire, snow to their colder moods;

Renege, affirm, and turn their halcyon beaks

With every gale and vary of their masters,

Knowing nought, like dogs, but following.

A plague upon your epileptic visage!

Smile you my speeches, as I were a fool?

Goose, if I had you upon Sarum plain,

I 'ld drive ye cackling home to Camelot.   90

Corn. What, art thou mad, old fellow?

Glou. How fell you out? say that.

Kent. No contraries hold more antipathy

Than I and such a knave.

Corn. Why dost thou call him knave? What's
his offence?

Kent. His countenance likes me not.

Corn. No more, perchance, does mine, nor his,
nor hers.

Kent. Sir, 't is my occupation to be plain:

I have seen better faces in my time

Than stands on any shoulder that I see   100

Before me at this instant.

Corn.   This is some fellow,

Who, having been praised for bluntness, doth affect
A saucy roughness, and constrains the garb
Quite from his nature : he cannot flatter, he,
An honest mind and plain, he must speak truth !
An they will take it, so ; if not, he 's plain.
These kind of knaves I know, which in this plain-
        ness
Harbour more craft and more corrupter ends
Than twenty silly ducking observants
That stretch their duties nicely.   110

   Kent. Sir, in good sooth, in sincere verity,
Under the allowance of your great aspect,
Whose influence, like the wreath of radiant fire
On flickering Phœbus' front, —

   Corn.   What mean'st by this ?

   Kent. To go out of my dialect, which you dis-
commend so much. I know, sir, I am no flatterer :
he that beguiled you in a plain accent was a plain
knave ; which for my part I will not be, though I
should win your displeasure to entreat me to 't.   120

   Corn. What was the offence you gave him ?

   Osw. I never gave him any :
It pleased the king his master very late
To strike at me, upon his misconstruction ;
When he, conjunct, and flattering his displeasure,
Tripp'd me behind ; being down, insulted, rail'd,
And put upon him such a deal of man,
That worthied him, got praises of the king
For him attempting who was self-subdued ;
And, in the fleshment of this dread exploit,   130
Drew on me here again.

   Kent.   None of these rogues and cowards

But Ajax is their fool.

Corn.   Fetch forth the stocks!
You stubborn ancient knave, you reverent braggart,
We 'll teach you —

Kent.   Sir, I am too old to learn:
Call not your stocks for me: I serve the king;
On whose employment I was sent to you:
You shall do small respect, show too bold malice
Against the grace and person of my master,
Stocking his messenger.

Corn.   Fetch forth the stocks! As I have life
          and honour,   140
There shall he sit till noon.

Reg.   Till noon! till night, my lord; and all
          night too.

Kent.   Why, madam, if I were your father's dog,
You should not use me so.

Reg.   Sir, being his knave, I will.

Corn.   This is a fellow of the self-same colour
Our sister speaks of.   Come, bring away the stocks!
                              [*Stocks brought out.*

Glou.   Let me beseech your grace not to do so:
His fault is much, and the good king his master
Will check him for 't: your purposed low correction
Is such as basest and contemned'st wretches   150
For pilferings and most common trespasses
Are punish'd with: the king must take it ill,
That he, so slightly valued in his messenger,
Should have him thus restrain'd.

Corn.   I 'll answer that.

Reg.   My sister may receive it much more worse,
To have her gentleman abused, assaulted,

For following her affairs.   Put in his legs.

                [Kent is put in the stocks.

Come, my good lord, away.

              [Exeunt all but Gloucester and Kent.

   Glou.   I am sorry for thee, friend; 't is the
     duke's pleasure,

Whose disposition, all the world well knows,   160

Will not be rubb'd nor stopp'd: I 'll entreat for
     thee.

   Kent.   Pray, do not, sir: I have watched and
     travell'd hard;

Some time I shall sleep out, the rest I 'll whistle.

A good man's fortune may grow out at heels:

Give you good morrow!

   Glou.   The duke 's to blame in this; 't will be
     ill-taken.   *[Exit.*

   Kent.   Good king, that must approve the com-
     mon saw,

Thou out of heaven's benediction comest

To the warm sun!

Approach, thou beacon to this under globe,   170

That by thy comfortable beams I may

Peruse this letter!   Nothing almost sees miracles

But misery: I know 't is from Cordelia,

Who hath most fortunately been inform'd

Of my obscured course; and shall find time

From this enormous state, seeking to give

Losses their remedies.   All weary and o'er-watch'd,

Take vantage, heavy eyes, not to behold

This shameful lodging.

Fortune, good night: smile once more; turn thy
     wheel!   *[Sleeps.* 180

SCENE III — *A wood*

Enter EDGAR

Edg.   I heard myself proclaim'd;
And by the happy hollow of a tree
Escaped the hunt.   No port is free; no place,
That guard, and most unusual vigilance,
Does not attend my taking.   Whiles I may 'scape,
I will preserve myself: and am bethought
To take the basest and most poorest shape
That ever penury, in contempt of man,
Brought near to beast: my face I 'll grime with
      filth:
Blanket my loins; elf all my hair in knots;   **10**
And with presented nakedness out-face
The winds and persecutions of the sky.
The country gives me proof and precedent
Of Bedlam beggars, who, with roaring voices,
Strike in their numb'd and mortified bare arms
Pins, wooden pricks, nails, sprigs of rosemary;
And with this horrible object, from low farms,
Poor pelting villages, sheep-cotes, and mills,
Sometime with lunatic bans, sometime with prayers,
Enforce their charity.   Poor Turlygod! poor Tom! **20**
That 's something yet: Edgar I nothing am. [*Exit.*

SCENE IV — *Before Gloucester's castle.   Kent*
in the stocks

Enter LEAR, Fool, *and* Gentleman

Lear.   'T is strange that they should so depart
      from home,
And not send back my messenger.

Gent.   As I learn'd,
The night before there was no purpose in them
Of this remove.

Kent.   Hail to thee, noble master!

Lear. Ha!
Makest thou this shame thy pastime?

Kent.   No, my lord.

Fool. Ha, ha! he wears cruel garters. Horses
are tied by the heads, dogs and bears by the neck,
monkeys by the loins, and men by the legs: when
a man's over-lusty at legs, then he wears wooden 10
nether-stocks.

Lear. What 's he that hath so much thy place
              mistook
To set thee here?

Kent.   It is both he and she;
Your son and daughter.

Lear. No.

Kent. Yes.

Lear. No, I say.

Kent. I say, yea.

Lear. No, no, they would not.

Kent. Yes, they have.   20

Lear. By Jupiter, I swear, no.

Kent. By Juno, I swear, ay.

Lear.   They durst not do 't;
They could not, would not do 't; 't is worse than
              murder,
To do upon respect such violent outrage:
Resolve me, with all modest haste, which way
Thou mightst deserve, or they impose, this usage,
Coming from us.

   Kent.   My lord, when at their home
I did commend your highness' letter to them,
Ere I was risen from the place that show'd
My duty kneeling, came there a reeking post,   30
Stew'd in his haste, half breathless, panting forth
From Goneril his mistress salutations;
Deliver'd letters, spite of intermission,
Which presently they read: on whose contents,
They summon'd up their meiny, straight took horse;
Commanded me to follow, and attend
The leisure of their answer; gave me cold looks:
And meeting here the other messenger,
Whose welcome, I perceived, had poison'd mine, —
Being the very fellow that of late   40
Display'd so saucily against your highness, —
Having more man than wit about me, drew:
He raised the house with loud and coward cries.
Your son and daughter found this trespass worth
The shame which here it suffers.

   Fool.   Winter 's not gone yet, if the wild-geese
fly that way.

              Fathers that wear rags
                 Do make their children blind;
              But fathers that bear bags   50
                 Shall see their children kind.
              Fortune, that arrant whore,
                 Ne'er turns the key to the poor.
But, for all this, thou shalt have as many dolours for
thy daughters as thou canst tell in a year.

   Lear.   O, how this mother swells up toward my
          heart!
Hysterica passio, down, thou climbing sorrow,

Thy element 's below !   Where is this daughter ?

Kent.   With the earl, sir, here within.

Lear.   Follow me not ;
Stay here.   [*Exit.* 60

Gent.   Made you no more offence but what you
speak of ?

Kent.   None.

How chance the king comes with so small a train ?

Fool.   An thou hadst been set i' the stocks for
that question, thou hadst well deserved it.

Kent.   Why, fool ?

Fool.   We 'll set thee to school to an ant, to
teach thee there 's no labouring i' the winter.   All
that follow their noses are led by their eyes but 70
blind men ; and there 's not a nose among twenty
but can smell him that 's stinking.   Let go thy hold
when a great wheel runs down a hill, lest it break
thy neck with following it ; but the great one that
goes up the hill, let him draw thee after.   When a
wise man gives thee better counsel, give me mine
again : I would have none but knaves follow it,
since a fool gives it.

> That sir which serves and seeks for gain,
>> And follows but for form,   80
> Will pack when it begins to rain,
>> And leave thee in the storm.
> But I will tarry ; the fool will stay,
>> And let the wise man fly :
> The knave turns fool that runs away ;
>> The fool no knave, perdy.

Kent.   Where learned you this, fool ?

Fool.   Not i' the stocks, fool.

Re-enter LEAR, *with* GLOUCESTER

 Lear. Deny to speak with me? They are sick?
   they are weary?
They have travell'd all the night? Mere fetches; 90
The images of revolt and flying off.
Fetch me a better answer.
 Glou.   My dear lord,
You know the fiery quality of the duke;
How unremoveable and fix'd he is
In his own course.
 Lear. Vengeance! plague! death! confusion!
Fiery? what quality? Why, Gloucester, Glouces-
   ter,
I 'ld speak with the Duke of Cornwall and his wife.
 Glou. Well, my good lord, I have inform'd them
   so.
 Lear. Inform'd them! Dost thou understand
   me, man?   100
 Glou. Ay, my good lord.
 Lear. The king would speak with Cornwall; the
   dear father
Would with his daughter speak, commands her
   service:
Are they inform'd of this? My breath and blood!
Fiery? the fiery duke? Tell the hot duke that —
No, but not yet: may be he is not well:
Infirmity doth still neglect all office
Whereto our health is bound; we are not ourselves
When nature, being oppress'd, commands the mind
To suffer with the body: I 'll forbear;   110
And am fall'n out with my more headier will,

To take the indisposed and sickly fit
For the sound man.   Death on my state! where-
    fore   [*Looking on Kent.*
Should he sit here?   This act persuades me
That this remotion of the duke and her
Is practice only.   Give me my servant forth.
Go tell the duke and 's wife I 'ld speak with them,
Now, presently : bid them come forth and hear me,
Or at their chamber-door I 'll beat the drum
Till it cry sleep to death.   120

 Glou.   I would have all well betwixt you. [*Exit.*
 Lear.   O me, my heart, my rising heart! but,
  down!
 Fool.   Cry to it, nuncle, as the cockney did to
the eels when she put 'em i' the paste alive;
she knapped 'em o' the coxcombs with a stick,
and cried "Down, wantons, down!"   'T was her
brother that, in pure kindness to his horse, but-
tered his hay.

 Enter Cornwall, Regan, Gloucester, *and* Servants

 Lear.   Good morrow to you both.
 Corn.   Hail to your grace!
         [*Kent is set at liberty.*
 Reg.   I am glad to see your highness. 130
 Lear.   Regan, I think you are; I know what
  reason
I have to think so: if thou shouldst not be glad,
I would divorce me from thy mother's tomb,
Sepulchring an adultress. [*To Kent*] O, are you
  free?
Some other time for that.   Beloved Regan,

Thy sister 's naught : O Regan, she hath tied
Sharp-tooth'd unkindness, like a vulture, here :

                         [Points to his heart.

I can scarce speak to thee; thou 'lt not believe
With how depraved a quality — O Regan !

   Reg.   I pray you, sir, take patience : I have hope 140
You less know how to value her desert
Than she to scant her duty.

   Lear.   Say, how is that?

   Reg.   I cannot think my sister in the least
Would fail her obligation : if, sir, perchance
She have restrain'd the riots of your followers,
'T is on such ground, and to such wholesome end,
As clears her from all blame.

   Lear.   My curses on her !

   Reg.   O, sir, you are old ;
Nature in you stands on the very verge
Of her confine : you should be ruled and led   150
By some discretion, that discerns your state
Better than you yourself.   Therefore, I pray you,
That to our sister you do make return ;
Say you have wrong'd her, sir.

   Lear.   Ask her forgiveness?
Do you but mark how this becomes the house :
"Dear daughter, I confess that I am old ; *[Kneeling.*
Age is unnecessary : on my knees I beg
That you 'll vouchsafe me raiment, bed, and food."

   Reg.   Good sir, no more ; these are unsightly
          tricks :
Return you to my sister.

   Lear.   *[Rising]* Never, Regan : 160
She hath abated me of half my train ;

Look'd black upon me; struck me with her tongue
Most serpent-like, upon the very heart:
All the stored vengeances of heaven fall
On her ingrateful top! Strike her young bones,
You taking airs, with lameness!

   Corn.   Fie, sir, fie!

   Lear.   You nimble lightnings, dart your blinding
          flames
Into her scornful eyes! Infect her beauty,
You fen-suck'd fogs, drawn by the powerful sun,
To fall and blast her pride!   170

   Reg.   O the blest gods! so will you wish on
          me,
When the rash mood is on.

   Lear.   No, Regan, thou shalt never have my
          curse:
Thy tender-hefted nature shall not give
Thee o'er to harshness: her eyes are fierce; but
          thine
Do comfort and not burn. 'T is not in thee
To grudge my pleasures, to cut off my train,
To bandy hasty words, to scant my sizes,
And in conclusion to oppose the bolt
Against my coming in: thou better know'st   180
The offices of nature, bond of childhood,
Effects of courtesy, dues of gratitude;
Thy half o' the kingdom hast thou not forgot,
Wherein I thee endow'd.

   Reg.   Good sir, to the purpose.

   Lear.   Who put my man i' the stocks?

                            [Tucket within.

   Corn.   What trumpet 's that?

 Reg. I know 't, my sister's : this approves her
   letter,
That she would soon be here.

Enter OSWALD

        Is your lady come?
 Lear. This is a slave, whose easy-borrow'd pride
Dwells in the fickle grace of her he follows.
Out, varlet, from my sight !
 Corn.   What means your grace? 190
 Lear. Who stock'd my servant? Regan, I
   have good hope
Thou didst not know on 't. Who comes here?
   O heavens,

Enter GONERIL

If you do love old men, if your sweet sway
Allow obedience, if yourselves are old,
Make it your cause ; send down, and take my part !
[*To Gon.*] Art not ashamed to look upon this
   beard ?
O Regan, wilt thou take her by the hand ?
 Gon. Why not by the hand, sir ? How have I
   offended ?
All 's not offence that indiscretion finds
And dotage terms so.
 Lear.   O sides, you are too tough ; 200
Will you yet hold ? How came my man i' the
   stocks ?
 Corn. I set him there, sir : but his own disorders
Deserved much less advancement.
 Lear.   You ! did you ?
 Reg. I pray you, father, being weak, seem so.

If, till the expiration of your month,
You will return and sojourn with my sister,
Dismissing half your train, come then to me:
I am now from home, and out of that provision
Which shall be needful for your entertainment.

   Lear. Return to her, and fifty men dismiss'd?   210
No, rather I abjure all roofs, and choose
To wage against the enmity o' the air;
To be a comrade with the wolf and owl, —
Necessity's sharp pinch! Return with her?
Why, the hot-blooded France, that dowerless took
Our youngest born, I could as well be brought
To knee his throne, and, squire-like, pension beg
To keep base life afoot. Return with her?
Persuade me rather to be slave and sumpter
To this detested groom.   [*Pointing at Oswald.*
   Gon.   At your choice, sir.   220
   Lear. I prithee, daughter, do not make me mad:
I will not trouble thee, my child; farewell:
We 'll no more meet, no more see one another:
But yet thou art my flesh, my blood, my daughter;
Or rather a disease that 's in my flesh,
Which I must needs call mine: thou art a boil,
A plague-sore, an embossed carbuncle,
In my corrupted blood. But I 'll not chide thee;
Let shame come when it will, I do not call it:
I do not bid the thunder-bearer shoot,   230
Nor tell tales of thee to high-judging Jove:
Mend when thou canst; be better at thy leisure:
I can be patient; I can stay with Regan,
I and my hundred knights.
   Reg.   Not altogether so:

I look'd not for you yet, nor am provided
For your fit welcome.   Give ear, sir, to my sister;
For those that mingle reason with your passion
Must be content to think you old, and so —
But she knows what she does.

    Lear.   Is this well spoken?

    Reg.   I dare avouch it, sir: what, fifty followers? 240
Is it not well?   What should you need of more?
Yea, or so many, sith that both charge and danger
Speak 'gainst so great a number?   How, in one
        house,
Should many people, under two commands,
Hold amity?   'T is hard; almost impossible.

    Gon.   Why might not you, my lord, receive
        attendance
From those that she calls servants or from mine?

    Reg.   Why not, my lord?   If then they chanced
        to slack you,
We could control them.   If you will come to me, —
For now I spy a danger, — I entreat you   250
To bring but five-and-twenty: to no more
Will I give place or notice.

    Lear.   I gave you all —

    Reg.   And in good time you gave it.

    Lear.   Made you my guardians, my depositaries;
But kept a reservation to be follow'd
With such a number.   What, must I come to you
With five-and-twenty, Regan?   said you so?

    Reg.   And speak 't again, my lord; no more with
        me.

    Lear.   Those wicked creatures yet do look well-
        favour'd,

When others are more wicked; not being the worst 260
Stands in some rank of praise. [*To Gon.*] I 'll go
　　with thee:
Thy fifty yet doth double five-and-twenty,
And thou art twice her love.
　　Gon. 　　　　　　　　　Hear me, my lord:
What need you five-and-twenty, ten, or five,
To follow in a house where twice so many
Have a command to tend you?
　　Reg. 　　　　　　　　　What need one?
　　Lear. O, reason not the need: our basest
　　　　beggars
Are in the poorest thing superfluous:
Allow not nature more than nature needs,
Man's life 's as cheap as beast's: thou art a lady; 270
If only to go warm were gorgeous,
Why, nature needs not what thou gorgeous wear'st,
Which scarcely keeps thee warm. But, for true
　　　　need, —
You heavens, give me that patience, patience I
　　　　need!
You see me here, you gods, a poor old man,
As full of grief as age; wretched in both!
If it be you that stirs these daughters' hearts
Against their father, fool me not so much
To bear it tamely; touch me with noble anger,
And let not women's weapons, water-drops, 　　280
Stain my man's cheeks! No, you unnatural hags,
I will have such revenges on you both,
That all the world shall — I will do such things, —
What they are, yet I know not; but they shall be
The terrors of the earth. You think I 'll weep;

No, I 'll not weep:
I have full cause of weeping ; but this heart
Shall break into a hundred thousand flaws,
Or ere I 'll weep.   O fool, I shall go mad !

> [*Exeunt Lear, Gloucester, Kent, and Fool.*
> *Storm and tempest.*

Corn.   Let us withdraw ; 't will be a storm.   290
Reg.   This house is little : the old man and his
   people
Cannot be well bestow'd.
Gon.   'T is his own blame ; hath put himself
   from rest,
And must needs taste his folly.
Reg.   For his particular, I 'll receive him gladly,
But not one follower.
Gon.   So am I purposed.
Where is my lord of Gloucester ?
Corn.   Follow'd the old man forth : he is re-
   turn'd.

Re-enter GLOUCESTER

Glou.   The king is in high rage.
Corn.   Whither is he going ?
Glou.   He calls to horse ; but will I know not
   whither.   300
Corn.   'T is best to give him way ; he leads
   himself.
Gon.   My lord, entreat him by no means to stay.
Glou.   Alack, the night comes on, and the bleak
   winds
Do sorely ruffle ; for many miles about
There 's scarce a bush.

Reg.   O, sir, to wilful men,
The injuries that they themselves procure
Must be their schoolmasters.   Shut up your doors,
He is attended with a desperate train;
And what they may incense him to, being apt
To have his ear abused, wisdom bids fear.   310

    Corn.   Shut up your doors, my lord; 't is a wild
        night :
My Regan counsels well : come out o' the storm.
                                [Exeunt.

ACT III

Scene I — *A heath*

Storm still.   Enter Kent *and a* Gentleman, *meeting*

    Kent.   Who 's there, besides foul weather?
    Gent.   One minded like the weather, most un-
        unquietly.
    Kent.   I know you.   Where 's the king?
    Gent.   Contending with the fretful element;
Bids the wind blow the earth into the sea,
Or swell the curled waters 'bove the main,
That things might change or cease; tears his white
        hair,
Which the impetuous blasts, with eyeless rage,
Catch in their fury, and make nothing of;
Strives in his little world of man to out-scorn   10
The to-and-fro-conflicting wind and rain.
This night, wherein the cub-drawn bear would
        couch,
The lion and the belly-pinched wolf

Keep their fur dry, unbonneted he runs,
And bids what will take all.

   Kent.   But who is with him?
   Gent. None but the fool; who labours to out-
       jest
His heart-struck injuries.

   Kent.   Sir, I do know you;
And dare, upon the warrant of my note,
Commend a dear thing to you.   There is division,
Although as yet the face of it be cover'd   20
With mutual cunning, 'twixt Albany and Corn-
       wall;
Who have — as who have not, that their great stars
Throned and set high? — servants, who seem no
       less,
Which are to France the spies and speculations
Intelligent of our state; what hath been seen,
Either in snuffs and packings of the dukes,
Or the hard rein which both of them have borne
Against the old kind king; or something deeper,
Whereof perchance these are but furnishings;
But, true it is, from France there comes a power   30
Into this scatter'd kingdom; who already,
Wise in our negligence, have secret feet
In some of our best ports, and are at point
To show their open banner.   Now to you:
If on my credit you dare build so far
To make your speed to Dover, you shall find
Some that will thank you, making just report
Of how unnatural and bemadding sorrow
The king hath cause to plain.
I am a gentleman of blood and breeding;   40

And, from some knowledge and assurance, offer
This office to you.

    Gent.   I will talk further with you.

    Kent.   No, do not.
For confirmation that I am much more
Than my out-wall, open this purse, and take
What it contains.   If you shall see Cordelia, —
As fear not but you shall, — show her this ring;
And she will tell you who your fellow is
That yet you do not know.   Fie on this storm!
I will go seek the king.   50

    Gent.   Give me your hand: have you no more to
         say?

    Kent.   Few words, but, to effect, more than all
         yet;
That, when we have found the king, — in which
         your pain
That way, I 'll this, — he that first lights on him
Holla the other.   *[Exeunt severally.*

SCENE II — *Another part of the heath.* *Storm still*

Enter LEAR *and* Fool

    Lear.   Blow, winds, and crack your cheeks!
         rage! blow!
You cataracts and hurricanoes, spout
Till you have drench'd our steeples, drown'd the
         cocks!
You sulphurous and thought-executing fires,
Vaunt-couriers to oak-cleaving thunderbolts,
Singe my white head! And thou, all-shaking
         thunder,

Smite flat the thick rotundity o' the world!
Crack nature's moulds, all germens spill at once,
That make ingrateful man!

Fool. O nuncle, court holy-water in a dry 10
house is better than this rain-water out o' door.
Good nuncle, in, and ask thy daughters' blessing: here's a night pities neither wise man nor
fool.

Lear. Rumble thy bellyful! Spit, fire! spout,
    rain!
Nor rain, wind, thunder, fire, are my daughters:
I tax not you, you elements, with unkindness;
I never gave you kingdom, call'd you children,
You owe me no subscription: then let fall
Your horrible pleasure; here I stand, your slave,
A poor, infirm, weak, and despised old man: 20
But yet I call you servile ministers,
That have with two pernicious daughters join'd
Your high engender'd battles 'gainst a head
So old and white as this. O! O! 't is foul!

Fool. He that has a house to put 's head in has
a good head-piece.

       The cod-piece that will house
         Before the head has any,
       The head and he shall louse;
         So beggars marry many.   30
       The man that makes his toe
         What he his heart should make
       Shall of a corn cry woe,
         And turn his sleep to wake.

For there was never yet fair woman but she made
mouths in a glass.

Lear. No, I will be the pattern of all patience; I
will say nothing.

Enter Kent

Kent. Who 's there?

Fool. Marry, here 's grace and a cod-piece; 40
that 's a wise man and a fool.

Kent. Alas, sir, are you here? things that love
night

Love not such nights as these; the wrathful skies
Gallow the very wanderers of the dark,
And make them keep their caves: since I was man,
Such sheets of fire, such bursts of horrid thunder,
Such groans of roaring wind and rain, I never
Remember to have heard: man's nature cannot
carry
The affliction nor the fear.

Lear.   Let the great gods,
That keep this dreadful pother o'er our heads,   50
Find out their enemies now. Tremble, thou
wretch,
That hast within thee undivulged crimes,
Unwhipp'd of justice: hide thee, thou bloody
hand;
Thou perjured, and thou simular man of virtue
That are incestuous: caitiff, to pieces shake,
That under covert and convenient seeming
Hast practised on man's life: close pent-up guilts
Rive your concealing continents, and cry
These dreadful summoners grace. I am a man
More sinn'd against than sinning.

Kent.   Alack, bare-headed! 60
Gracious my lord, hard by here is a hovel;

Some friendship will it lend you 'gainst the tem-
    pest:
Repose you there; while I to this hard house —
More harder than the stones whereof 't is raised;
Which even but now, demanding after you,
Denied me to come in — return, and force
Their scanted courtesy.

    Lear.   My wits begin to turn.
Come on, my boy: how dost, my boy? art cold?
I am cold myself. Where is this straw, my fellow?
The art of our necessities is strange,   70
That can make vile things precious. Come, your
    hovel.
Poor fool and knave, I have one part in my heart
That 's sorry yet for thee.

    Fool. [*Singing*] He that has and a little tiny wit,—
      With hey, ho, the wind and the rain, —
    Must make content with his fortunes fit,
      For the rain it raineth every day.
    Lear. True, my good boy. Come, bring us to
    this hovel.   [*Exeunt Lear and Kent.*
    Fool. This is a brave night to cool a courtezan.
I 'll speak a prophecy ere I go: 80
    When priests are more in word than matter;
    When brewers mar their malt with water;
    When nobles are their tailors' tutors;
    No heretics burn'd, but wenches' suitors;
    When every case in law is right;
    No squire in debt, nor no poor knight;
    When slanders do not live in tongues;
    Nor cutpurses come not to throngs;
    When usurers tell their gold i' the field;

And bawds and whores do churches build;   90
Then shall the realm of Albion
Come to great confusion:
Then comes the time, who lives to see 't,
That going shall be used with feet.
This prophecy Merlin shall make; for I live before
     his time.   [*Exit.*

Scene III — *Gloucester's castle*

Enter Gloucester *and* Edmund

Glou. Alack, alack, Edmund, I like not this unnatural dealing. When I desired their leave that I might pity him, they took from me the use of mine own house; charged me, on pain of their perpetual displeasure, neither to speak of him, entreat for him, nor any way sustain him.

Edm. Most savage and unnatural!

Glou. Go to; say you nothing. There 's a division betwixt the dukes; and a worse matter than that: I have received a letter this night; 't is 10 dangerous to be spoken; I have locked the letter in my closet: these injuries the king now bears will be revenged home; there 's part of a power already footed: we must incline to the king. I will seek him, and privily relieve him: go you and maintain talk with the duke, that my charity be not of him perceived: if he ask for me, I am ill, and gone to bed. Though I die for it, as no less is threatened me, the king my old master must be relieved. There is some strange thing toward, Edmund; pray 20 you, be careful.   [*Exit.*

Edm. This courtesy, forbid thee, shall the duke
Instantly know; and of that letter too:
This seems a fair deserving, and must draw me
That which my father loses; no less than all:
The younger rises when the old doth fall. [*Exit.*

SCENE IV — *The heath. Before a hovel*

Enter LEAR, KENT, *and* Fool

Kent. Here is the place, my lord; good my
    lord, enter:
The tyranny of the open night 's too rough
For nature to endure. [*Storm still.*
Lear. Let me alone.
Kent. Good my lord, enter here.
Lear. Wilt break my heart?
Kent. I had rather break mine own. Good my
    lord, enter.
Lear. Thou think'st 't is much that this con-
    tentious storm
Invades us to the skin: so 't is to thee;
But where the greater malady is fixed,
The lesser is scarce felt. Thou 'ldst shun a bear;
But if thy flight lay toward the raging sea,   10
Thou 'ldst meet the bear i' the mouth. When the
    mind 's free,
The body 's delicate: the tempest in my mind
Doth from my senses take all feeling else
Save what beats there. Filial ingratitude!
Is it not as this mouth should tear this hand
For lifting food to 't? But I will punish home:
No, I will weep no more. In such a night

To shut me out! Pour on; I will endure.
In such a night as this! O Regan, Goneril!
Your old kind father, whose frank heart gave
     all, —	20
O, that way madness lies; let me shun that;
No more of that.

    Kent.	Good my lord, enter here.

    Lear. Prithee, go in thyself; seek thine own
     ease:
This tempest will not give me leave to ponder
On things would hurt me more. But I'll go in.
[*To the Fool*] In, boy; go first. You houseless
     poverty, —
Nay, get thee in. I'll pray, and then I'll sleep.
                  [*Fool goes in.*
Poor naked wretches, whereso'er you are,
That bide the pelting of this pitiless storm,
How shall your houseless heads and unfed sides,	30
Your loop'd and window'd raggedness, defend
     you
From seasons such as these? O, I have ta'en
Too little care of this! Take physic, pomp;
Expose thyself to feel what wretches feel,
That thou mayst shake the superflux to them,
And show the heavens more just.

    Edg. [*Within*] Fathom and half, fathom and half!
Poor Tom!	[*The Fool runs out from the hovel.*

    Fool. Come not in here, nuncle, here's a spirit.
Help me, help me!	40

    Kent. Give me thy hand. Who's there?

    Fool. A spirit, a spirit: he says his name's
poor Tom.

Kent. What art thou that dost grumble there i' the straw? Come forth.

Enter EDGAR *disguised as a madman*

Edg. Away! the foul fiend follows me!
Through the sharp hawthorn blows the cold wind.
Hum! go to thy cold bed, and warm thee.

Lear. Hast thou given all to thy two daughters?
And art thou come to this? 50

Edg. Who gives any thing to poor Tom? whom
the foul fiend hath led through fire and through
flame, through ford and whirlpool, o'er bog and
quagmire; that hath laid knives under his pillow,
and halters in his pew; set ratsbane by his porridge;
made him proud of heart, to ride on a bay trotting-
horse over four-inched bridges, to course his own
shadow for a traitor. Bless thy five wits! Tom's
a-cold, — O, do de, do de, do de. Bless thee from 60
whirlwinds, star-blasting, and taking! Do poor
Tom some charity, whom the foul fiend vexes:
there could I have him now, — and there, — and
there again, and there. [*Storm still.*

Lear. What, have his daughters brought him
to this pass?
Couldst thou save nothing? Didst thou give them
all?

Fool. Nay, he reserved a blanket, else we had
been all shamed.

Lear. Now, all the plagues that in the pendulous
air
Hang fated o'er men's faults light on thy daughters! 70

Kent. He hath no daughters, sir.

Lear.   Death, traitor! nothing could have sub-
dued nature
To such a lowness but his unkind daughters.
Is it the fashion that discarded fathers
Should have thus little mercy on their flesh?
Judicious punishment! 't was this flesh begot
Those pelican daughters.

Edg.   Pillicock sat on Pillicock-hill:
Halloo, halloo, loo, loo!

Fool.   This cold night will turn us all to fools and 80
madmen.

Edg.   Take heed o' the foul fiend: obey thy
parents; keep thy word justly; swear not; commit not with man's sworn spouse; set not thy sweet
heart on proud array. Tom 's a-cold.

Lear.   What hast thou been?

Edg.   A serving-man, proud in heart and mind;
that curled my hair; wore gloves in my cap; served
the lust of my mistress' heart, and did the act of
darkness with her; swore as many oaths as I spake 90
words, and broke them in the sweet face of heaven:
one that slept in the contriving of lust, and waked
to do it: wine loved I deeply, dice dearly; and in
woman out-paramoured the Turk: false of heart,
light of ear, bloody of hand; hog in sloth, fox in
stealth, wolf in greediness, dog in madness, lion in
prey. Let not the creaking of shoes nor the rus-
tling of silks betray thy poor heart to woman: keep
thy foot out of brothels, thy hand out of plackets, 100
thy pen from lenders' books, and defy the foul fiend.
Still through the hawthorn blows the cold wind:
Says suum, mun, ha, no, nonny.

Dolphin my boy, my boy, sessa! let him trot by.
[Storm still.

Lear. Why, thou wert better in thy grave than to answer with thy uncovered body this extremity of the skies. Is man no more than this? Consider him well. Thou owest the worm no silk, the beast no hide, the sheep no wool, the cat no perfume. Ha! here 's three on 's are sophisticated! Thou 110 art the thing itself: unaccommodated man is no more but such a poor, bare, forked animal as thou art. Off, off, you lendings! come, unbutton here. *[Tearing off his clothes.*

Fool. Prithee, nuncle, be contented; 't is a naughty night to swim in. Now a little fire in a wild field were like an old lecher's heart; a small spark, all the rest on's body cold. Look, here comes a walking fire.

Enter GLOUCESTER, *with a torch*

Edg. This is the foul fiend Flibbertigibbet: he 120 begins at curfew, and walks till the first cock; he gives the web and the pin, squints the eye, and makes the hare-lip; mildews the white wheat, and hurts the poor creature of earth.

S. Withold footed thrice the old;
He met the night-mare, and her nine-fold;
Bid her alight,
And her troth plight,
And, aroint thee, witch, aroint thee!

Kent. How fares your grace? 130
Lear. What 's he?
Kent. Who 's there? What is 't you seek?

Glou. What are you there? Your names?

Edg. Poor Tom; that eats the swimming frog, the toad, the tadpole, the wall-newt and the water; that in the fury of his heart, when the foul fiend rages, eats cow-dung for sallets; swallows the old rat and the ditch-dog; drinks the green mantle of the standing-pool; who is whipped from tithing to 140 tithing, and stock-punished, and imprisoned; who hath had three suits to his back, six shirts to his body, horse to ride, and weapon to wear;

But mice and rats, and such small deer,

Have been Tom's food for seven long year.

Beware my follower. Peace, Smulkin; peace, thou fiend!

Glou. What, hath your grace no better company?

Edg. The prince of darkness is a gentleman: Modo he's call'd, and Mahu.

Glou. Our flesh and blood is grown so vile, my lord, 150

That it doth hate what gets it.

Edg. Poor Tom's a-cold.

Glou. Go in with me: my duty cannot suffer To obey in all your daughters' hard commands: Though their injunction be to bar my doors, And let this tyrannous night take hold upon you, Yet have I ventured to come seek you out, And bring you where both fire and food is ready.

Lear. First let me talk with this philosopher. What is the cause of thunder? 160

Kent. Good my lord, take his offer; go into the house.

Lear. I 'll talk a word with this same learned
    Theban.
What is your study?

Edg. How to prevent the fiend, and to kill ver-
    min.

Lear. Let me ask you one word in private.

Kent. Importune him once more to go, my lord;
His wits begin to unsettle.

Glou.   Canst thou blame him? [*Storm still.*
His daughters seek his death; ah, that good Kent!
He said it would be thus, poor banish'd man!
Thou say'st the king grows mad; I 'll tell thee,
    friend,   170
I am almost mad myself: I had a son,
Now outlaw'd from my blood; he sought my life,
But lately, very late: I loved him, friend;
No father his son dearer: truth to tell thee,
The grief hath crazed my wits. What a night's
    this!
I do beseech your grace, —

Lear.   O, cry you mercy, sir.
Noble philosopher, your company.

Edg. Tom 's a-cold.

Glou. In, fellow, there, into the hovel: keep thee
    warm.

Lear. Come, let 's in all.

Kent.   This way, my lord.

Lear.   With him; 180
I will keep still with my philosopher.

Kent. Good my lord, soothe him; let him take
    the fellow.

Glou. Take him you on.

> *Kent.* Sirrah, come on; go along with us.
>
> *Lear.* Come, good Athenian.
>
> *Glou.* No words, no words: hush.
>
> *Edg.* Child Rowland to the dark tower came,
>
>   His word was still, — Fie, foh, and fum,
>
>   I smell the blood of a British man. [*Exeunt.*

SCENE V — *Gloucester's castle*

Enter CORNWALL *and* EDMUND

Corn. I will have my revenge ere I depart his house.

Edm. How, my lord, I may be censured, that nature thus gives way to loyalty, something fears me to think of.

Corn. I now perceive, it was not altogether your brother's evil disposition made him seek his death; but a provoking merit, set a-work by a re-proveable badness in himself.

Edm. How malicious is my fortune, that I must 10 repent to be just! This is the letter he spoke of, which approves him an intelligent party to the advantages of France. O heavens! that this treason were not, or not I the detector!

Corn. Go with me to the duchess.

Edm. If the matter of this paper be certain, you have mighty business in hand.

Corn. True or false, it hath made thee Earl of Gloucester. Seek out where thy father is, that he may be ready for our apprehension. 20

Edm. [*Aside*] If I find him comforting the king, it will stuff his suspicion more fully. — I will persevere in my course of loyalty, though the conflict be sore between that and my blood.

Corn. I will lay trust upon thee; and thou shalt find a dearer father in my love. [*Exeunt.*

SCENE VI — *A chamber in a farmhouse adjoining the castle*

Enter GLOUCESTER, LEAR, KENT, FOOL, *and* EDGAR

Glou. Here is better than the open air; take it thankfully. I will piece out the comfort with what addition I can; I will not be long from you.

Kent. All the power of his wits have given sway to his impatience: the gods reward your kindness! [*Exit Gloucester.*

Edg. Fraterretto calls me; and tells me Nero is an angler in the lake of darkness. Pray, innocent, and beware the foul fiend.

Fool. Prithee, nuncle, tell me whether a mad- 10 man be a gentleman or a yeoman?

Lear. A king, a king!

Fool. No, he 's a yeoman that has a gentleman to his son; for he 's a mad yeoman that sees his son a gentleman before him.

Lear. To have a thousand with red burning spits Come hissing in upon 'em, —

Edg. The foul fiend bites my back.

Fool. He 's mad that trusts in the tameness of a wolf, a horse's health, a boy's love, or a whore's 20 oath.

Lear. It shall be done; I will arraign them straight.

[*To Edgar*]   Come, sit thou here, most learned
         justicer;

[*To the Fool*]   Thou, sapient sir, sit here.   Now,
         you she foxes!

  Edg.   Look, where he stands and glares!   Wantest thou eyes at trial, madam?

         Come o'er the bourn, Bessy, to me, —

  Fool.   Her boat hath a leak,

          And she must not speak

         Why she dares not come over to thee.   30

  Edg.   The foul fiend haunts poor Tom in the
voice of a nightingale.   Hopdance cries in Tom's
belly for two white herring.   Croak not, black
angel; I have no food for thee.

  Kent.   How do you, sir?   Stand you not so
         amazed:

Will you lie down and rest upon the cushions?

  Lear.   I 'll see their trial first.   Bring in the
         evidence.

[*To Edgar*]   Thou robed man of justice, take thy
         place;

[*To the Fool*]   And thou, his yoke-fellow of equity,

Bench by his side: [*To Kent*] you are o' the com-
         mission,   40

Sit you too.

  Edg.   Let us deal justly.

         Sleepest or wakest thou, jolly shepherd?

         Thy sheep be in the corn;

         And for one blast of thy minikin mouth,

         Thy sheep shall take no harm.

Pur! the cat is gray.

  Lear.   Arraign her first; 't is Goneril.   I here

take my oath before this honourable assembly, she
kicked the poor king her father.   50

Fool. Come hither, mistress. Is your name
Goneril?

Lear. She cannot deny it.

Fool. Cry you mercy, I took you for a joint-
stool.

Lear. And here's another, whose warp'd looks
        proclaim
What store her heart is made on. Stop her
        there!
Arms, arms, sword, fire! Corruption in the place!
False justicer, why hast thou let her 'scape?

Edg. Bless thy five wits!   60

Kent. O pity! Sir, where is the patience now,
That you so oft have boasted to retain?

Edg. [*Aside*] My tears begin to take his part
        so much,
They 'll mar my counterfeiting.

Lear. The little dogs and all,
Tray, Blanch, and Sweet-heart, see, they bark at
        me.

Edg. Tom will throw his head at them. Avaunt,
you curs!

>   Be thy mouth or black or white,
>   Tooth that poisons if it bite;   70
>   Mastiff, greyhound, mongrel grim,
>   Hound or spaniel, brach or lym,
>   Or bobtail tike or trundle-tail,
>   Tom will make them weep and wail:
>   For, with throwing thus my head,
>   Dogs leap the hatch, and all are fled.

Do de, de, de.   Sessa!   Come, march to wakes and
fairs and market-towns.   Poor Tom, thy horn is
dry.

Lear.   Then let them anatomize Regan; see 80
what breeds about her heart.   Is there any cause
in nature that makes these hard hearts?   [*To
Edgar*]   You, sir, I entertain for one of my hundred;
only I do not like the fashion of your garments:
you will say they are Persian attire; but let them
be changed.

Kent.   Now, good my lord, lie here and rest
awhile.

Lear.   Make no noise, make no noise; draw the
curtains: so, so, so.   We'll go to supper i' the 90
morning.   So, so, so.

Fool.   And I'll go to bed at noon.

Re-enter GLOUCESTER

Glou.   Come hither, friend: where is the king
   my master?

Kent.   Here, sir; but trouble him not, his wits
   are gone.

Glou.   Good friend, I prithee, take him in thy
   arms;
I have o'erheard a plot of death upon him:
There is a litter ready; lay him in 't.
And drive towards Dover, friend, where thou shalt
   meet
Both welcome and protection.   Take up thy
   master:
If thou shouldst dally half an hour, his life, 100
With thine, and all that offer to defend him,

Stand in assured loss: take up, take up;
And follow me, that will to some provision
Give thee quick conduct.

    Kent.   Oppressed nature sleeps:
This rest might yet have balm'd thy broken
        sinews,
Which, if convenience will not allow,
Stand in hard cure.   [*To the Fool*] Come, help to
        bear thy master:
Thou must not stay behind.

    Glou.   Come, come, away.
                    [*Exeunt all but Edgar.*

    Edg. When we our betters see bearing our
        woes,
We scarcely think our miseries our foes.   110
Who alone suffers suffers most i' the mind,
Leaving free things and happy shows behind:
But then the mind much sufferance doth
        o'erskip
When grief hath mates, and bearing fellow-
        ship.
How light and portable my pain seems now,
When that which makes me bend makes the king
        bow;
He childed as I father'd! Tom, away!
Mark the high noises, and thyself bewray
When false opinion, whose wrong thought defiles
        thee,
In thy just proof repeals and reconciles thee.   120
What will hap more to-night, safe 'scape the
        king!
Lurk, lurk.   [*Exit.*

Scene VII — *Gloucester's castle*

Enter Cornwall, Regan, Goneril, Edmund,
and Servants

Corn. Post speedily to my lord your husband;
show him this letter: the army of France is landed.
Seek out the villain Gloucester.

[*Exeunt some of the Servants.*

Reg. Hang him instantly.

Gon. Pluck out his eyes.

Corn. Leave him to my displeasure. Edmund,
keep you our sister company: the revenges we are
bound to take upon your traitorous father are not
fit for your beholding. Advise the duke, where
you are going, to a most festinate preparation: 10
we are bound to the like. Our posts shall be swift
and intelligent betwixt us. Farewell, dear sister:
farewell, my lord of Gloucester.

Enter Oswald

How now! where 's the king?

Osw. My lord of Gloucester hath convey'd him
        hence:
Some five or six and thirty of his knights,
Hot questrists after him, met him at gate;
Who, with some other of the lords dependants,
Are gone with him towards Dover; where they boast
To have well-armed friends.

Corn.   Get horses for your mistress. 20

Gon. Farewell, sweet lord, and sister.

Corn. Edmund, farewell.

[*Exeunt Goneril, Edmund, and Oswald.*

Go seek the traitor Gloucester,
Pinion him like a thief, bring him before us.

                        [Exeunt other Servants.

Though well we may not pass upon his life
Without the form of justice, yet our power
Shall do a courtesy to our wrath, which men
May blame, but not control. Who 's there? the
        traitor?

    Enter GLOUCESTER, *brought in by two or three*

Reg.   Ingrateful fox! 't is he.
Corn.   Bind fast his corky arms.
Glou.   What mean your graces? Good my
        friends, consider   **30**
You are my guests: do me no foul play, friends.
Corn.   Bind him, I say.   *[Servants bind him.*
Reg.   Hard, hard. O filthy traitor!
Glou.   Unmerciful lady as you are, I'm none.
Corn.   To this chair bind him. Villain, thou
        shalt find —   *[Regan plucks his beard.*
Glou.   By the kind gods, 't is most ignobly done
To pluck me by the beard.
Reg.   So white, and such a traitor!
Glou.   Naughty lady,
These hairs, which thou dost ravish from my chin,
Will quicken, and accuse thee: I am your host:
With robbers' hands my hospitable favours   **40**
You should not ruffle thus. What will you do?
Corn.   Come, sir, what letters had you late from
        France?
Reg.   Be simple answerer, for we know the
        truth.

Corn. And what confederacy have you with the
    traitors
Late footed in the kingdom?

Reg. To whose hands have you sent the lunatic
    king?
Speak.

Glou. I have a letter guessingly set down,
Which came from one that 's of a neutral heart,
And not from one opposed.

Corn.   Cunning.

Reg.   And false.

Corn. Where hast thou sent the king?   **50**

Glou. To Dover.

Reg. Wherefore to Dover? Wast thou not
    charged at peril —

Corn. Wherefore to Dover? Let him first
    answer that.

Glou. I am tied to the stake, and I must stand
    the course.

Reg. Wherefore to Dover, sir?

Glou. Because I would not see thy cruel nails
Pluck out his poor old eyes; nor thy fierce sister
In his anointed flesh stick boarish fangs.
The sea, with such a storm as his bare head
In hell-black night endured, would have buoy'd up, **60**
And quench'd the stelled fires:
Yet, poor old heart, he holp the heavens to rain.
If wolves had at thy gate howl'd that stern time,
Thou shouldst have said "Good porter, turn the
    key."
All cruels else subscribed: but I shall see
The winged vengeance overtake such children.

Corn. See 't shalt thou never. Fellows, hold the chair.

Upon these eyes of thine I 'll set my foot.

Glou. He that will think to live till he be old,

Give me some help! O cruel! O you gods! 70

Reg. One side will mock another; the other too.

Corn. If you see vengeance, —

First Serv. Hold your hand, my lord:

I have served you ever since I was a child;

But better service have I never done you

Than now to bid you hold.

Reg. How now, you dog!

First Serv. If you did wear a beard upon your chin,

I 'd shake it on this quarrel. What do you mean?

Corn. My villain! *[They draw and fight.*

First Serv. Nay, then, come on, and take the chance of anger.

Reg. Give me thy sword. A peasant stand up thus! 80

[Takes a sword, and runs at him behind.

First Serv. O, I am slain! My lord, you have one eye left

To see some mischief on him. O! *[Dies.*

Corn. Lest it see more, prevent it. Out, vile jelly!

Where is thy lustre now?

Glou. All dark and comfortless. Where 's my son Edmund?

Edmund, enkindle all the sparks of nature,

To quit this horrid act.

Reg. Out, treacherous villain!

Thou call'st on him that hates thee: it was he
That made the overture of thy treasons to us;
Who is too good to pity thee.   90

  Glou. O my follies! then Edgar was abused.
Kind gods, forgive me that, and prosper him!

  Reg. Go thrust him out at gates, and let him
       smell
His way to Dover.   *[Exit one with Gloucester.*
              How is 't, my lord? how look you?

  Corn. I have received a hurt: follow me, lady;
Turn out that eyeless villain; throw this slave
Upon the dunghill. Regan, I bleed apace:
Untimely comes this hurt: give me your arm.
             [Exit Cornwall led by Regan.

  Sec. Serv. I'll never care what wickedness I do,
If this man come to good.

  Third Serv.   If she live long, 100
And in the end meet the old course of death,
Women will all turn monsters.

  Sec. Serv. Let 's follow the old earl, and get the
       Bedlam
To lead him where he would: his roguish madness
Allows itself to any thing.

  Third Serv. Go thou: I'll fetch some flax and
       whites of eggs
To apply to his bleeding face. Now, heaven help
       him!   *[Exeunt severally.*

ACT IV

SCENE I — *The heath*

Enter EDGAR

Edg. Yet better thus, and known to be con-
        temn'd
Than still contemn'd and flatter'd. To be worst,
The lowest and most dejected thing of fortune,
Stands still in esperance, lives not in fear:
The lamentable change is from the best;
The worst returns to laughter. Welcome, then,
Thou unsubstantial air that I embrace!
The wretch that thou hast blown unto the worst
Owes nothing to thy blasts. But who comes here?

Enter GLOUCESTER, *led by an* Old Man

My father, poorly led? World, world, O world!   10
But that thy strange mutations make us hate thee,
Life would not yield to age.

   Old Man. O, my good lord, I have been your
tenant, and your father's tenant, these fourscore
years.

   Glou. Away, get thee away; good friend, be
        gone:
Thy comforts can do me no good at all;
Thee they may hurt.

   Old Man. Alack, sir, you cannot see your way.

   Glou. I have no way, and therefore want no
        eyes;   20
I stumbled when I saw: full oft 't is seen,
Our means secure us, and our mere defects

Prove our commodities. O dear son Edgar,
The food of thy abused father's wrath!
Might I but live to see thee in my touch,
I 'ld say I had eyes again!

    Old Man.   How now! Who 's there?

    Edg. [*Aside*] O gods! Who is 't can say "I am
        at the worst"?

I am worse than e'er I was.

    Old Man.   'T is poor mad Tom.

    Edg. [*Aside.*] And worse I may be yet: the
        worst is not

So long as we can say "This is the worst."   30

    Old Man. Fellow, where goest?

    Glou.   Is it a beggar-man?

    Old Man. Madman and beggar too.

    Glou. He has some reason, else he could not beg.
I' the last night's storm I such a fellow saw;
Which made me think a man a worm: my son
Came then into my mind; and yet my mind
Was then scarce friends with him: I have heard
    more since.
As flies to wanton boys, are we to the gods;
They kill us for their sport.

    Edg.   [*Aside*] How should this be?
Bad is the trade that must play fool to sorrow,   40
Angering itself and others. — Bless thee, master!

    Glou. Is that the naked fellow?

    Old Man.   Ay, my lord.

    Glou. Then, prithee, get thee gone: if, for my
        sake,
Thou wilt o'ertake us, hence a mile or twain,
I' the way toward Dover, do it for ancient love;

And bring some covering for this naked soul,
Who I 'll entreat to lead me.

> *Old Man.*　　　　　　　　　Alack, sir, he is mad.
> *Glou.*　'T is the times' plague, when madmen
> > lead the blind.

Do as I bid thee, or rather do thy pleasure;
Above the rest, be gone.　　　　　　　　　　　50

> *Old Man.*　I 'll bring him the best 'parel that I
> > have,

Come on 't what will.　　　　　　　　　*[Exit.*

> *Glou.*　Sirrah, naked fellow, —
> *Edg.*　Poor Tom 's a-cold. [*Aside*] I cannot daub
> > it further.
> *Glou.*　Come hither, fellow.
> *Edg.*　[*Aside*] And yet I must. — Bless thy sweet
> > eyes, they bleed.
> *Glou.*　Know'st thou the way to Dover?
> *Edg.*　Both stile and gate, horse-way and foot-

path.　Poor Tom hath been scared out of his good
wits: bless thee, good man's son, from the foul 60
fiend! five fiends have been in poor Tom at once;
of lust, as Obidicut: Hobbididance, prince of dumb-
ness; Mahu, of stealing; Modo, of murder; Flibbertigibbet, of mopping and mowing, who since
possesses chambermaids and waiting-women.　So,
bless thee, master!

> *Glou.*　Here, take this purse, thou whom the
> > heavens' plagues

Have humbled to all strokes: that I am wretched
Makes thee the happier: heavens, deal so still!
Let the superfluous and lust-dieted man,　　　70
That slaves your ordinance, that will not see

Because he doth not feel, feel your power quickly;
So distribution should undo excess,
And each man have enough. Dost thou know
   Dover?

 Edg. Ay, master.

 Glou. There is a cliff, whose high and bending
   head
Looks fearfully in the confined deep:
Bring me but to the very brim of it,
And I 'll repair the misery thou dost bear
With something rich about me: from that place 80
I shall no leading need.

 Edg.   Give me thy arm:
Poor Tom shall lead thee.   [*Exeunt.*

Scene II — *Before the Duke of Albany's palace*

Enter Goneril *and* Edmund

 Gon. Welcome, my lord: I marvel our mild husband
Not met us on the way.

Enter Oswald

       Now, where 's your master?

 Osw. Madam, within; but never man so
   changed.
I told him of the army that was landed;
He smiled at it: I told him you were coming;
His answer was "The worse": of Gloucester's
   treachery,
And of the loyal service of his son,
When I inform'd him, then he call'd me sot,
And told me I had turn'd the wrong side out:

What most he should dislike seems pleasant to him; 10
What like, offensive.

Gon. [*To Edm.*] Then shall you go no further.
It is the cowish terror of his spirit,
That dares not undertake: he 'll not feel wrongs
Which tie him to an answer. Our wishes on the way
May prove effects.   Back, Edmund, to my brother;
Hasten his musters and conduct his powers:
I must change arms at home, and give the distaff
Into my husband's hands. This trusty servant
Shall pass between us: ere long you are like to hear,
If you dare venture in your own behalf,   20
A mistress's command. Wear this; spare speech;
[*Giving a favour.*
Decline your head: this kiss, if it durst speak,
Would stretch thy spirits up into the air:
Conceive, and fare thee well.

Edm.   Yours in the ranks of death.
Gon.   My most dear Gloucester!
[*Exit Edmund.*
O, the difference of man and man!
To thee a woman's services are due:
My fool usurps my body.

Osw.   Madam, here comes my lord.   [*Exit.*

Enter ALBANY

Gon. I have been worth the whistle.
Alb.   O Goneril!
You are not worth the dust which the rude wind   30
Blows in your face. I fear your disposition:
That nature, which contemns it origin,
Cannot be border'd certain in itself;

She that herself will sliver and disbranch
From her material sap, perforce must wither
And come to deadly use.

   Gon. No more; the text is foolish.

   Alb. Wisdom and goodness to the vile seem
      vile:
Filths savour but themselves. What have you
      done?
Tigers, not daughters, what have you perform'd?   40
A father, and a gracious aged man,
Whose reverence even the head-lugg'd bear would
      lick,
Most barbarous, most degenerate! have you
      madded.
Could my good brother suffer you to do it?
A man, a prince, by him so benefited!
If that the heavens do not their visible spirits
Send quickly down to tame these vile offences,
It will come,
Humanity must perforce prey on itself,
Like monsters of the deep.

   Gon.   Milk-liver'd man!   50
That bear'st a cheek for blows, a head for wrongs:
Who hast not in thy brows an eye discerning
Thine honour from thy suffering; that not know'st
Fools do those villains pity who are punish'd
Ere they have done their mischief. Where 's thy
      drum?
France spreads his banners in our noiseless land,
With plumed helm thy state begins to threat;
Whiles thou, a moral fool, sit'st still, and criest
"Alack, why does he so?"

Alb.   See thyself, devil!
Proper deformity seems not in the fiend   60
So horrid as in woman.

Gon.   O vain fool!

Alb.   Thou changed and self-cover'd thing, for
    shame,
Be-monster not thy feature. Were 't my fitness
To let these hands obey my blood,
They are apt enough to dislocate and tear
Thy flesh and bones: howe'er thou art a fiend,
A woman's shape doth shield thee.

Gon.   Marry, your manhood! mew!

Enter a Messenger

Alb.   What news?

Mess.   O, my good lord, the Duke of Cornwall's
    dead;   70
Slain by his servant, going to put out
The other eye of Gloucester.

Alb.   Gloucester's eyes!

Mess.   A servant that he bred, thrill'd with re-
    morse,
Opposed against the act, bending his sword
To his great master; who, thereat enraged,
Flew on him, and amongst them fell'd him dead;
But not without that harmful stroke, which since
Hath pluck'd him after.

Alb.   This shows you are above,
You justicers, that these our nether crimes
So speedily can venge! But, O poor Gloucester!   80
Lost he his other eye?

Mess.   Both, both, my lord.

This letter, madam, craves a speedy answer;
'T is from your sister.

   Gon. [*Aside*] One way I like this well;
But being widow, and my Gloucester with her,
May all the building in my fancy pluck
Upon my hateful life: another way,
The news is not so tart. — I 'll read, and answer.

                                 [*Exit.*

   Alb. Where was his son when they did take his
      eyes?

   Mess. Come with my lady hither.

   Alb.   He is not here. 90

   Mess. No, my good lord; I met him back again.

   Alb. Knows he the wickedness?

   Mess. Ay, my good lord; 't was he inform'd
      against him;
And quit the house on purpose, that their punish-
      ment
Might have the freer course.

   Alb.   Gloucester, I live
To thank thee for the love thou show'dst the king,
And to revenge thine eyes. Come hither, friend:
Tell me what more thou know'st.   [*Exeunt.*

SCENE III — *The French camp near Dover*

Enter KENT *and a* Gentleman

   Kent. Why the King of France is so suddenly
gone back know you the reason?

   Gent. Something he left imperfect in the state,
which since his coming forth is thought of; which
imports to the kingdom so much fear and danger,

that his personal return was most required and necessary.

Kent. Who hath he left behind him general?

Gent. The Marshall of France, Monsieur La Far. 10

Kent. Did your letters pierce the queen to any demonstration of grief?

Gent. Ay, sir; she took them, read them in my
presence;
And now and then an ample tear trill'd down
Her delicate cheek: it seem'd she was a queen
Over her passion; who, most rebel-like,
Sought to be king o'er her.

Kent. O, then it moved her.

Gent. Not to a rage: patience and sorrow
strove
Who should express her goodliest. You have seen
Sunshine and rain at once: her smiles and tears 20
Were like, a better way: those happy smilets,
That play'd on her ripe lip, seem'd not to know
What guests were in her eyes; which parted thence,
As pearls from diamonds dropp'd. In brief,
Sorrow would be a rarity most beloved,
If all could so become it.

Kent. Made she no verbal question?

Gent. 'Faith, once or twice she heaved the name
of "father"
Pantingly forth, as if it press'd her heart;
Cried "Sisters! sisters! Shame of ladies! sisters!
Kent! father! sisters! What, i' the storm? i' the
night? 30
Let pity not be believed!" There she shook
The holy water from her heavenly eyes,

And clamour moisten'd: then away she started
To deal with grief alone.

    Kent.   It is the stars,
The stars above us, govern our conditions;
Else one self mate and mate could not beget
Such different issues. You spoke not with her
    since?

    Gent. No.

    Kent. Was this before the king return'd?

    Gent.   No, since.

    Kent. Well, sir, the poor distress'd Lear 's i'
    the town;   40
Who sometime, in his better tune, remembers
What we are come about, and by no means
Will yield to see his daughter.

    Gent.   Why, good sir?

    Kent. A sovereign shame so elbows him: his
    own unkindness,
That stripp'd her from his benediction, turn'd her
To foreign casualties, gave her dear rights
To his dog-hearted daughters, these things sting
His mind so venomously, that burning shame
Detains him from Cordelia.

    Gent.   Alack, poor gentleman!

    Kent. Of Albany's and Cornwall's powers you
    heard not?   50

    Gent. 'T is so, they are afoot.

    Kent. Well, sir, I 'll bring you to our master
    Lear,
And leave you to attend him: some dear cause
Will in concealment wrap me up awhile;
When I am known aright, you shall not grieve

Lending me this acquaintance.   I pray you, go
Along with me.   [*Exeunt.*

SCENE IV — *The same.   A tent*

Enter, with drum and colours, CORDELIA,
Doctor, *and* Soldiers

    Cor.   Alack, 't is he : why, he was met even now
As mad as the vex'd sea ; singing aloud ;
Crown'd with rank fumiter and furrow-weeds,
With hor-docks, hemlock, nettles, cuckoo-flowers,
Darnel, and all the idle weeds that grow
In our sustaining corn.   A century send forth ;
Search every acre in the high-grown field,
And bring him to our eye.   [*Exit an Officer.*]   What
            can man's wisdom
In the restoring his bereaved sense ?
He that helps him take all my outward worth.   10
    Doct.   There is means, madam :
Our foster-nurse of nature is repose,
The which he lacks ; that to provoke in him,
Are many simples operative, whose power
Will close the eye of anguish.
    Cor.   All blest secrets,
All you unpublish'd virtues of the earth,
Spring with my tears ! be aidant and remediate
In the good man's distress !   Seek, seek for him ;
Lest his ungovern'd rage dissolve the life
That wants the means to lead it.

                    Enter a Messenger
    Mess.   News, madam ; 20
The British powers are marching hitherward.

Cor. 'T is known before; our preparation
       stands
In expectation of them. O dear father,
It is thy business that I go about;
Therefore great France
My mourning and important tears hath pitied.
No blown ambition doth our arms incite,
But love, dear love, and our aged father's right:
Soon may I hear and see him !   [*Exeunt.*

Scene V — *Gloucester's castle*

Enter REGAN *and* OSWALD

Reg.   But are my brother's powers set forth?
Osw.   Ay, madam.
Reg.   Himself in person there?
Osw.   Madam, with much ado:
Your sister is the better soldier.
Reg.   Lord Edmund spake not with your lord at
       home?
Osw.   No, madam.
Reg.   What might import my sister's letter to
       him?
Osw.   I know not, lady.
Reg.   'Faith, he is posted hence on serious
       matter.
It was great ignorance, Gloucester's eyes being out,
To let him live: where he arrives he moves   10
All hearts against us: Edmund, I think, is gone,
In pity of his misery, to dispatch
His nighted life; moreover, to descry
The strength o' the enemy.

Osw.   I must needs after him, madam, with my
    letter.

Reg.   Our troops set forth to-morrow : stay with
    us ;

The ways are dangerous.

Osw.   I may not, madam :

My lady charged my duty in this business.

Reg.   Why should she write to Edmund ?   Might
    not you

Transport her purposes by word ?   Belike,   20

Something — I know not what : I 'll love thee
    much,

Let me unseal the letter.

Osw.   Madam, I had rather —

Reg.   I know your lady does not love her hus-
    band ;

I am sure of that : and at her late being here

She gave strange œillades and most speaking looks

To noble Edmund.   I know you are of her bosom.

Osw.   I, madam ?

Reg.   I speak in understanding ;   you are, I
    know 't :

Therefore I do advise you, take this note :

My lord is dead ; Edmund and I have talk'd ;   30

And more convenient is he for my hand

Than for your lady's : you may gather more.

If you do find him, pray you, give him this ;

And when your mistress hears thus much from you,

I pray, desire her call her wisdom to her.

So, fare you well.

If you do chance to hear of that blind traitor,

Preferment falls on him that cuts him off.

  Osw. Would I could meet him, madam! I
    should show
What party I do follow.
  Reg.   Fare thee well. [*Exeunt.* 40

   Scene VI — *Fields near Dover*

Enter GLOUCESTER, *and* EDGAR *dressed like a peasant*

  Glou. When shall we come to the top of that
    same hill?
  Edg. You do climb up it now: look, how we
    labour.
  Glou. Methinks the ground is even.
  Edg.   Horrible steep.
Hark, do you hear the sea?
  Glou.   No, truly.
  Edg. Why, then, your other senses grow im-
    perfect
By your eyes' anguish.
  Glou.   So may it be, indeed:
Methinks thy voice is alter'd; and thou speak'st
In better phrase and matter than thou didst.
  Edg. You 're much deceived: in nothing am I
    changed
But in my garments.
  Glou.   Methinks you 're better spoken. 10
  Edg. Come on, sir; here 's the place: stand
    still. How fearful
And dizzy 't is, to cast one's eyes so low!
The crows and choughs that wing the midway
    air
Show scarce so gross as beetles: half way down

Hangs one that gathers samphire, dreadful trade!
Methinks he seems no bigger than his head:
The fishermen, that walk upon the beach,
Appear like mice; and yond tall anchoring bark,
Diminish'd to her cock; her cock, a buoy
Almost too small for sight: the murmuring surge,   20
That on the unnumber'd idle pebbles chafes,
Cannot be heard so high.   I 'll look no more,
Lest my brain turn, and the deficient sight
Topple down headlong.

   Glou.   Set me where you stand.

   Edg.   Give me your hand: you are now within
      a foot
Of the extreme verge: for all beneath the moon
Would I not leap upright.

   Glou.   Let go my hand.
Here, friend, 's another purse; in it a jewel
Well worth a poor man's taking: fairies and gods
Prosper it with thee!   Go thou farther off;   30
Bid me farewell, and let me hear thee going.

   Edg.. Now fare you well, good sir.

   Glou.   With all my heart.

   Edg.   Why I do trifle thus with his despair
Is done to cure it.

   Glou.   [*Kneeling*] O you mighty gods!
This world I do renounce, and, in your sights,
Shake patiently my great affliction off:
If I could bear it longer, and not fall
To quarrel with your great opposeless wills,
My snuff and loathed part of nature should
Burn itself out.   If Edgar live, O, bless him!   40
Now, fellow, fare thee well.   [*He falls forward.*

 Edg.   Gone, sir : farewell.
And yet I know not how conceit may rob
The treasury of life, when life itself
Yields to the theft : had he been where he thought,
By this had thought been past. Alive or dead ?
Ho, you sir ! friend ! Hear you, sir ! speak !
Thus might he pass indeed : yet he revives.
What are you, sir ?
 Glou.   Away, and let me die.
 Edg. Hadst thou been aught but gossamer,
   feathers, air,
So many fathom down precipitating,   50
Thou 'dst shiver'd like an egg : but thou dost
   breathe ;
Hast heavy substance; bleed'st not; speak'st;
   art sound.
Ten masts at each make not the altitude
Which thou hast perpendicularly fell :
Thy life 's a miracle. Speak yet again.
 Glou. But have I fall'n, or no ?
 Edg. From the dread summit of this chalky
   bourn.
Look up a-height; the shrill-gorged lark so far
Cannot be seen or heard : do but look up.
 Glou. Alack, I have no eyes.   60
Is wretchedness deprived that benefit,
To end itself by death ? 'T was yet some comfort,
When misery could beguile the tyrant's rage,
And frustrate his proud will.
 Edg.   Give me your arm :
Up : so. How is 't? Feel you your legs? You
   stand.

Glou. Too well, too well.

Edg.   This is above all strangeness.
Upon the crown o' the cliff, what thing was that
Which parted from you?

Glou.   A poor unfortunate beggar.

Edg. As I stood here below, methought his eyes
Were two full moons; he had a thousand noses,   70
Horns whelk'd and waved like the enridged sea:
It was some fiend; therefore, thou happy father,
Think that the clearest gods, who make them
          honours
Of men's impossibilities, have preserved thee.

  Glou. I do remember now: henceforth I'll bear
Affliction till it do cry out itself
"Enough, enough," and die. That thing you
          speak of,
I took it for a man; often 't would say
"The fiend, the fiend": he led me to that place.

  Edg. Bear free and patient thoughts. But who
          comes here?
                                                      80

Enter LEAR, *fantastically dressed with wild flowers*

The safer sense will ne'er accommodate
His master thus.

  Lear. No, they cannot touch me for coining;
I am the king himself.

  Edg. O thou side-piercing sight!

  Lear. Nature's above art in that respect.
There's your press-money. That fellow handles
his bow like a crow-keeper: draw me a clothier's
yard. Look, look, a mouse! Peace, peace; this
piece of toasted cheese will do 't. There's my 90

gauntlet; I 'll prove it on a giant. Bring up the brown bills. O, well flown, bird! i' the clout, i' the clout: hewgh! Give the word.

Edg.   Sweet marjoram.

Lear.   Pass.

Glou.   I know that voice.

Lear.   Ha! Goneril, with a white beard! They flattered me like a dog; and told me I had white hairs in my beard ere the black ones were there. To say "ay" and "no" to every thing that I said!— 100 "Ay" and "no" too was no good divinity. When the rain came to wet me once, and the wind to make me chatter; when the thunder would not peace at my bidding; there I found 'em, there I smelt 'em out. Go to, they are not men o' their words: they told me I was every thing; 't is a lie, I am not ague-proof.

Glou.   The trick of that voice I do well remember: Is 't not the king?

Lear.   Ay, every inch a king: When I do stare, see how the subject quakes.   110 I pardon that man's life. What was thy cause? Adultery? Thou shalt not die: die for adultery! No: The wren goes to 't, and the small gilded fly Does lecher in my sight. Let copulation thrive; for Gloucester's bastard son Was kinder to his father than my daughters Got 'tween the lawful sheets. To 't, luxury, pell-mell! for I lack soldiers. Behold yond simpering dame,   120

Whose face between her forks presages snow;
That minces virtue, and does shake the head
To hear of pleasure's name;
The fitchew, nor the soiled horse, goes to 't
With a more riotous appetite.
Down from the waist they are Centaurs,
Though women all above:
But to the girdle do the gods inherit,
Beneath is all the fiends';
There 's hell, there 's darkness, there 's the sul-
      phurous pit, 130
Burning, scalding, stench, consumption; fie, fie,
fie! pah! pah! Give me an ounce of civet, good
apothecary, to sweeten my imagination: there 's
money for thee.

    Glou. O, let me kiss that hand!

    Lear. Let me wipe it first; it smells of mortality.

    Glou. O ruin'd piece of nature! This great
        world
Shall so wear out to nought. Dost thou know me?

    Lear. I remember thine eyes well enough.
Dost thou squiny at me? No, do thy worst, blind 140
Cupid; I 'll not love. Read thou this challenge;
mark but the penning of it.

    Glou. Were all the letters suns, I could not see
      one.

    Edg. I would not take this from report; it is,
And my heart breaks at it.

    Lear. Read.

    Glou. What, with the case of eyes?

    Lear. O, ho, are you there with me? No eyes
in your head, nor no money in your purse? Your

eyes are in a heavy case, your purse in a light: yet 150
you see how this world goes.

Glou. I see it feelingly.

Lear. What, art mad? A man may see how this
world goes with no eyes. Look with thine ears:
see how yond justice rails upon yond simple thief.
Hark, in thine ear: change places; and, handy-
dandy, which is the justice, which is the thief?
Thou hast seen a farmer's dog bark at a beggar?

Glou. Ay, sir.   160

Lear. And the creature run from the cur?
There thou mightst behold the great image of au-
thority: a dog 's obeyed in office.
Thou rascal beadle, hold thy bloody hand!
Why dost thou lash that whore? Strip thine own
      back;
Thou hotly lust'st to use her in that kind
For which thou whipp'st her. The usurer hangs
      the cozener.
Through tatter'd clothes small vices do appear;
Robes and furr'd gowns hide all. Plate sin with
      gold,
And the strong lance of justice hurtless breaks; 170
Arm it in rags, a pigmy's straw does pierce it.
None does offend, none, I say, none; I 'll able 'em;
Take that of me, my friend, who have the power
To seal the accuser's lips. Get thee glass eyes;
And, like a scurvy politician, seem
To see the things thou dost not. Now, now, now,
      now:
Pull off my boots: harder, harder: so.

Edg. O, matter and impertinency mix'd!

Reason in madness!

    Lear.   If thou wilt weep my fortunes, take my
         eyes.   180

I know thee well enough; thy name is Gloucester:

Thou must be patient; we came crying hither:

Thou know'st, the first time that we smell the air,

We wawl and cry.   I will preach to thee : mark.

   Glou.   Alack, alack the day!

    Lear.   When we are born, we cry that we are
         come

To this great stage of fools: this' a good block;

It were a delicate stratagem, to shoe

A troop of horse with felt: I 'll put 't in proof;

And when I have stol'n upon these sons-in-law,   190

Then, kill, kill, kill, kill, kill, kill!

Enter a Gentleman, *with* Attendants

   Gent.   O, here he is; lay hand upon him.   Sir,

Your most dear daughter —

    Lear.   No rescue?   What, a prisoner?   I am
         even

The natural food of fortune.   Use me well;

You shall have ransom.   Let me have surgeons;

I am cut to the brains.

   Gent.   You shall have any thing.

    Lear.   No seconds?   all myself?

Why, this would make a man a man of salt,

To use his eyes for garden water-pots,   200

Ay, and laying autumn's dust.

   Gent.   Good sir, —

    Lear.   I will die bravely, like a smug bridegroom.
         What!

I will be jovial: come, come; I am a king,
My masters, know you that.

Gent.   You are a royal one, and we obey you.

Lear.   Then there 's life in 't.   Nay, if you get
it, you shall get it with running.   Sa, sa, sa, sa.

[Exit running; Attendants follow.

Gent.   A sight most pitiful in the meanest wretch,
Past speaking of in a king!   Thou hast one
        daughter,
Who redeems nature from the general curse   210
Which twain have brought her to.

Edg.   Hail, gentle sir.

Gent.   Sir, speed you: what 's your will?

Edg.   Do you hear aught, sir, of a battle toward?

Gent.   Most sure and vulgar: every one hears
        that,
Which can distinguish sound.

Edg.   But, by your favour,
How near 's the other army?

Gent.   Near and on speedy foot; the main descry
Stands on the hourly thought.

Edg.   I thank you, sir: that 's all.

Gent.   Though that the queen on special cause
        is here,
Her army is moved on.

Edg.   I thank you, sir.   [*Exit Gent.* 220

Glou.   You ever-gentle gods, take my breath
        from me;
Let not my worser spirit tempt me again
To die before you please!

Edg.   Well pray you, father.

Glou.   Now, good sir, what are you?

   Edg.   A most poor man, made tame to fortune's
       blows;
Who, by the art of known and feeling sorrows,
Am pregnant to good pity.   Give me your hand,
I 'll lead you to some biding.
   Glou.   Hearty thanks:
The bounty and the benison of heaven
To boot, and boot!

Enter OSWALD

   Osw.   A proclaim'd prize!   Most happy!   230
That eyeless head of thine was first framed flesh
To raise my fortunes.   Thou old unhappy traitor,
Briefly thyself remember: the sword is out
That must destroy thee.
   Glou.   Now let thy friendly hand
Put strength enough to 't.   [*Edgar interposes.*
   Osw.   Wherefore, bold peasant,
Darest thou support a publish'd traitor?   Hence;
Lest that the infection of his fortune take
Like hold on thee.   Let go his arm.
   Edg.   Chill not let go, zir, without vurther
'casion.   240
   Osw.   Let go, slave, or thou diest!
   Edg.   Good gentleman, go your gait, and let
poor volk pass.   An chud ha' bin zwaggered out
of my life, 't would not ha' bin zo long as 't is by
a vortnight.   Nay, come not near th' old man;
keep out, che vor ye, or ise try whether your
costard or my ballow be the harder: chill be plain
with you.
   Osw.   Out, dunghill!

Edg.　Chill pick your teeth, zir: come; no 250
matter vor your foins.

　　　　　　[*They fight, and Edgar knocks him down.*

Osw.　Slave, thou hast slain me: villain, take
　　　my purse:
If ever thou wilt thrive, bury my body;
And give the letters which thou find'st about me
To Edmund earl of Gloucester; seek him out
Upon the British party: O, untimely death!

　　　　　　　　　　　　　　　　　　[*Dies.*

Edg.　I know thee well: a serviceable villain
As duteous to the vices of thy mistress
As badness would desire.

Glou.　　　　　　　　What, is he dead?

Edg.　Sit you down, father; rest you.　　260
Let 's see these pockets: the letters that he
　　　speaks of
May be my friends.　He 's dead; I am only sorry
He had no other death's-man.　Let us see:
Leave, gentle wax; and, manners, blame us not:
To know our enemies' minds, we 'ld rip their hearts;
Their papers, is more lawful.

[*Reads*] "Let our reciprocal vows be remembered.
You have many opportunities to cut him off: if
your will want not, time and place will be fruitfully
offered.　There is nothing done, if he return the 270
conqueror: then am I the prisoner, and his bed
my gaol; from the loathed warmth whereof deliver
me, and supply the place for your labour.

　　　　"Your — wife, so I would say —

　　　　　　　　　　"Affectionate servant,

　　　　　　　　　　　　"GONERIL."

O undistinguish'd space of woman's will!
A plot upon her virtuous husband's life;
And the exchange my brother! Here, in the sands, 280
Thee I 'll rake up, the post unsanctified
Of murderous lechers: and in the mature time
With this ungracious paper strike the sight
Of the death-practised duke: for him 't is well
That of thy death and business I can tell.

    Glou. The king is mad: how stiff is my vile
        sense,
That I stand up, and have ingenious feeling
Of my huge sorrows! Better I were distract:
So should my thoughts be sever'd from my griefs,
And woes by wrong imaginations lose   290
The knowledge of themselves.

    Edg.   Give me your hand:
                           [*Drum afar off.*
Far off, methinks, I hear the beaten drum:
Come, father, I 'll bestow you with a friend.
                             [*Exeunt.*

SCENE VII — *A tent in the French camp.* LEAR *on
    a bed asleep, soft music playing;* Gentleman,
    and others attending

Enter CORDELIA, KENT, *and* Doctor

    Cor. O thou good Kent, how shall I live and
        work,
To match thy goodness? My life will be too short,
And every measure fail me.

    Kent. To be acknowledged, madam, is o'erpaid.
All my reports go with the modest truth;

Nor more nor clipp'd, but so.

Cor.   Be better suited:
These weeds are memories of those worser hours:
I prithee, put them off.

Kent.   Pardon me, dear madam;
Yet to be known shortens my made intent:
My boon I make it, that you know me not   **10**
Till time and I think meet.

    Cor.   Then be 't so, my good lord. [*To the
Doctor*] How does the king?

    Doct.   Madam, sleeps still.

    Cor.   O you kind gods,
Cure this great breach in his abused nature!
The untuned and jarring senses, O, wind up
Of this child-changed father!

    Doct.   So please your majesty
That we may wake the king: he hath slept long.

    Cor.   Be govern'd by your knowledge, and pro-
ceed
I' the sway of your own will.   Is he array'd?   **20**

    Gent.   Ay, madam; in the heaviness of his sleep
We put fresh garments on him.

    Doct.   Be by, good madam, when we do awake
him
I doubt not of his temperance.

    Cor.   Very well.

    Doct.   Please you, draw near. Louder the
music there!

    Cor.   O my dear father! Restoration hang
Thy medicine on my lips; and let this kiss
Repair those violent harms that my two sisters
Have in thy reverence made!

Kent.   Kind and dear princess!

Cor. Had you not been their father, these white
    flakes   30

Had challenged pity of them. Was this a face

To be opposed against the warring winds?

To stand against the deep dread-bolted thunder?

In the most terrible and nimble stroke

Of quick, cross lightning? to watch — poor
    perdu! —

With this thin helm? Mine enemy's dog,

Though he had bit me, should have stood that night

Against my fire; and wast thou fain, poor father,

To hovel thee with swine, and rogues forlorn,

In short and musty straw? Alack, alack!   40

'T is wonder that thy life and wits at once

Had not concluded all. He wakes; speak to him.

Doct. Madam, do you; 't is fittest.

Cor. How does my royal lord? How fares your
    majesty?

Lear. You do me wrong to take me out o' the
    grave:

Thou art a soul in bliss; but I am bound

Upon a wheel of fire, that mine own tears

Do scald like molten lead.

Cor.   Sir, do you know me?

Lear. You are a spirit, I know: when did you
    die?

Cor. Still, still, far wide!   50

Doct. He 's scarce awake: let him alone awhile.

Lear. Where have I been? Where am I? Fair
    daylight?

I am mightily abused. I should e'en die with pity,

To see another thus.   I know not what to say.
I will not swear these are my hands: let 's see;
I feel this pin prick.   Would I were assured
Of my condition!

    Cor.   O, look upon me, sir,
And hold your hands in benediction o'er me:
No, sir, you must not kneel.

    Lear.   Pray, do not mock me:
I am a very foolish fond old man,   60
Fourscore and upward, not an hour more nor less;
And, to deal plainly,
I fear I am not in my perfect mind.
Methinks I should know you, and know this man;
Yet I am doubtful: for I am mainly ignorant
What place this is; and all the skill I have
Remembers not these garments; nor I know not
Where I did lodge last night.   Do not laugh at me;
For, as I am a man, I think this lady
To be my child Cordelia.

    Cor.   And so I am, I am.   70

    Lear. Be your tears wet? yes, 'faith.   I pray,
        weep not:
If you have poison for me, I will drink it.
I know you do not love me; for your sisters
Have, as I do remember, done me wrong:
You have some cause, they have not.

    Cor.   No cause, no cause.

    Lear. Am I in France?

    Kent.   In your own kingdom, sir.

    Lear. Do not abuse me.

    Doct. Be comforted, good madam: the great
        rage,

You see, is kill'd in him : and yet it is danger
To make him even o'er the time he has lost.   80
Desire him to go in : trouble him no more
Till further settling.

 Cor. Will 't please your highness, walk?

 Lear.   You must bear with me :
Pray you now, forget and forgive : I am old and
    foolish.

     [Exeunt all but Kent and Gentleman.

 Gent. Holds it true, sir, that the Duke of Cornwall was so slain?

 Kent. Most certain, sir.

 Gent. Who is conductor of his people?

 Kent. As 't is said, the bastard son of Gloucester.

 Gent. They say Edgar, his banished son, is with 90
the Earl of Kent in Germany.

 Kent. Report is changeable. 'T is time to look
about ; the powers of the kingdom approach apace.

 Gent. The arbitrement is like to be bloody.
Fare you well, sir.   *[Exit.*

 Kent. My point and period will be thoroughly
    wrought,
Or well or ill, as this day's battle 's fought. *[Exit.*

ACT V

SCENE I — *The British camp near Dover*

Enter, with drum and colours, EDMUND, REGAN,
Gentlemen, *and* Soldiers

 Edm. Know of the duke if his last purpose hold,
Or whether since he is advised by aught

To change the course : he 's full of alteration
And self-reproving : bring his constant pleasure.

                    [To a Gentleman, who goes out.

    Reg.   Our sister's man is certainly miscarried.

    Edm.   'T is to be doubted, madam.

    Reg.   Now, sweet lord,
You know the goodness I intend upon you :
Tell me -- but truly — but then speak the truth,
Do you not love my sister ?

    Edm.   In honour'd love.

    Reg.   But have you never found my brother's
        way   10
To the forfended place ?

    Edm.   That thought abuses you.

    Reg.   I am doubtful that you have been conjunct
And bosom'd with her, as far as we call hers.

    Edm.   No, by mine honour, madam.

    Reg.   I never shall endure her : dear my lord,
Be not familiar with her.

    Edm.   Fear me not :
She and the duke her husband !

  Enter, with drum and colours, Albany, Goneril,
              and Soldiers

    Gon.   [*Aside*] I had rather lose the battle than
        that sister
Should loosen him and me.

    Alb.   Our very loving sister, well be-met.   20
Sir, this I hear ; the king is come to his daughter,
With others whom the rigour of our state
Forced to cry out.   Where I could not be honest,
I never yet was valiant : for this business,

It toucheth us, as France invades our land,
Not bolds the king, with others, whom, I fear,
Most just and heavy causes make oppose.

 Edm. Sir, you speak nobly.

 Reg.   Why is this reason'd?

 Gon. Combine together 'gainst the enemy;
For these domestic and particular broils   30
Are not the question here.

 Alb.   Let 's then determine
With the ancient of war on our proceedings.

 Edm. I shall attend you presently at your
   tent.

 Reg. Sister, you 'll go with us?

 Gon. No.

 Reg. 'T is most convenient; pray you, go with
   us.

 Gon. [*Aside*] O, ho, I know the riddle. — I
   will go.

As they are going out, enter EDGAR *disguised*

 Edg. If e'er your grace had speech with man
   so poor,
Hear me one word.

 Alb.   I 'll overtake you.   Speak.
      [*Exeunt all but Albany and Edgar.*

 Edg. Before you fight the battle, ope this letter. 40
If you have victory, let the trumpet sound
For him that brought it: wretched though I
   seem,
I can produce a champion that will prove
What is avouched there.   If you miscarry,
Your business of the world hath so an end,

And machination ceases.   Fortune love you!

    Alb.   Stay till I have read the letter.

    Edg.   I was forbid it.

When time shall serve, let but the herald cry,

And I 'll appear again.

    Alb.   Why, fare thee well :   I will o'erlook thy

        paper.   *[Exit Edgar.* 5⊙

Re-enter EDMUND

    Edm.   The enemy 's in view; draw up your

        powers.

Here is the guess of their true strength and forces

By diligent discovery ; but your haste

Is now urged on you.

    Alb.   We will greet the time. *[Exit.*

    Edm.   To both these sisters have I sworn my

        love;

Each jealous of the other, as the stung

Are of the adder.   Which of them shall I take?

Both? one? or neither?   Neither can be enjoy'd,

If both remain alive : to take the widow

Exasperates, makes mad her sister Goneril ;   60

And hardly shall I carry out my side,

Her husband being alive.   Now then we 'll use

His countenance for the battle; which being done,

Let her who would be rid of him devise

His speedy taking off.   As for the mercy

Which he intends to Lear and to Cordelia,

The battle done, and they within our power,

Shall never see his pardon; for my state

Stands on me to defend, not to debate.   *[Exit.*

SCENE II — *A field between the two camps*

Alarum within. Enter, with drum and colours, LEAR,
CORDELIA, *and* Soldiers, *over the stage; and exeunt*

Enter EDGAR *and* GLOUCESTER

Edg.   Here, father, take the shadow of this tree
For your good host; pray that the right may thrive:
If ever I return to you again,
I 'll bring you comfort.
  Glou.   Grace go with you, sir!
                                           [*Exit Edgar.*
      Alarum and retreat within. Re-enter EDGAR

Edg.   Away, old man; give me thy hand; away!
King Lear hath lost, he and his daughter ta'en:
Give me thy hand; come on.
  Glou.   No farther, sir; a man may rot even here.
  Edg.   What, in ill thoughts again? Men must
          endure
Their going hence, even as their coming hither: 10
Ripeness is all: come on.
  Glou.   And that 's true too. [*Exeunt.*

SCENE III — *The British camp near Dover*

Enter, in conquest, with drum and colours, EDMUND;
  LEAR *and* CORDELIA, *prisoners;* Captain, Soldiers, &c.

Edm.   Some officers take them away: good
          guard,
Until their greater pleasures first be known
That are to censure them.
  Cor.   We are not the first

Who, with best meaning, have incurr'd the worst.
For thee, oppressed king, am I cast down;
Myself could else out-frown false fortune's frown.
Shall we not see these daughters and these sisters?

Lear.   No, no, no, no! Come, let 's away to
    prison:
We two alone will sing like birds i' the cage:
When thou dost ask me blessing, I 'll kneel down,   10
And ask of thee forgiveness: so we 'll live,
And pray, and sing, and tell old tales, and laugh
At gilded butterflies, and hear poor rogues
Talk of court news; and we 'll talk with them too,
Who loses and who wins; who 's in, who 's out;
And take upon 's the mystery of things,
As if we were God's spies: and we 'll wear out,
In a wall'd prison, packs and sects of great ones,
That ebb and flow by the moon.

    Edm.   Take them away.

    Lear.   Upon such sacrifices, my Cordelia,   20
The gods themselves throw incense. Have I
    caught thee?
He that parts us shall bring a brand from heavens,
And fire us hence like foxes. Wipe thine eyes;
The good-years shall devour them, flesh and fell,
Ere they shall make us weep: we 'll see 'em starve
    first.

Come.   [*Exeunt Lear and Cordelia, guarded.*

    Edm.   Come hither, captain; hark.
Take thou this note [*giving a paper*]; go follow them
    to prison:
One step I have advanced thee; if thou dost
As this instructs thee, thou dost make thy way

To noble fortunes: know thou this, that men   30
Are as the time is: to be tender-minded
Does not become a sword: thy great employment
Will not bear question: either say thou 'lt do 't,
Or thrive by other means.

    Capt.   I 'll do 't, my lord.

    Edm.   About it; and write happy when thou
         hast done.
Mark, I say, instantly; and carry it so
As I have set it down.

    Capt.   I cannot draw a cart, nor eat dried oats;
If it be man's work, I 'll do 't.   [*Exit.*

  Flourish.   *Enter* ALBANY, GONERIL, REGAN, *another*
            Captain, *and* Soldiers

    Alb.   Sir, you have shown to-day your valiant
         strain,   40
And fortune led you well: you have the captives
That were the opposites of this day's strife:
We do require them of you, so to use them
As we shall find their merits and our safety
May equally determine.

    Edm.   Sir, I thought it fit
To send the old and miserable king
To some retention and appointed guard;
Whose age has charms in it, whose title more,
To pluck the common bosom on his side,
And turn our impress'd lances in our eyes   50
Which do command them. With him I sent the
         queen;
My reason all the same; and they are ready
To-morrow, or at further space, to appear

Where you shall hold your session.   At this time
We sweat and bleed : the friend hath lost his friend ;
And the best quarrels, in the heat, are cursed
By those that feel their sharpness :
The question of Cordelia and her father
Requires a fitter place.

Alb.   Sir, by your patience,
I hold you but a subject of this war,   6●
Not as a brother.

Reg.   That 's as we list to grace him.
Methinks our pleasure might have been demanded,
Ere you had spoke so far.   He led our powers ;
Bore the commission of my place and person ;
The which immediacy may well stand up,
And call itself your brother.

Gon.   Not so hot :
In his own grace he doth exalt himself,
More than in your addition.

Reg.   In my rights,
By me invested, he compeers the best.

Gon.   That were the most, if he should husband
            you.   70

Reg.   Jesters do oft prove prophets.

Gon.   Holla, holla !
That eye that told you so look'd but a-squint.

Reg.   Lady, I am not well ; else I should answer
From a full-flowing stomach.   General,
Take thou my soldiers, prisoners, patrimony ;
Dispose of them, of me ; the walls are thine :
Witness the world, that I create thee here
My lord and master.

Gon.   Mean you to enjoy him ?

Alb. The let-alone lies not in your good will.

Edm. Nor in thine, lord.

Alb.   Half-blooded fellow, yes. 80

Reg. [*To Edmund*] Let the drum strike, and
  prove my title thine.

Alb. Stay yet; hear reason. Edmund, I arrest
  thee

On capital treason; and, in thine attaint,

This gilded serpent [*pointing to Goneril*]. For your
  claim, fair sister,

I bar it in the interest of my wife;

'T is she is sub-contracted to this lord,

And I, her husband, contradict your bans.

If you will marry, make your loves to me,

My lady is bespoke.

Gon.   An interlude!

Alb. Thou art arm'd, Gloucester: let the trumpet sound: 90

If none appear to prove upon thy head

Thy heinous, manifest, and many treasons,

There is my pledge [*throwing down a glove*]; I 'll
  prove it on thy heart,

Ere I taste bread, thou art in nothing less

Than I have here proclaim'd thee.

Reg.   Sick, O, sick!

Gon. [*Aside*] If not, I 'll ne'er trust medicine.

Edm. There 's my exchange [*throwing down a
  glove*]: what in the world he is

That names me traitor, villain-like he lies:

Call by thy trumpet: he that dares approach,

On him, on you, who not? I will maintain 100

My truth and honour firmly.

Alb. A herald, ho !

Edm. A herald, ho, a herald !

Alb. Trust to thy single virtue ; for thy soldiers,
All levied in my name, have in my name
Took their discharge.

Reg. My sickness grows upon me.

Alb. She is not well ; convey her to my tent.

[*Exit Regan, led.*

Enter a Herald

Come hither, herald, — Let the trumpet sound, —
And read out this.

Capt. Sound, trumpet ! [*A trumpet sounds.*

Her. [*Reads*] "If any man of quality or degree 110
within the lists of the army will maintain upon
Edmund, supposed Earl of Gloucester, that he is
a manifold traitor, let him appear by the third
sound of the trumpet : he is bold in his defence."

Edm. Sound ! [*First trumpet.*

Her. Again ! [*Second trumpet.*

Her. Again ! [*Third trumpet.*

[*Trumpet answers within.*

Enter Edgar, *at the third sound, armed, with a
trumpet before him*

Alb. Ask him his purposes, why he appears
Upon this call o' the trumpet.

Her. What are you ?
Your name, your quality ? and why you answer 120
This present summons ?

Edg. Know, my name is lost ;
By treason's tooth bare-gnawn and canker-bit :
Yet am I noble as the adversary

I come to cope.

    Alb.   Which is that adversary?

    Edg.   What 's he that speaks for Edmund Earl
          of Gloucester?

    Edm.   Himself: what say'st thou to him?

    Edg.   Draw thy sword,
That, if my speech offend a noble heart,
Thy arm may do thee justice: here is mine.
Behold, it is the privilege of mine honours,
My oath, and my profession: I protest,   130
Maugre thy strength, youth, place, and eminence,
Despite thy victor sword and fire-new fortune,
Thy valour and thy heart, thou art a traitor;
False to thy gods, thy brother, and thy father;
Conspirant 'gainst this high-illustrious prince;
And, from the extremest upward of thy head
To the descent and dust below thy foot,
A most toad-spotted traitor. Say thou "No,"
This sword, this arm, and my best spirits, are bent
To prove upon thy heart, whereto I speak,   140
Thou liest.

    Edm.   In wisdom I should ask thy name;
But, since thy outside looks so fair and warlike
And that thy tongue some say of breeding breathes,
What safe and nicely I might well delay
By rule of knighthood, I disdain and spurn:
Back do I toss these treasons to thy head;
With the hell-hated lie o'erwhelm thy heart;
Which, for they yet glance by and scarcely bruise,
This sword of mine shall give them instant way,
Where they shall rest for ever. Trumpets, speak! 150
        [*Alarums. They fight. Edmund falls.*

Alb.　Save him, save him !

Gon.　　　　　This is practice, Gloucester :
By the law of arms thou wast not bound to answer
An unknown opposite ; thou art not vanquish'd,
But cozen'd and beguiled.

Alb.　　　　　Shut your mouth, dame,
Or with this paper shall I stop it.　Hold, sir ;
Thou worse than any name, read thine own evil :
No tearing, lady ; I perceive you know it.

　　　　　　　　[*Gives the letter to Edmund.*

Gon.　Say, if I do, the laws are mine, not thine :
Who can arraign me for 't ?

Alb.　　　　　Most monstrous ! oh !
Know'st thou this paper ?

Gon.　　　Ask me not what I know.　[*Exit.* 160

Alb.　Go after her : she 's desperate ; govern her.

Edm.　What you have charged me with, that have I done ;
And more, much more ; the time will bring it out :
'T is past, and so am I.　But what art thou
That hast this fortune on me ?　If thou 'rt noble,
I do forgive thee.

Edg.　　　　　Let 's exchange charity.
I am no less in blood than thou art, Edmund ;
If more, the more thou hast wrong'd me.
My name is Edgar, and thy father's son.
The gods are just, and of our pleasant vices 170
Make instruments to plague us :
The dark and vicious place where thee he got
Cost him his eyes.

Edm.　　　　Thou hast spoken right, 't is true ;

The wheel is come full circle; I am here.

Alb. Methought thy very gait did prophesy
A royal nobleness: I must embrace thee:
Let sorrow split my heart, if ever I
Did hate thee or thy father!

Edg.   Worthy prince, I know 't.

Alb. Where have you hid yourself?
How have you known the miseries of your father? 180

Edg. By nursing them, my lord. List a brief
          tale;
And when 't is told, O, that my heart would burst!
The bloody proclamation to escape,
That follow'd me so near, — O, cur lives' sweetness!
That we the pain of death would hourly die
Rather than die at once! — taught me to shift
Into a madman's rags; to assume a semblance
That very dogs disdain'd: and in this habit
Met I my father with his bleeding rings,
Their precious stones new lost; became his guide, 190
Led him, begg'd for him, saved him from despair;
Never, — O fault! — reveal'd myself unto him,
Until some half-hour past, when I was arm'd:
Not sure, though hoping, of this good success,
I ask'd his blessing, and from first to last
Told him my pilgrimage: but his flaw'd heart, —
Alack, too weak the conflict to support! —
'Twixt two extremes of passion, joy and grief,
Burst smilingly.

Edm.   This speech of yours hath moved me,
And shall perchance do good: but speak you on; 200
You look as you had something more to say.

Alb. If there be more, more woeful, hold it in;

For I am almost ready to dissolve,
Hearing of this.

    Edg.   This would have seem'd a period
To such as love not sorrow; but another,
To amplify too much, would make much more,
And top extremity.
Whilst I was big in clamour came there in a
    man,
Who, having seen me in my worst estate,
Shunn'd my abhorr'd society; but then, finding   210
Who 't was that so endured, with his strong arms
He fasten'd on my neck, and bellow'd out
As he 'ld burst heaven; threw him on my father;
Told the most piteous tale of Lear and him
That ever ear received: which in recounting
His grief grew puissant, and the strings of life
Began to crack: twice then the trumpets sounded,
And there I left him tranced.

    Alb.   But who was this?
    Edg.   Kent, sir, the banish'd Kent; who in dis-
        guise
Follow'd his enemy king, and did him service   220
Improper for a slave.

       Enter a Gentleman, *with a bloody knife*

    Gent.   Help, help, O, help!
    Edg.   What kind of help?
    Alb.   Speak, man.
    Edg.   What means that bloody knife?
    Gent.   'T is hot, it smokes;
It came even from the heart of — O, she's dead!
    Alb.   Who dead? speak, man.

Gent. Your lady, sir, your lady: and her sister
By her is poisoned; she hath confess'd it.

Edm. I was contracted to them both: all three
Now marry in an instant.

Edg.   Here comes Kent.

Alb. Produce their bodies, be they alive or dead: 230
This judgement of the heavens, that makes us
       tremble,
Touches us not with pity.   [*Exit Gentleman.*

Enter Kent

                  O, is this he?
The time will not allow the compliment
Which very manners urges.

Kent.   I am come
To bid my king and master aye good night.
Is he not here?

Alb.   Great thing of us forgot!
Speak, Edmund, where 's the king? and where 's
       Cordelia?
See'st thou this object, Kent?

       [*The bodies of Goneril and Regan are brought in.*

Kent. Alack, why thus?

Edm.   Yet Edmund was beloved:
The one the other poison'd for my sake,   240
And after slew herself.

Alb. Even so. Cover their faces.

Edm. I pant for life: some good I mean to do,
Despite of mine own nature. Quickly send,
Be brief in it, to the castle; for my writ
Is on the life of Lear and on Cordelia:
Nay, send in time.

Alb. Run, run, O, run!

Edg. To who, my lord? Who hath the office? send

Thy token of reprieve.

Edm. Well thought on: take my sword, 250
Give it the captain.

Alb. Haste thee for thy life. [*Exit Edgar.*

Edm. He hath commission from thy wife and me

To hang Cordelia in the prison, and

To lay the blame upon her own despair,

That she fordid herself.

Alb. The gods defend her! Bear him hence
awhile. [*Edmund is borne off.*

Re-enter LEAR, *with* CORDELIA *dead in his arms;*
EDGAR, Captain, *and others following*

Lear. Howl, howl, howl, howl! O, you are
men of stones:

Had I your tongues and eyes, I 'ld use them so

That heaven's vault should crack. She 's gone for
ever!

I know when one is dead, and when one lives; 260

She 's dead as earth. Lend me a looking-glass;

If that her breath will mist or stain the stone,

Why, then she lives.

Kent. Is this the promised end?

Edg. Or image of that horror?

Alb. Fall, and cease!

Lear. This feather stirs: she lives! if it be so,

It is a chance which does redeem all sorrows

That ever I have felt.

Kent. [*Kneeling*] O my good master!

Lear. Prithee, away.

Edg.   'T is noble Kent, your friend.

Lear. A plague upon you, murderers, traitors
          all!

I might have saved her; now she 's gone for ever! 270
Cordelia, Cordelia! stay a little.   Ha!
What is 't thou say'st?   Her voice was ever soft,
Gentle, and low, an excellent thing in woman.
I kill'd the slave that was a-hanging thee.

Capt. 'T is true, my lords, he did.

Lear.   Did I not, fellow?
I have seen the day, with my good biting falchion
I would have made them skip: I am old now,
And these same crosses spoil me.   Who are you?
Mine eyes are not o' the best: I 'll tell you straight.

Kent. If fortune brag of two she loved and
          hated,   280
One of them we behold.

Lear. This is a dull sight.   Are you not Kent?

Kent.   The same,
Your servant Kent.   Where is your servant Caius?

Lear. He 's a good fellow, I can tell you that;
He 'll strike, and quickly too: he 's dead and rotten.

Kent. No, my good lord; I am the very man, —

Lear. I 'll see that straight.

Kent. That, from your first of difference and
          decay,
Have follow'd your sad steps.

Lear.   You are welcome hither.

Kent. Nor no man else: all 's cheerless, dark,
          and deadly.   290

Your eldest daughters have fordone themselves,
And desperately are dead.

   Lear.   Ay, so I think.

   Alb.   He knows not what he says: and vain it is
That we present us to him.

   Edg.   Very bootless.

Enter a Captain

   Capt.   Edmund is dead, my lord.

   Alb.   That 's but a trifle here.
You lords and noble friends, know our intent.
What comfort to this great decay may come
Shall be applied: for us, we will resign,
During the life of this old majesty,
To him our absolute power: [*To Edgar and Kent*]
         you, to your rights;   300
With boot, and such addition as your honours
Have more than merited. All friends shall taste
The wages of their virtue, and all foes
The cup of their deservings. O, see, see!

   Lear.   And my poor fool is hang'd! No, no, no
         life!
Why should a dog, a horse, a rat, have life,
And thou no breath at all? Thou 'lt come no
         more,
Never, never, never, never, never!
Pray you, undo this button: thank you, sir.
Do you see this? Look on her, look, her lips,   310
Look there, look there!   [*Dies.*

   Edg.   He faints! My lord, my lord!

   Kent.   Break, heart; I prithee, break!

   Edg.   Look up, my lord.

Kent. Vex not his ghost : O, let him pass ! he
          hates him much
That would upon the rack of this tough world
Stretch him out longer.

Edg.   He is gone, indeed.

Kent. The wonder is, he hath endured so long :
He but usurp'd his life.

Alb.   Bear them from hence.   Our present busi-
          ness
Is general woe. [*To Kent and Edgar*] Friends of
          my soul, you twain
Rule in this realm, and the gored state sustain.   320

Kent. I have a journey, sir, shortly to go ;
My master calls me, I must not say no.

Edg. The weight of this sad time we must obey ;
Speak what we feel, not what we ought to say.
The oldest hath borne most : we that are young
Shall never see so much, nor live so long.

                          [*Exeunt, with dead march.*

NOTES

ABBREVIATIONS

Abbott	Abbott's *Shakespearian Grammar*.
F1	First Folio (1623) of Shakespeare's plays.
F2	Second Folio (1632).
F3	Third Folio (1663 and 1664).
F4	Fourth Folio (1685).
Ff	The four Folios.
Kellner . . .	Kellner's *Historical Outlines of English Syntax*.
O. E.	Old English (Anglo-Saxon).
M. E. . . .	Middle English.
E. E.	Elizabethan English.
Mod. E. . . .	Modern English.
Q1	First Quarto (1608) of *King Lear*.
Q2	Second Quarto (1608 [?]1619).
Qq	The two Quartos.

For the meaning of words not given in these notes, the student is referred to the Glossary at the end of the volume.

The numbering of the lines corresponds to that of the Globe edition; this applies also to the scenes in prose.

Dramatis Personæ. This list is not in the Quartos or Folios. It was first given by Rowe (1709).

The division into acts and scenes is not marked in the Quartos.

ACT I — SCENE 1

The first scene of *King Lear* is of unusual importance. It both enacts the events on which the whole play is founded and brings out prominently the characters of all the principal actors. As a general rule the first scene is confined to giving information necessary for the understanding of the story; or it may, as in *Macbeth*, symbolize the drama. But in *King Lear* we are introduced at once, without any preparation, to the circumstance on which the story turns. The play as a whole is the representation of the effects of its opening incidents. Goethe considered this scene " irrational " in its want of preparation.

1. *affected*, had affection for, favored — the common meaning in Shakespeare. Cf. *Twelfth Night,* ii. 5. 28, " Maria once told me she did affect me."

5. *equalities are so weighed*, . . . , their shares are so balanced that close scrutiny will not show one to be better than the other. For *curiosity,* see Glossary.

11. *brazed*, hardened. Cf. " brazen-faced."

18. *proper*, handsome, as frequently in E. E.

20. *some year*, a year or so, about a year. See i. 2. 5.

32. *deserving*, *i.e.* to be better known by you.

33. *out*, abroad, in foreign lands. Cf. *Two Gentlemen of Verona,* i. 3. 7, " Put forth their sons to seek preferment out."

37. *our darker purpose*, our more secret design. Lear makes a full statement of what is already known by Kent and Gloucester.

39. *fast intent*, fixed intention; synonymous with " constant will " in l. 44.

41–46. *while we . . . now*. Omitted in the Qq.

54. *challenge*, claim as due : " where there are both the claims of nature (*i.e.* of birth) and merit." Cf. iv. 7. 31.

56. *wield the matter*, express.

62. *Beyond all manner of so much*, beyond all such comparisons.

65. *shadowy*, shady.

73. *names my very deed of love*, states exactly my love; expresses my love in very deed.

76. *the most precious square of sense*, the most exquisitely sensitive part of our nature.

77. *felicitate*, made happy. Regan's protestations are as forced as Goneril's. Her stilted phraseology betokens her insincerity. It is in ominous contrast to the simplicity of all that Cordelia can bring herself to say.

80. *more ponderous*. So the Ff. The Qq read *more richer.* The double comparative and superlative (*e.g.* l. 219) were commonly used in E. E. to give emphasis.

83. *validity*, value, worth; not in the modern sense of " good title."

85. *Although the last, not least.* This phrase occurs also in *Julius Cæsar*, iii. 1. 189, " Though last, not least in love " ; and there are several other instances of it in Elizabethan literature.

The Ff read, " Our last and least," which is preferred by some editors ; while the Qq have " Although the last, not least in our dear love," but omit from *to whose young love* to *interess'd.* The usual reading of this passage is therefore founded on both texts.

86. *milk*: referring to the rich pasture land of Burgundy.

87. *interess'd.* See Glossary for unusual words.

92. *Nothing will come of nothing.* Cf. i. 4. 145–146, and the proverb, *Ex nihilo nihil fit.*

95. *bond*, bounden duty, obligation.

97. *Good my lord*, a common form of transposition when the possessive is unemphatic. Cf. l. 122 and iii. 2. 61. The transposition occurs most commonly when the address begins a sentence ; contrast ii. 1. 111, iv. 2. 70 and 91.

102. *all*, exclusively, only. So also l. 106.

109. All that Cordelia says has the sincerity and abrupt simplicity inevitable on being goaded to give expression to feelings too heartfelt for words. It has been remarked by some critics that Cordelia's conduct bears in its tactless obstinacy traces of her father's headstrong nature. Coleridge, for instance, says : " There is something of disgust at the ruthless hypocrisy of her sisters, and some little faulty admixture of pride and sullenness in Cordelia's ' Nothing ' ; and her tone is well contrived, indeed, to lessen the glaring absurdity of Lear's conduct." But the prevailing note of her character is simplicity and truth. She feels so deeply that she is unable to frame a formal statement of her love for her father, and she is the less able to do so from her abhorrence of her sisters' rank insincerity.

110. Wounded vanity is the cause of Lear's anger. He had already determined on a division of his kingdom among his three daughters. He says definitely, on his very entrance, " we *have* divided in three our kingdom," and Kent and Gloucester have already discussed two of the shares. But that his vanity may be ministered unto, he wishes to hear the professions of his daughters' love. " The trial is but a trick," says Coleridge ; " the grossness of the old king's rage is in part the natural result of a silly trick suddenly and most unexpectedly baffled and disappointed."

112. *Hecate,* the goddess in classical mythology of enchantments and sorcery. In the Middle Ages she was regarded as the queen of witches. Cf. *Macbeth,* ii. 1. 52 and iii. 5. The word is pronounced as a dissyllable in Shakespeare.

113. *operation of the orbs,* influence of the stars.

116. *property,* equivalent to " identity." Cf. *proper,* iv. 2. 60.

119. *generation,* generally said to mean " offspring," as in the phrase " generation of vipers," *St. Matthew,* iii. 7, etc. It is plausibly suggested by Mr. W. J. Craig, however, that *generation* may here mean parents, as *progeny* does in *Coriolanus,* i. 8. 12. " Though Purchas in his *Pilgrimes* has a curious passage mentioning different kinds of cannibalism, he does not mention eating of children by their parents, nor do I know any reference to it. On the other hand, Herodotus tells us that the Scythians ate their aged and impotent relations, and Chapman in *Byron's Tragedy,* iv. 1, has the following passage : ' to teach . . . The Scythians to inter not *eat* their parents.' "

125–126. *to set my rest On her kind nursery.* This appears to have a double meaning. " To set one's rest " is a phrase used in the game of primero, meaning " to stake all upon the cards in one's hand," and hence it came to mean generally to stake one's all. *To set my rest on her kind nursery* would therefore mean " to rely absolutely on her care." But it is probable that Shakespeare had the simpler interpretation also in view, viz. " to find rest for my old age with her." There is a similar usage in *Romeo and Juliet,* v. 3. 110, " O here Will I set up my everlasting rest " ; and in this the phrase cannot well have the first meaning exclusively.

126. *nursery,* nursing.

Hence, and avoid my sight! Addressed to Cordelia.

130. *digest,* divide, dispose of. See Glossary.

131. Let her pride find her a husband, as she won't have a dowry to do so.

133. *effects,* signs, manifestations. Cf. ii. 4. 182.

138. *additions,* titles, as commonly in Shakespeare. Cf. ii. 2. 26 and v. 3. 68.

141. *This coronet* : referring to the one originally intended for Cordelia.

145. *make from,* get out of the way of.

146. *the fork,* the barbed arrow-head.

147. " Almost the first burst of that noble tide of passion which runs through the play is in the remonstrance of Kent to his royal master on the injustice of his sentence against his youngest daughter: ' Be Kent unmannerly, when Lear is mad!' This manly plainness, which draws down on him the displeasure of the unadvised king, is worthy of the fidelity with which he adheres to his fallen fortunes " (Hazlitt).

151. *Reverse thy doom* (change your sentence) is the reading of the Qq; the Ff have *Reserve thy state*, retain your royal power.

153. *answer my life my judgement*, let my life answer for my judgment.

161. *blank*, literally the white centre of a target.

163. *swear'st*, adjurest, swearest by. For the omission of the preposition, cf. ii. 2. 88, and see Abbott, § 200.

175. *our potency made good*, our royal authority being maintained.

" Kent's opposition . . . displays Lear's moral incapability of resigning the sovereign power in the very act of disposing of it " (Coleridge).

177. *diseases*, discomforts, absence of ease.

187. *approve*, justify, confirm, as commonly in E. E. Cf. ii. 2. 167, ii. 4. 187, and iii. 5. 12.

191. *Here's France and Burgundy*. For the common Shakespearean use of a singular verb preceding a plural subject, see Abbott, § 335.

193-194. *you who . . . Hath.* A singular verb often follows a relative whose antecedent is plural. Cf. *stirs*, ii. 4. 277, and see Abbott, § 247.

199. *so, i.e.* " dear," with the meaning " of high price."

201. *that little seeming substance.* A difficult phrase. Johnson takes *seeming* in the sense of *beautiful*, *little seeming* being thus equivalent to *ugly;* Steevens and Schmidt give it the sense of *specious;* while Wright understands it to mean *in appearance.* The second interpretation is the best. There appears to be little point in " that substance which is but little in appearance," and Johnson's explanation is forced.

203. *like*, please, as commonly in E. E. Cf. ii. 2. 96.

205. *owes*, possesses.

209. *makes not up*, does not decide. " There is no choice on such conditions."

212. *make such a stray*, stray so far.

213. *To match.* For the omission of *as*, see Abbott, § 281, and cf. l. 220.

beseech. i.e. I beseech. " The Elizabethan authors objected to scarcely any ellipsis, provided the deficiency could be easily supplied from the context." See Abbott, §§ 399–401. Cf. ii. 4. 42 and v. 1. 68.

218. *argument*, theme, subject; as commonly in E. E.

223. *monsters it*, makes it monstrous. A similar use occurs in *Coriolanus*, ii. 2. 81: "idly sit To hear my nothings monster'd."

224. *Fall'n into taint*, (must have) fallen into decay.

227. *for*, because.

234. *still-soliciting*, ever-begging. Cf. i. 4. 353, ii. 4. 107, and *The Tempest*, i. 2. 229, " the still-vex'd Bermoothes."

242. *regards*, considerations. Cf. l. 251.

243. *the entire point*, the sole consideration, the object of pure love.

253–264. France's tender declaration appears the more beautiful by contrast with the prosaic selfish remarks of his rival, who has amply merited Cordelia's " Peace be with Burgundy ! "

261. *waterish*, well-watered; used in contempt.

262. *unprized*, beyond price. " The suffix *-ed* in past participles had in E. E. gone far to acquire the sense of ' what may be done ' in addition to that of ' what has been done.' For the most part this heightened meaning occurs in combination with a *negative prefix* " (Herford). Cf. *untented*, i. 4. 322; *unnumber'd*, iv. 6. 21; and *undistinguish'd*, iv. 6. 278. *Unprized* may, however, be used here in the simple sense of " not prized."

264. *here* and *where* are used as nouns.

271. Cordelia from the first has seen through her sisters' deceit; but pity for her father, despite the wrong he has done her, at last forces her to speak plainly. Note how she has gradually worked herself up to this declaration.

The jewels of our father, in apposition with " you."

with wash'd eyes, *i.e.* with tears.

275. *professed*, full of professions. For this active sense of the past participle, cf. *better spoken*, iv. 6. 10, and see Kellner, § 408.

277. *prefer*, recommend, direct; as commonly in Shakespeare.

279. As Hazlitt remarks, the true character of the two eldest daughters, who have not spoken since the very beginning of the love test, breaks out in Regan's answer to Cordelia, " their hatred of advice being in proportion to their determination to do wrong, and to their hypocritical pretensions to do right." But most striking of all is Goneril's odious self-righteousness in telling her sister " You have obedience scanted."

281. *At*, used in statements of price or value ; hence, " as an alms of fortune."

282. This line presents some difficulty. It is best rendered thus, " And well deserve that absence of affection from your father which you have shown towards him." It is possible, however, to take *want* as referring specifically to the dowry, and in this case, as Wright says, *the want that you have wanted* would be an instance of a verb and its cognate accusative.

286–312. The closing dialogue of this scene shows Goneril to be the stronger and more assertive of the two sisters. It is she who broaches the discussion of their position, and declares, when Regan purposes merely to " think " on their policy, that they must strike while the iron is hot. But the dialogue is also of considerable importance in the structure of the play, as it serves to prepare us for Lear's fate. The very waywardness to which they owe their fortunes they make a reason for their treacherous design to deprive him of authority. Lear's faults, it appears, are not due to senility, though this has aggravated them, for he " hath ever but slenderly known himself," and " the best and soundest years of his life have been but rash."

Note the change from verse to prose. We pass with it from the higher plane of passion to that of underhand scheming.

295. *grossly*, plainly, evidently.

304. *like*, likely. Cf. iv. 2. 19.

310. *offend*, harm.

SCENE 2

In the second scene we turn to the minor web of the play, the Gloucester story, which has already been indicated by the opening conversation of the previous scene. This underplot is in striking parallelism with the main story, and each in turn acts as a foil to the other. See Introduction, p. xv.

1. *Thou, nature, art my goddess*, as he is a natural son.

3. *Stand in the plague of custom*, be subject to the injustice of custom.

4. *curiosity*, scruples. See Glossary.

6. *Lag of*, later than.

8. *generous*: used in the obsolete sense of " gallant," " noble," " natural to one of noble birth or spirit."

21. *top the*. The commonly accepted emendation of the old reading *to the*. It is supported by several other passages in Shakespeare, *e.g.* v. 3. 207.

24. *subscribed*, surrendered; literally " signed away." Cf. *subscription*, iii. 2. 18.

25. *exhibition*, allowance.

26. *Upon the gad*, suddenly, as if pricked by a gad (*i.e.* a goad). Cf. " upon the spur of the moment."

32. *terrible*, terrified.

48. *policy and reverence of age*, *i.e.* policy of reverencing age. Cf. other instances of this figure of speech — hendiadys — in ll. 191–192, " image and horror," and i. 4. 364, " This milky gentleness and course."

49. *the best of our times*, the best part of our lives, as in i. 1. 298 and i. 2. 122.

53. *suffered*, allowed, endured.

89. *where*, whereas, as commonly in Shakespeare.

93. *wrote*. Cf. *mistook*, ii. 4. 12; *fell*, iv. 6. 54; and see Abbott, §§ 343, 344.

94. *pretence of danger*, dangerous intention. Cf. i. 4. 75.

106. *wind me into him*, worm yourself into his confidence. *Me* is an ethical dative. Cf. iv. 6. 88.

107–108. *I would unstate myself*, . . . I should give up my position and dignity in order to be certain how matters stand.

109. *convey*, discharge, carry out; commonly with a notion of secrecy.

111–127. As Wright has pointed out, this passage may have been suggested by the eclipses of the sun and moon in September and October, 1605. See Introduction, p. ix.

There is perhaps a reference to the Gunpowder Plot (Nov. 5, 1605) in the words " in palaces, treason " and " machinations, hollowness, treachery."

113–114. *though the wisdom of nature* . . . " Though natural philosophy can give account of eclipses, yet we feel their consequences " (Johnson).

119–124. *This villain* . . . *graves*. Omitted in the Qq.

120–121. *bias of nature*, *i.e.* natural bias or inclination.

126–127. Gloucester's superstitiousness has made him an easy prey to Edmund's cunning. His reference to the injustice done to Kent gives point to the folly of his own credulity. Lear was no more unjust to the " noble and true-hearted Kent " than Gloucester himself is to Edgar.

128. *foppery,* folly, the original meaning of *fop* being a "fool." Cf. *foppish,* i. 4. 182.

133-134. *spherical predominance,* synonymous with "planetary influence."

136. *divine thrusting on,* impulse from above.

146. *pat he comes like the catastrophe* . . . An allusion to the clumsy structure of the early comedies, in which the conclusion seemed to come by chance at the very moment it was wanted.

148. *Tom o' Bedlam.* See ii. 3. 14. Thanks to Edmund's treachery, Tom o' Bedlam is yet to be Edgar's cue.

157. *succeed,* ensue, turn out; used, like the noun success, indifferently of good or bad consequences. Cf. "this good success," v. 3. 194.

157-166. *as of* . . . *Come, come.* Omitted in the Ff.

161. *diffidences,* suspicions, distrust; now used only of distrust of one's self.

161-162. *dissipation of cohorts.* Probably corrupt; the phrase does not suit the context, and neither of the words occurs elsewhere in Shakespeare. Of the emendations that have been suggested, the best is "disputation of consorts" (Craig).

164-165. *a sectary astronomical,* a devotee of astrology.

178-179. *with the mischief* . . . *allay,* would scarcely be allayed even by doing harm to your person.

181-187. *I pray you* . . . *Armed, brother!* Omitted in the Qq.

185. *ye* is strictly a nominative, but it is frequently used in E. E., and especially by the dramatists, instead of the objective *you.* Cf. i. 4. 324 and ii. 2. 50.

191-192. *image and horror.* See note on l. 48, above.

198. *practices,* plots, artifices; a common sense in E. E. Cf. ii. 1. 75, 109, etc., and *practised,* iii. 2. 57, etc.

SCENE 3

This scene takes up the main thread of the story and follows directly on the closing dialogue of scene 1. In the interval Goneril is fully instated in her new power, and has gained confidence in her ability to deprive Lear of the remnants of his authority.

1. *for chiding of.* See note on ii. 1. 41.

10. *answer,* answer for. Cf. i. 1. 153.

20. *With checks as flatteries*, . . . The line is best rendered, " With rebukes instead of flatteries, when flatteries are seen to feed their folly." *As* has the force of " instead of " rather than of " as well as." *They* in the second half of the line is sometimes taken to refer to " old fools," *i.e.* " when old fools are seen to be deceived." Possibly the line is corrupt. Ll. 16–20 are omitted in the Ff.

24. Goneril has more initiative than her sister. It is she who " breeds occasion " to humble Lear completely, and she dictates her sister's policy also.

SCENE 4

Lear comes to realize the position in which he has placed himself. Hitherto he has appeared merely hasty, wayward, and imperious, but now we begin to see the better elements of his character. The pathos of his lot is emphasized by the solicitude of Kent and the significant utterances of the Fool, and he wins our sympathy.

2. *defuse*, confuse, hence disguise; an obsolete form of *diffuse*.

12. *What dost thou profess?* What is thy profession? Note the play on the word in Kent's reply.

16. *converse*, associate; the common meaning in Shakespeare.

18. *to eat no fish*. Warburton explained this as a reference to the Roman Catholic custom of eating fish on Fridays. " In Queen Elizabeth's time the Papists were esteemed enemies to the government. Hence the proverbial phrase of ' He's an honest man and eats no fish,' to signify he's a friend to the government and a Protestant." Capell explained it as meaning that Kent was " no lover of such meagre diet as fish." Cf. *2 Henry IV*, iv. 3. 99; but this gives the phrase little point. If Warburton's explanation is correct, Kent uses this phrase as an indirect way of expressing his loyalty.

26. *Who*. See Abbott, § 274. Cf. iv. i. 47.

35. *curious*, complicated. See Glossary.

51. *clotpoll*, blockhead, " clod-pate." The form " clodpole " occurs in *Twelfth Night*, iii. 4. 208.

59. *roundest*, plainest. Cf. *Othello*, 1. 3. 90, " a round unvarnished tale "; and *Twelfth Night*, ii. 3. 102, " I must be round with you."

64. For the construction, see note on iii. 2. 13.

72–78. We have here the first indication of Lear's finer qualities. Though hasty in temper, he is at least generous. Sooner than believe in any purposed unkindness, he blames his own suspicions.

73. *faint*, cold, indifferent, half-hearted.

75. *pretence*, offer. It is commonly synonymous with *purpose* (*e.g.* i. 2. 95), but here it has a stronger force.

77–78. *this two days*, a common Shakespearean usage.

81. In Lear's " No more of that," etc., we detect the first hint of his regret for his treatment of Cordelia.

107. The Fool plays a very important part in *King Lear*. He is not to be regarded as an accessory suited to the public taste, and he has a higher function than merely to relieve the intensity of the situation. His rambling remarks do relax the strain on our feelings, but their chief effect is, by reason of their deep significance, to heighten the pathos. See Introduction p. xvii.

coxcomb, the Fool's cap.

111. *you were best*, a common construction in E. E. It is a corrupted survival of an O. E. usage, in which *you* is the dative and the whole phrase is impersonal. That Shakespeare used *you* as a nominative may be seen from such lines as " I were better to be eaten to death," *2 Henry IV*, i. 2. 245, and " She were better love a dream," *Twelfth Night*, ii. 2. 27. Cf. iii. 4. 105.

114. *on's*, a euphonic contraction of *of his*. See Abbott, § 182. Cf. i. 5. 20, and *on't*, l. 168 below.

117. *nuncle*, the customary address of a fool to his master; a contraction of *mine uncle*.

125. *Lady the brach*, *i.e.* the bitch-hound. Cf. iii. 6. 72.

131. *showest*, seemest to have. Cf. *shows* (appears), l. 265.

133. *owest*, *i.e.* ownest. Cf. i. 1. 205.

134. *goest*, *i.e.* walkest, as often in Shakespeare.

135. *Learn more than thou trowest.* Don't believe all you hear.

136. *Set*, stake, offer wagers at dice. Cf. *Richard II*, iv. 1. 57, " Who sets me else? by heaven I'll throw at all " (*i.e.* who else lays down stakes, challenges me). The meaning seems to be, " offer lower wagers than your dice-throws bring to you, than you win at a throw," or " stake lower than the chances of your game."

143–144. *Can you make no use of nothing?* The Fool suggests that his lines have a significance which Lear has not realized. Kent is the first to see that " this is not altogether fool."

154–169. *That lord . . . snatching.* Omitted in the Ff. Johnson suggests that there was perhaps a political reason in their omission, " as they seemed to censure the monopolies "; but this objection does not apply to the Fool's verses.

The first two verses are explained by a passage in the old play, *King Leir*. See Introduction, pp. xiii.

167. *monopoly.* " A satire on the gross abuses of monopolies at that time, and the corruption and avarice of the courtiers, who commonly went shares with the patentee " (Warburton).

out, taken out, granted to me.

176–177. *thou borest thy ass on thy back.* An allusion to Æsop's fable.

179. *like myself, i.e.* like a fool. He again insists on his seriousness.

181–184. " There never was a time when fools were less in favour; and the reason is, that they were never so little wanted, for wise men now supply their place " (Johnson).

182. *foppish,* foolish. Cf. *foppery,* i. 2. 128.

191–192. These two lines, like several others farther on, are probably taken from an old song. Steevens points out a similar couplet in Heywood's *Rape of Lucrece* (1608):

> " When Tarquin first in court began,
>   And was approved king,
> Some men for sudden joy 'gan weep,
>   But I for sorrow sing."

208. *frontlet,* literally a band worn on the forehead; here used metaphorically for " frown."

211–212. *an O,* a mere cipher, of no value unless joined to a figure.

219. *shealed,* shelled. This form survives in Scotch and in provincial English.

221. *other, i.e.* others. *Other* is now plural only when it is used attributively (*e.g.* other men). In O. E. *other* was used in both numbers, the plural form being *othre.* The final *e* was dropped in time; hence the E. E. plural form *other,* which is found in the authorized version of the Bible along with the modern form *others* (see *St. Luke*, xxiii. 32).

227. *put on*, encourage. Cf. note on ii. 1. 101.

228. *allowance*, approval.

229–233. *nor the redresses sleep*. . . , nor would the punishment (for the riotous conduct of your retinue) fail to be put into operation, which punishment, given to preserve soundly the peace of the commonwealth, might in its course give you an affront that would be a shame under other circumstances, but which under these necessarily would be called a well chosen procedure.

230. *tender*, care, tendance. Cf. *1 Henry IV*, v. 4. 49, " thou makest some tender of my life."

weal, commonwealth.

233. The somewhat embarrassed syntax and the indirect expressions betoken Goneril's hesitation. Her statements have been direct enough while she merely objected to Lear's conduct. Now for the first time she threatens him to his face.

236. *it*. This possessive form is of fairly common occurrence in E. E. Cf. iv. 2. 32. The ordinary neuter possessive in E. E. is *his*. *Its* is not found in Spenser, and occurs very seldom in Shakespeare (*e.g. Henry VIII*, i. 1. 18), but it began about this time to replace *his*. For the form *it*, cf. the West Midland uninflected genitive *hit*. See Abbott, § 228.

Sir Joshua Reynolds remarks on the incoherent words with which Shakespeare often finishes this Fool's speeches: " We may suppose that they had a custom of taking off the edge of too sharp a speech by covering it hastily with the end of an old song, or any glib nonsense that came into mind." This may apply to " Whoop, Jug! I love thee " in l. 245; but in the present case there is a very pertinent meaning in the " glib nonsense."

237. A similar figure of speech occurs in Spenser's story of Lear, *Faërie Queene*, ii. 10. 30. See Appendix A.

245. *Jug*, a colloquial name for a sweetheart or mistress, derivatively a substitute for the feminine name Joan or Joanna. According to Steevens, " Whoop, Jug! I love thee " is a quotation from an old song.

248. *notion*, understanding, intellect; the only meaning of the word in Shakespeare.

Lear's awakening is so sudden that he can hardly believe his senses. This reference to his intellect is prophetic. It is the first hint of his madness.

252–254. On hearing the Fool's reply, Lear says he should like to know if he is only Lear's shadow. His marks of sovereignty, his knowledge, and his reason all tell him that he is Lear himself, and therefore the father of Goneril, but he may be falsely persuaded to that effect. This passage is omitted in the Ff.

Note the change, from this juncture, in Lear's attitude toward the Fool.

255. *Which*, whom. See Abbott, § 266.

258. *admiration*, astonishment, wonder.

265. *Shows*, appears.

epicurism, sensuality, though found in E. E. also in the specialized sense of " gluttony."

267. *graced*, honorable.

269. Goneril admits her own masterfulness. Her threats are no longer hesitating or cloaked in obscure phraseology.

271. *depend*, attend on you, be dependants. For the construction, see Abbott, § 354.

277. Goneril's objection to the conduct of Lear's servants is no doubt justified. We are ready to believe that, on the principle of like master like man, they are impetuous and noisy. Goneril has the ability to avail herself of every opportunity of criticism, and to turn every fault, however small, into an excuse for her conduct.

283. *sea-monster*. Cf. iv. 2. 50. This is often said to be the hippopotamus, which in Egyptian tradition was a monster of impiety and ingratitude. But as the hippopotamus does not live in the *sea*, some commentators think the reference is to the whale. Mr. Craig suggests that Shakespeare had not " any special kind of monster in his thoughts, but was thinking of those monsters of classical mythology slain by Hercules and by Perseus in defence of beauty — these stories were then very popular." Cf. *Merchant of Venice*, iii. 2. 57.

285. *choice and rarest*, *i.e.* choicest and rarest, the superlative form applying to both; a common construction in E. E.

290. *engine*, *i.e.* an engine of torture, the rack.

294. *dear*, precious. *Dear* is used regularly in E. E. to express extremeness or intensity: thus " my dearest foe " = my greatest foe.

302. *derogate*, deteriorated, debased.

305. *thwart*, perverse.

disnatured, unnatural.

316. With characteristic masterfulness and deceit, Goneril had given orders for the number of Lear's followers to be decreased before desiring him " a little to disquantity his train." Before the threat was uttered, it had been carried out.

322. *untented*, incurable; literally, not to be probed by a tent. See i. 1. 262.

324. *Beweep*, *i.e.* if you beweep.

328. *comfortable*, ready to comfort. Cf. ii. 2. 171.

334. Albany appears, at the beginning of the play, to be a mere puppet in the hands of Goneril. He has his qualms of conscience at her conduct, but is very reluctant to pass any criticism, and he is stopped short before he can do more than suggest his disapproval. But events show that he is not wanting in moral force.

345–356. *This man . . . unfitness*, omitted in the Qq.

347. *At point*, in readiness, fully equipped. Cf. iii. 1. 33.

348. *buzz*, whisper, rumor.

353. *taken*, *i.e.* by the harms.

360. *full*, the adjective for the adverb. Cf. iv. 6. 3.

366. *attask'd*, taken to task, blamed. The Ff read " at task."

369. Malone compares Shakespeare's *Sonnets*, ciii :

> " Were it not sinful then, striving to mend,
>   To mar the subject that before was well? "

371. *the event*, the issue; time will show.

SCENE 5

This scene contains little of importance to the action of the story. Its purpose is to convey a fuller sense of Lear's misfortune; and this is achieved by the subtle prattle of the Fool (who knows better than Lear how Regan will act), Lear's own involuntary reference to Cordelia (l. 24), and, above all, his foreboding of madness.

1. *Gloucester*, probably the city, not the earl, whose castle was in its vicinity.

2. *Acquaint my daughter no further*. Contrast Goneril's instruction to Oswald in the preceding scene.

8. *brains*, used in the singular, as elsewhere occasionally in Shakespeare. Cf. *All's Well*, iii. 2. 16, " The brains of my Cupid's knocked out."

11–12. *I.e.* as you have no brains, you run no risk of kibes and therefore of needing to wear slippers.

kibes, sores on the heels; also chilblains.

15. *kindly* : used equivocally with the two meanings " with kindness " and " after her nature."

crab, crab apple.

25. *I did her wrong.* " This and Lear's subsequent ejaculations to himself are in verse; his distracted replies to the Fool in prose " (Herford).

36. *Be* : generally used in E. E. to express doubt (*a*) in questions, and (*b*) after verbs of thinking. See Abbott, § 299.

38. *the seven stars,* the Pleiades.

43. *To take't again perforce!* " He is meditating on the resumption of his royalty." This is the interpretation of Johnson, which is better than that of Steevens, to the effect that he is thinking of his daughter's having so violently deprived him of the privileges she had agreed to grant him.

50. " The mind's own anticipation of madness! The deepest tragic notes are often struck by a half sense of an impending blow " (Coleridge).

ACT II — SCENE 1

The minor thread of the story is again taken up, and is now interwoven with the principal one. Edmund, after succeeding in his plot to turn his father against Edgar, fitly joins the party of Regan and Cornwall.

1. *Save thee,* i.e. God save thee — a common form of salutation.

8. *news* : used indifferently in E. E. in the singular (as in 89, 90) and plural (as here).

9. *ear-kissing,* whispered. *arguments,* cf. i. 1. 218.

12. *toward,* near at hand. Cf. iii. 3. 20 and iv. 6. 213.

One of Lear's objects in dividing his kingdom, it will be remembered, was " that future strife may be prevented now " (i. 1. 46).

19. *of a queasy question,* requiring delicate handling; *queasy,* strictly " squeamish," " sickly."

20. *briefness,* promptitude.

28. *Upon his party.* The usual explanation of this line is that Edmund, in order to confuse his brother and alarm him to a speedy flight, asks Edgar whether he has not spoken against the Duke of Cornwall, and then, reversing the question, asks whether he has not spoken against the Duke of Albany. *Upon his party* elsewhere in Shakespeare invariably means " on his side " (cf. iv. 6. 256). But this is not an insuperable obstacle to the simpler interpretation, " Have you said nothing upon the party formed by him against the Duke of Albany?"

33. *Yield . . . here.* Spoken loudly, so that Gloucester may hear.

41. Edmund knows how to turn to account Gloucester's superstitiousness.

Mumbling of. The preposition *of* shows *mumbling* to have the force of a verbal noun. The full construction would be *on mumbling of;* cf. *for chiding of,* i. 3. 1. But in E. E. the verbal noun was influenced by the present participle; hence the omission of the anterior preposition here, and of the posterior preposition in v. 3. 274, *a-hanging thee.*

48. *bend*, direct. Cf. iv. 2. 74.

51. *loathly*, with abhorrence, loathingly.

52. *motion*, a fencing term for " attack," " thrust."

54. *lanced* (for the Quarto's *lancht*). The Ff have *latch'd,* caught.

61. *arch*, master, chief; a substantival use of the adjective.

67. *pight*, determined, resolved; an old past tense of *pitch.* Cf. *Troilus and Cressida,* v. 10. 24:

> " You vile abominable tents,
> Thus proudly pight upon our Phrygian plains."

curst, angry, sharp; the same word as *cursed.*

69. *Thou unpossessing bastard.* " Thus the secret poison in Edmund's own heart steals forth; and then observe poor Gloucester's 'Loyal and *natural* boy,' as if praising the crime of Edmund's birth " (Coleridge).

unpossessing: since a bastard cannot inherit.

75. *practice*. Cf. note on i. 2. 198.

77. *If they not thought*: a common construction in E. E. The auxiliary was not required when the negative preceded the verb. See Abbott, § 305, and cf. iv. 2. 2.

79. *fasten'd*, determined.

80. *got*, *i.e.* begot. Cf. iii. 4. 151.

87. *capable*, legally able to inherit. The *New English Dictionary* gives the following quotation from Guillim's *Heraldry* (1610), " Bastards are not capable of their fathers patrimony."

99. *consort*, company, set; accented on the last syllable.

101. *put on*, incited to.

102. *expense*, the spending, expenditure.

103. Regan takes her cue from Goneril. She is perhaps even more repulsive than her sister, for she is cringingly spiteful, and lacks courage as well as initiative. " Regan is not, in fact, a greater monster than Goneril, but she has the power of casting more venom " (Coleridge).

108. *'Twas my duty*: the crowning touch of Edmund's sublime hypocrisy.

109. *bewray*, reveal, with no sense of perfidy, as now. Cf. iii. 6. 118.

his practice, Edgar's plot.

113. *make your own purpose . . .*, carry out your own design, availing yourself as you please of my power.

115. *virtue and obedience doth*. A singular verb is common in E. E. after two nouns which enforce the same idea or are not meant to be thought of separately. Cf. iii. 4. 150 and 158.

121–130. Regan interposes to explain on her own account the reason of their visit. It is not necessary to hold that Regan interrupts Cornwall, much less that the interruption is " characteristic." She could not behave to Cornwall in the overbearing manner that Goneril does to Albany. Cornwall's remark is complete in itself, and Regan merely takes it up and adds to it, as she is the person mainly concerned in their visit. It was to her that both her father and sister had written. Moreover, we are distinctly told in the following scene that it is the Duke's disposition " not to be rubb'd nor stopp'd." Cf. also ii. 4. 94–96.

121. *threading dark-eyed night*. Note the pun. There is another instance of it in *King John*, v. 4. 11, " Unthread the rude eye of rebellion."

122. *poise*, weight, moment.

125. *which*. The antecedent is some such word as " letters " understood. The relative is used with great freedom in E. E.

127. *attend dispatch*, await to be dispatched. Cf. ii. 4. 36.

SCENE 2

The events of this scene are not important in themselves, though they emphasize Regan's and Cornwall's hostility to Lear. They are essentially preparatory to the fourth scene of this act.

1. *dawning*, morning.

9. *Lipsbury pinfold*. This phrase remains unexplained. The suggestion received with most favor is that " It may be a coined name, and it is just possible that it might mean the teeth, as being the pinfold within the *lips* "(Nares); cf. ἔρκος ὀδόντων. This explanation, however, is not entirely satisfactory. There is probably an allusion to some place of which record has been lost.

16–17. *three-suited*. . . . Some of Kent's allusions are explained by a passage in Ben Jonson's *Silent Woman*, iii. 1, in which a rich wife rails at her husband in the following terms: " Who gives you your maintenance, I pray you? Who allows you your horse-meat, and man's meat? your three suits of apparel a year? your four pair of stockings, one silk, three worsted? " Cf. also Middleton's *Phœnix*, iv. 3 (quoted by Steevens): " How's this? Am I used like a hundred-pound gentleman? " *Three-suited*, menials being generally allowed three suits a year; *hundred-pound*, a term of reproach implying poverty; *worsted-stocking*, likewise implying poverty or menial employment, silk stockings being invariably worn by people who could afford them.

18. *lily-livered*. Cf. iv. 2. 50, " Milk-livered man." The liver being regarded as the seat of courage, a bloodless liver was said to betoken cowardice. Cf. *2 Henry IV*, iv. 3. 113: " left the liver white and pale, which is the badge of pusillanimity and cowardice."

action-taking, settling disputes by law rather than by the sword; hence likewise " cowardly," " mean-spirited."

19. *glass-gazing*, looking in the mirror, foppish.

superserviceable, above his work (Wright). Johnson and Schmidt give " over-officious."

20. *one-trunk-inheriting*, possessing enough for one trunk only. For *inheriting*, see Glossary.

26. *addition*. See note on i. 1. 138.

34–35. *sop o' the moonshine*: perhaps an allusion to an old dish of eggs cooked in oil, called " eggs in moonshine," referred to in Gabriel Harvey's *Pierce's Supererogation* (1593) and other contemporary works.

35. *cullionly*, rascally, wretched, like a cullion.

35–36. *barber-monger*, a frequenter of barbers' shops, a fop.

39. *vanity the puppet*. " Vanity " was a common character in the old *Moralities*.

41. *carbonado,* slash, hack; literally, make into a carbonado, *i.e.* a piece of flesh cut crosswise and grilled.

42. *come your ways,* come on.

45. *neat,* foppish, spruce.

48. *With you.* Kent purposely takes Edmund's "matter" in the sense of "cause of quarrel."

goodman, a familiar name of address, used contemptuously.

49. *flesh,* initiate in bloodshed; primarily, to initiate in the taste of flesh, as hunting-dogs.

59. *disclaims in,* disowns.

69–70. *zed! thou unnecessary letter.* Cf. Ben Jonson's *English Grammar* (ed. Gifford and Cunningham, iii, p. 435): "*Z* is a letter often heard amongst us, but seldom seen," its place being commonly taken in writing by *S*. The letter *Z* was often omitted in the dictionaries of the time.

71. *unbolted, i.e.* unsifted; hence, coarse. "Unbolted mortar is mortar made of unsifted lime, and to break the lumps it is necessary to tread it by men in wooden shoes" (Tollet).

81. *intrinse,* intricate.

84. *turn their halcyon beaks* . . . An allusion to the old idea that the kingfisher, if hung up by the neck, always turned so as to face straight against the wind.

87. *epileptic,* distorted with a grin.

88. *Smile,* smile at. See note on i. 1. 163.

89–90. *Goose . . . Camelot.* Large flocks of geese were bred on Sarum Plain near Cadbury, in Somersetshire, the traditional site of Camelot; and defeated knights were required to report at King Arthur's Court there; but the connection between these allusions is obscure.

98. The keynote of Kent's character, and the source of all his troubles. Cf. ii. 4. 42.

101. *some,* with the force of the indefinite article, a survival of the O. E. *sum.*

103. *constrains the garb Quite from his nature,* carries the assumed manner to a wholly unnatural extent.

107. *These kind of knaves.* See Kellner, §§ 167–172.

109. *observants,* obsequious courtiers. Similarly *observance* = homage (*As You Like It,* v. 2. 102), and *observe* = to show respect to, as in "the observed of all observers" (*Hamlet,* iii. 1. 162). Note that *observants* is accented on the first syllable.

110. *nicely,* punctiliously. See Glossary.

112. *aspect*, accented on the second syllable, as always in Shakespeare. Both *aspect* and *influence* have an astrological reference.

120. *win your displeasure*, etc., *i.e.* win you in your displeasure to ask me to be a plain knave (*i.e.* a flatterer).

124. *upon his misconstruction*, through his misunderstanding me.

125. *conjunct*, in agreement with him. Cf. v. 1. 12.

128. *worthied him*, made him appear worthy.

129. *For him attempting who was self-subdued*, for attacking one who had not really been subdued by him, but who had fallen.

130. *in the fleshment of*, being fleshed with, made eager. Cf. note on l. 50.

133. *Ajax is their fool*: either, Ajax is a fool compared with them, *i.e.* is outdone by them in bragging; or, a man like the plain, blunt Ajax is the kind of man these rogues and cowards always try to make a fool of.

145. *colour*, sort, kind.

148–152. *His fault . . . punish'd with*. Omitted in the Ff, which read for l. 152, " The king his master needs must take it ill."

161. *rubb'd*, hindered, obstructed; a term in the game of bowls, the noun *rub* signifying anything that hinders a bowl's course. Cf. *King John*, iii. 4. 128:

" For even the breath of what I mean to speak
    Shall blow each dust, each straw, each little rub,
    Out of the path."

162. *watched*, kept awake. Cf. " o'er-watch'd," l. 177.

164. *out at heels*. Cf. " out at elbows."

167. *approve*, confirm, prove the truth of. Cf. i. 1. 186.

168–169. *out of heaven's . . . sun*, a proverbial expression for a change from better to worse. The earliest known instance of it occurs in the *Proverbs of John Heywood*, 1546 (ed. Sharman, 1874, p. 115):

" In your running from him to me, yee runne
    Out of God's blessing into the warme sunne."

Cf. also Lyly's *Euphues* (ed. Arber, pp. 196 and 320). But the origin of this " common saw " is not known. Hanmer said it was applied to those who are turned out of house and home to the open weather, and Johnson suggested that it was used of men dismissed from a hospital or house of charity. A recent explanation — that " the proverb refers to the haste of the congregation to leave the shelter of the church immediately after the priest's benediction, running from God's blessing into the warm sun " — need not be treated seriously. For the idea of the proverb, cf. *Psalms*, lii. 8.

175–177. Many explanations of this difficult sentence have been suggested. Some hold that the lines are a portion of Cordelia's letter read aloud by Kent. Others correct the syntax, reading " she'll " for " shall "; and taking " state-seeking " as a compound word. Others, again, accept the incompleteness of the sentence and ascribe it to Kent's being " weary and o'erwatched," the halting syntax indicating that Kent is dropping off to sleep. The text is apparently corrupt, and some words or lines may have been omitted.

SCENE 3

" Edgar's assumed madness serves the great purpose of taking off part of the shock which would otherwise be caused by the true madness of Lear " (Coleridge).

Bedlam beggars or *Tom o' Bedlams* (i. 2. 148), also known as *Abraham-men*, were convalescent or harmless patients of Bedlam asylum who were turned out to wander or beg. The custom was in vogue in Shakespeare's time, but appears to have ceased about the middle of the seventeenth century. (See note, iii. 6. 78–79.) The following account of an Abraham-man, quoted by Steevens from Dekker's *Bell-man of London*, 1608, is an interesting parallel to Shakespeare's description of Edgar: " He sweares he hath been in Bedlam, and will talke frantickely of purpose: you see pinnes stuck in sundry places of his naked flesh, especially in his armes, which paine he gladly puts himself to, only to make you believe he is out of his wits. He calls himselfe by the name of *Poore Tom*, and comming near any body cries out, *Poor Tom is a-cold*. Of these Abraham-men, some be exceeding merry, and doe nothing but sing songs fashioned out of their own braines: some will dance, others will doe nothing but either laugh or weepe; others are dogged and so sullen both in loke and speech, that spying but a small company in a house, they boldly and bluntly enter, compelling the servants through fear to give them what they demand."

1, 3. *proclaim'd, port.* Cf. ii. 1. 62 and 82.

6. *am bethought,* am minded, intend.

10. *elf,* mat, tangle, — as an elf might do.

17. *object,* appearance.

20. *Turlygod,* apparently a common name for a Bedlam beggar; perhaps an English variation of *Turlupin,* the name of a similar class of beggars in France in the fourteenth century.

SCENE 4

This great scene brings us to the crisis of Lear's anguish.

Finding Regan and Cornwall unexpectedly absent from their own home, Lear has followed them to Gloucester's castle.

7. *cruel,* with a play upon *crewel,* worsted; apparently a common pun at the time.

11. *nether-stocks,* literally stockings; another pun. Cf. *1 Henry IV,* ii. 4. 130, " I'll sew nether stocks and mend them and foot them too." Breeches appear to have been called " over-stocks " or " upper-stocks."

24. *upon respect,* deliberately, upon consideration.

25. *Resolve,* inform, satisfy. Cf. *resolution,* i. 2. 108.

28. *commend,* deliver. See Glossary.

33. *spite of intermission,* though my business was thus interrupted.

34. *on,* in accordance with, on the ground of; this sense, which is very common in Shakespeare, arises from the temporal sense " immediately after." Cf. iii. 7. 77.

42. Admirable as is Kent's character in point of honesty and manliness, he is an unfortunate messenger for Lear to have chosen. He has Lear's hastiness and want of tact in an exaggerated degree, and he only prejudices his master's cause. In a sense all Lear's friends are his enemies, as they play into Goneril's and Regan's hands.

46-53. *Winter's . . . year.* Omitted in the Qq.

52. *dolours*: another pun, suggested by (money) " bags " in l. 50. The same pun occurs in *The Tempest,* ii. 1. 18–19 and *Measure for Measure,* i. 2. 50.

54, 55. *mother* and *Hysterica passio* were the popular and medical names for the complaint now known as hysteria. The use of these terms was probably suggested by a passage in Harsnet's *Declaration of Popish Impostures,* 1603, to which Shakespeare is otherwise indebted in this play. Lear's anguish of heart makes him ascribe to himself the complaint which, according to Harsnet, " riseth of a winde in the bottome of the belly, and proceeding with a great swelling, causeth a very painful collicke in the stomach, and an extraordinary giddiness in the head " (quoted by Bishop Percy). Hence Lear's words, " climbing sorrow " and " swells up towards my heart."

63. *How chance* was a common construction in questions for " how chances it that." " Here chance takes no inflection and almost assumes the character of an adverb " (*New Eng. Dict.*). Cf. *Merry Wives*, v. 5. 230, " How chance you went not with Master Slender? "

68–69. *school to an ant . . . winter.* See *Proverbs*, vi. 6–8. A king's followers are only summer friends; Lear has " so small a train " because he is in adversity.

72. *stinking*, referring likewise to Lear's adversity. Malone quotes in illustration *All's Well*, v. 2. 4, etc.: " I am now, sir, muddied in fortune's mood, and smell somewhat strong of her strong displeasure. . . . Truly fortune's displeasure is but sluttish, if it smell so strongly as thou speakest of."

79. *sir*, man; frequently so used as a common noun in Shakespeare.

85–86. After referring to the wise man flying, the Fool adds that the wise man who is such a knave as to run away is in reality a fool, while on the other hand the fool who remains is no knave. The antecedent to *that* is *knave*.

89. *Deny*, refuse.

90. *fetches*, subterfuges, tricks. Note the play on the word in l. 92.

106–110. Lear's generous attempt to excuse Cornwall suggests that he is mellowing with his misfortunes. The " fiery quality " that he complains of is one of his own strongest characteristics, and he himself was " unremovable and fixed " when he disinherited Cordelia and banished Kent. His misfortunes have so far dazed him that he almost seems to be learning self-control. But the sight of Kent, and the thought of the indignity thus done him in his messenger, throw him back on his old impetuosity.

107. *office*, duty.

111. *more headier.* For the double comparative, see note on i. 1. 80. The comparative has here merely an intensive force, " more headier " meaning " very heady," " too heady." Cf. *Cymbeline*, iii. 4. 164, " the harder heart." Heady = impetuous.

112. *To take*, for taking. This gerundial infinitive is common in E. E.

115. *remotion*, removal.

120. *cry sleep to death*, put an end to sleep.

123. *cockney*, a pampered, affected woman. The context suggests that the word is used also in the sense of " cook "; but there is no evidence to show that it had ever any such meaning. See Glossary.

137. An allusion to the story of Prometheus, who was chained to a rock on Mount Caucasus, where a vulture fed on his liver.

141–142. The literal meaning is the opposite of what is intended. The sense, however, is clear, — You rather fail to value, are more likely to undervalue.

142–147. *Say, how . . . blame*. Omitted in the Qq.

157. *unnecessary*, of no account, useless.

165. *top*, head.

***young bones*,** a fairly common phrase in Elizabethan literature for an " unborn child."

166. *taking*, malignant, infecting, blasting; " used of the malignant influence of superhuman powers " (Schmidt). Cf. iii. 4. 61, and *Hamlet*, i. 1. 163:

> " then no planets strike,
> No fairy takes, nor witch hath power to charm."

174. *tender-hefted*, tenderly fitted, delicately framed. *Heft* is an old form for *haft*, a handle.

181. *bond of childhood*. Lear himself is now constrained to refer to the " bond of childhood." Cf. Cordelia's words, i. 1. 95.

182. *Effects*, manifestations. Cf. i. 1. 133.

184. So far Regan has said nothing to incense Lear. She has been cold and heartless, but she wants the courage to show herself in her true light before the arrival of her sister. Once she has Goneril's presence to support her, she can screw herself up to actions which are a maddening sequel to the praises Lear has just uttered.

186. *approves*. See note on ii. 2. 167.

194. *Allow*, approve of.

" When Lear calls upon the heavens to avenge his cause, ' for they are old like him,' there is nothing extravagant or impious in this sublime identification of his age with theirs; for there is no other image which could do justice to the agonising sense of his wrongs and his despair" (Hazlitt).

203. *much less advancement*, a much less respectable punishment.

219. *sumpter*, literally a packhorse; used in the secondary sense of "drudge."

248. *slack*, neglect, be careless in their attendance on.

259-261. *I.e.* Goneril, wicked as she is, appears well favored in comparison with Regan; it is something to be said for Goneril that there is another even more wicked.

267. "Observe that the tranquillity which follows the first stunning of the blow permits Lear to reason" (Coleridge).

268. *superfluous*, possessed of more than what is necessary.

289. The disjointed syntax, the short words, and their directness show Lear's difficulty in expressing himself. In this awful picture of passion the very structure of the lines reflects the incoherence of Lear's rage. He begins by asking Heaven for patience, but in the next breath asks to be touched with noble anger, and, struggling against his gentler impulses, defiantly threatens the "terrors of the earth."

295. *For his particular*, as to him himself. Cf. *Troilus and Cressida*, ii. 2. 9, "As far as toucheth my particular," *i.e.* as far as I myself am concerned.

308. *a desperate train*. Not a fair description of Lear's present attendants, Kent and the Fool. But see iii. 7. 16-17.

309. *incense*, incite, provoke.

ACT III — SCENE 1

So far, everything has gone well with Regan and Goneril. In this scene we have the first hint of their retribution, in the announcement that the King of France has planned an invasion. But though the tide is turning against Regan and Goneril, Lear's lot becomes only more pitiable. The agitation and tempest in his own mind are symbolized in the raging of the elements.

6. *main*, apparently in the uncommon sense of *mainland*, though other instances of this use have been pointed out in E. E., but not in Shakespeare.

7-15. *tears . . . take all*. Omitted in the Ff.

10. *little world of man*. An allusion to the old theory according to which man — the "microcosm" or little world —

was an epitome of the universe or great world — the " macrocosm." This theory was the basis of the astrological belief, so often alluded to in this play, in the connection of the movements of the planets with the fortunes of men.

12. *cub-drawn, i.e.* " with udders all drawn dry," " sucked and hungry," as in *As You Like It*, iv. 2. 115, 127.

18. *upon the warrant of my note*, on the strength of my information.

19. *dear*, important, momentous; cf. i. 4. 294.

22–29. *who have . . . furnishings*. Omitted in the Qq.

23–24. *who, Which*. See Abbott, § 266.

24. *speculations*, observers; an instance of abstract for concrete. Cf. iii. 4. 26.

25. *Intelligent*, informative, giving information. Cf. iii. 7. 12.

26. *snuffs*, resentments, quarrels. " To take in snuff " was a regular phrase (used elsewhere in Shakespeare) for " to take offence at."

packings, plottings. Cf. *packs* (confederacies), v. 3. 18, and the use of the verb (= to arrange or manipulate fraudulently), as in the phrases " to pack a jury," " to pack cards."

29. *furnishings*, outward signs.

30–42. *But, true . . . to you*. Omitted in the Ff.

43. *I will talk further with you*. An attempt to postpone or evade the matter. But Kent refuses to be put off.

47. *fear*, doubt. Cf. v. 1. 16.

53–54. *in which your pain That way, I'll this, i.e.* your work of search lies that way, while I'll go this.

SCENE 2

2. *hurricanoes*, waterspouts.

3. *cocks*, weathercocks.

4. *thought-executing*, doing execution with the speed of thought.

8. *germens*, seeds of life.

10. *court holy-water*, a proverbial phrase for flattery, fair words, " soft sawder." Cf. the French *eau bénite de cour*.

13. *here's a night pities*. This construction is frequently explained as due to the omission of the relative (see Abbott, § 244); but it is really a survival of the construction called ἀπὸ κοινοῦ, in which one subject serves for two predicates, and from which the relative clause was developed. See Kellner, §§ 109–111. Cf. i. 4. 64–65, iii. 4. 110–111, and iv. 3. 34–35.

18. *subscription*, submission. Cf. *subscribed*, i. 2. 24.

23. *battles*, battalions, as commonly in E. E.

27–34. It is difficult to draw a satisfactory meaning from these verses, though the Fool's remarks have generally a deep significance. The best explanation is that by Furness: " A man who prefers or cherishes a mean member in place of a vital one shall suffer enduring pain where others would suffer merely a twinge. Lear had preferred Regan and Goneril to Cordelia."

48–49. It is too great for man to suffer or to dread.

54. *simular man*, *i.e.* a simulator. This is the reading of the Ff; the Qq omit *man*, which makes *simular* a noun.

57. *practised.* See note on i. 2. 198.

58. *concealing continents*, shrouds of secrecy. For this use of *continent* in the sense of " that which contains," cf. *Antony and Cleopatra*, iv. 14. 40, " Heart, once be stronger than thy continent."

58–59. *cry These dreadful summoners grace.* A common construction. Cf. " cry you mercy," iii. 4. 176 and iii. 6. 54. *grace*, mercy.

60. *More sinn'd against than sinning.* Cf. the similar statement of Œdipus in the *Œdipus Coloneus* of Sophocles, ll. 266–267:

$$\epsilon\pi\epsilon\grave{\iota} \; \tau\acute{a} \; \gamma' \; \check{\epsilon}\rho\gamma a \; \mu o \upsilon$$
$$\pi\epsilon\pi o \nu\theta\acute{o}\tau' \; \acute{\epsilon}\sigma\tau\grave{\iota} \; \mu\hat{a}\lambda\lambda o\nu \; \mathring{\eta} \; \delta\epsilon\delta\rho a\kappa\acute{o}\tau a.$$

(" Since mine acts, at least, have been in suffering rather than in doing.")

66. *Denied*, did not allow. Cf. note on ii. 4. 89.

67. *My wits begin to turn.* Note the succession of Lear's statements as to his mental condition and their increasing definiteness. In i. 4. 248–249 he says:

" Either his notion weakens, his discernings
    Are lethargied — Ha ! waking ? 'tis not so ";

in i. 5. 50–51:

" O, let me not be mad, not mad, sweet heaven !
    Keep me in temper : I would not be mad ! ";

in ii. 4. 221:

" I prithee, daughter, do not make me mad ";

in ii. 4. 289:

> " O fool, I shall go mad ! "

Now he says definitely, " My wits begin to turn."

74–77. Apparently a variation of the first verse of the Clown's song at the end of *Twelfth Night*:

> " When that I was and a little tiny boy,
>   With hey, ho, the wind and the rain,
> A foolish thing was but a toy,
>   For the rain it raineth every day."

80–95. Omitted in the Qq, and probably an actor's interpolation. The verses are modelled on some well-known lines commonly called " Chaucer's Prophecy." They are referred to as by Chaucer in Puttenham's *Art of English Poesie* (ed. Arber, p. 232), but are certainly not his. See Skeat's *Chaucer*, vol. i, p. 46, where they are reprinted from Caxton. There is in the Bodleian (see Professor Skeat's letter to the *Athenæum*, December 19, 1896) a MS. copy of this very prophecy with the heading " Prophecia Merlini doctoris perfecti." In *1 Henry IV*, iii. 1. 150, Shakespeare speaks of " the dreamer Merlin and his prophecies." Some of Merlin's prophecies are given in Holinshed.

SCENE 3

The Gloucester plot is again taken up and interwoven more closely with the main story. Hitherto Gloucester has only hinted disapproval of Goneril's and Regan's conduct (ii. 4. 303), but now he definitely throws in his lot with Lear. He confides in Edmund, and so plays into the hands of his enemies. The parallelisms in the two stories become more marked.

13. *home*, to the utmost, thoroughly. Cf. iii. 4. 16.

power already footed. See iii. 1. 30–32.

20. *toward*, near at hand. Cf. ii. 1. 12.

22. *forbid thee*, which you were forbidden to do him.

SCENE 4

" O, what a world's convention of agonies is here ! All external nature in a storm, all moral nature convulsed, — the real madness of Lear, the feigned madness of Edgar, the babbling of the Fool, the desperate fidelity of Kent — surely such a scene was never conceived before or since! Take it but as a picture for the eye only, it is more terrific than any which a Michael Angelo, inspired by a Dante, could have conceived, and which none but a Michael Angelo could have executed. Or let it have been uttered to the blind, the howlings of nature would seem converted into the voice of conscious humanity. This scene ends with the first symptoms of positive derangement; and the intervention of the fifth scene is particularly judicious, — the interruption allowing an interval for Lear to appear in full madness in the sixth scene " (Coleridge).

28-36. Lear's affliction incites compassion in him for the poorest of his subjects. The finer elements in his character are brought out by his sufferings. " Expose thyself to feel what wretches feel " is utterly alien to the Lear of the first scene. Compare Gloucester's similar remark after he too has suffered (iv. 1. 70-72).

31. *loop'd*, full of holes, loop-holed. Cf. *1 Henry IV*, iv. 1. 71:

" Stop all sight-holes, every loop from whence
    The eye of reason may pry in upon us."

37. *Fathom and half,* as if he were taking soundings at sea, the idea being suggested apparently by the rain.

47. *Through the sharp hawthorn blows the cold wind.* Probably a line from an old song or ballad. Cf. Percy's *Friar of Orders Grey*, l. 87.

48. *go to thy cold bed and warm thee.* This phrase occurs also in *The Taming of the Shrew,* Induction, l. 10. It was apparently proverbial.

54-55. *laid knives . . . pew.* This passage likewise (cf. ii. 4. 54-55) seems to owe something to Harsnet's *Declaration of Popish Impostures,* 1603. Malone quotes from it a story of how an apothecary, in order to tempt a girl to suicide, " having brought with him . . . a new halter, and two blades of knives, did leave the same upon the gallerie floore in her maister's house "; and how " it was reported that the devil layd them in the gallery that some of those that were possessed might either hang themselves with the halter or kill themselves with the blades."

58. *four-inched,* four inches broad.

59. *five wits,* not the *five senses,* but " common wit, imagination, fantasy, estimation, and memory," according to a line in Stephen Hawes's *Pastime of Pleasure* (quoted by Malone). The two terms are often confounded, but Shakespeare keeps them distinct. Thus *Sonnets*, cxli :

> " But my five wits nor my five senses can
> Dissuade one foolish heart from serving thee."

Cf. iii. 6. 60 and *Twelfth Night*, iv. 2. 92.

61. *star-blasting*, being " struck " or blighted by the influence of the stars.

taking. See note on ii. 4. 166.

72. " What a bewildered amazement, what a wrench of the imagination, that cannot be brought to conceive of any other cause of misery than that which has bowed it down, and absorbs all other sorrow in its own ! His sorrow, like a flood, supplies the sources of all other sorrow." And again, " It is the mere natural ebullition of passion, urged nearly to madness, and that will admit no other cause of dire misfortune but its own, which swallows up all other griefs " (Hazlitt).

77. *pelican daughters*. An allusion to the legend that young pelicans fed upon their parents' blood. The story occurs in the mediæval Bestiaries, among others in the *Ancren Riwle*. Cf. *Hamlet*, iv. 5. 146, and *Richard II*, ii. 1. 126. A similar allusion occurs in the old play of *King Leir:*

> " I am as kind as is the pelican
> That kills it selfe to save her yong ones lives."

78. *Pillicock* — here suggested by " pelican " — was a term of endearment meaning " my pretty boy." There is perhaps an allusion to the old rhyme :

> " Pillicock, Pillicock sat on a hill,
> If he's not gone, he sits there still."

(Quoted by Collier from *Gammer Gurton's Garland*.)

88. *wore gloves in my cap*, as his mistress's favors.

103. *Dolphin my boy*. Apparently another allusion to a song. The same phrase occurs in Ben Jonson's *Bartholomew Fair*, v. 3, " He shall be Dauphin my boy." Steevens adduced a stanza from which he said it was taken :

> " Dolphin, my boy, my boy,
> Cease, let him trot by ;
> It seemeth not that such a foe
> From me or you would fly."

This was a stanza, he said, from a very old ballad written on some battle fought in France, and repeated to him by an old gentleman. Unfortunately, no trace of this ballad is discoverable. *Dolphin* is an old form of *Dauphin*.

sessa, on! an exhortation to speed. Cf. iii. 6. 77.

109. *the cat*, *i.e.* the civet-cat.

116. *naughty*, bad, disagreeable. See Glossary.

120. *Flibbertigibbet.* The name of a fiend, probably suggested, like Smulkin, Modo, Mahu, and Frateretto (iii. 6. 7) below, by a passage in Harsnet's *Declaration of Popish Impostures.* The word, however, was fairly common at the time, though in different forms, *e.g.* " flebergebet," and it was used in the sense of a gossiping or frivolous woman. Cf. Scott's *Kenilworth*, ch. x.

122. *the web and the pin*, an old name for cataract. Cf. *Winter's Tale*, i. 2. 291:

> " and all eyes
> Blind with the web and pin but theirs."

125. *S. Withold*, Saint Vitalis, who was invoked against nightmare. The Ff have Swithold, a reading preserved by several editors.

old, *i.e.* wold, a down. *Old* is a common provincial pronunciation; the form is often found in E. E.

126. *nine-fold*, " nine familiars, in the form of ' foals ' " (Herford).

129. *aroint thee*, begone, away with thee. The origin of the word is unknown. Cf. *Macbeth*, i. 3. 6.

136. *wall-newt*, the lizard.

water, water-newt.

138. *sallets*, salads; a common form in E. E.

139. *ditch-dog*, a dead dog thrown into a ditch.

144–145. A quotation from the romance of *Sir Bevis of Hamptoun:*

> " Rattes and myce and suche small dere
> Was his meate that seven yere."

deer. See Glossary.

164. *prevent*, with the old sense of anticipating, and so defeating by forestalling.

169. *He said*. See i. 1. 157–159.

172. *outlaw'd from my blood*. One of the legal consequences of outlawry is " corruption of blood," *i.e.* inability to inherit or bequeath. Cf. *1 Henry VI*, iii. 1. 159 :

> " Our pleasure is
> That Richard be restored to his blood."

In Gloucester's words " he sought my life," Edgar has the first explanation of his father's attitude.

176. *O, cry you mercy*, I beg your pardon; a common phrase in the Elizabethan dramatists. Cf. iii. 2. 58.

182. *soothe*, humor, as frequently in Shakespeare.

187. *Child Rowland* . . . These lines may perhaps be taken from the ballad of " Child Rowland and Burd Ellen," fragments of which are given in Child's *English and Scottish Ballads*, 1861, vol. i. Two of the lines (p. 251) are :

> " With *fi, fi, fo,* and *fum*
> I smell the blood of a Christian man."

For *British*, see Introduction, p. ix.

SCENE 5

Edmund now appears at the height of his villainy and of his fortune. He has already supplanted his elder brother in his father's regard and has been declared heir; he now supplants his father himself and is made, by Cornwall, Earl of Gloucester.

3. *censured*, judged (not necessarily judged adversely). This is the usual meaning in Shakespeare. Cf. the similar tendency in the word *criticism*.

4–5. *something fears me*, frightens me somewhat.

8. *provoking merit, set-a-work* . . ., a strenuous merit (in Edgar) incited by a reprehensible badness in Gloucester.

12. *approves him*, proves him to be. Cf. note on i. 1. 187.

intelligent, well-informed, though it may have the same force as in iii. 1. 25 and iii. 7. 12.

18. Edmund's plans have succeeded. Cf. iii. 2. 24–25.

21. *comforting*, assisting. See Glossary.

SCENE 6

4. *have*, plural by attraction.

7. *Frateretto*. See note on iii. 4. 120.

7–8. *Nero . . . darkness*. Said to be an allusion to Rabelais, *Gargantua and Pantagruel*, ii. 30, where Nero is described as a fiddler and Trajan as an angler. There is another reference to Rabelais in *As You Like It*, iii. 2. 238, " You must borrow me Gargantua's mouth."

8. *innocent*, a mild term for simpleton, fool.

13–15. *No, he's a yeoman . . . him.* Omitted in the Qq. It has been surmised that in writing this passage Shakespeare was humorously thinking of his own experience. In 1599 his family had been granted a coat of arms by the College of Heralds. Probably it was Shakespeare himself who suggested to his father that these insignia of the gentleman be applied for. His father however, does not fall into the Fool's category of " mad yeoman "; for the application was in John Shakespeare's name, and consequently William was not made " a gentleman before him."

18–59. *The foul fiend . . . let her 'scape?* Omitted in the Ff.

20. *horse's health*, the horse being specially liable to disease. Cf. *Taming of the Shrew*, iii. 2. 50–56.

25–26. *Wantest thou eyes. . . .* This is a doubtful passage, possibly corrupt. It may mean " Dost thou want to be stared at by the fiend while thou art on trial," or " Canst thou not see the fiend at thy trial ? "

27. *Come o'er the bourn, Bessy.* The first line of a ballad by William Birche, written in 1558, the year of the queen's accession, and entitled *A Songe betwene the Quenes Majestie and Englande.* It is printed in full in the *Harleian Miscellany*, vol. x, p. 260, edition of 1813. The first lines are:

> " Come over the born, Bessy,
> Come over the born, Bessy,
> Swete Bessey come over to me."

bourn, brook; a variant of *burn*.

32. *Hopdance* : probably suggested by " Hoberdidance," the name of another fiend in Harsnet's *Declaration*. *Hobbididance* (iv. 1. 62) apparently is another form of the same word.

33. *white herring*, fresh herring.

40. *Bench*, sit on the judge's bench.

43–46. *Sleepest or wakest thou . . .?* Apparently another snatch of a song.

45. *minikin*, dainty, pretty.

47. *Pur!* Perhaps only an imitation of the noise made by a cat, though, as Malone pointed out, *Purre* is the name of one of the devils mentioned in Harsnet's book.

54-55. *I took you for a joint-stool*, a proverbial expression, of which the precise meaning is not now known.

57. *store.* Some editions read " stone," others " stuff."

60. *five wits.* See note on iii. 4. 59.

61-62. See ii. 4. 233 and 274, and iii. 2. 37.

65. " When he exclaims in the mad scene ' The little dogs ' etc., it is passion lending occasion to imagination to make every creature in league against him, conjuring up ingratitude and insult in their least-looked-for and most galling shapes, searching every thread and fibre of his heart, and finding out the last remaining image of respect or attachment in the bottom of his breast only to torture and kill it ! " And again, " All nature was, as he supposed, in a conspiracy against him, and the most trivial and insignificant creatures concerned in it were the most striking proofs of its malignity and extent " (Hazlitt).

72. *brach*: cf. note on i. 4. 125.

lym, a bloodhound; called also a *lyam* or *lime-hound*, " from the *leam* or leash in which he was held till he was let slip."

73. *trundle-tail*, a dog with a curled tail.

78-79. *thy horn is dry.* The allusion is explained by the following passage in Aubrey's *Natural History of Wiltshire* (quoted by Halliwell-Phillipps): " Till the breaking out of the Civill Warres, *Tom o' Bedlams* did trauell about the countery. They had been poore distracted men that had been putt into Bedlam, where recovering to some sobernesse, they were licentiated to goe a begging. . . . They wore about their necks a great horn of an oxe in a string or bawdric, which, when they came to an house for almes, they did wind; and they did putt the drink given them into this horn, whereto they did putt a stopple." Edgar's meaning, of course, is that he has come to the end of his rôle.

85. *Persian*, *i.e.* rich and gorgeous; spoken ironically. Cf. Horace's " Persicos apparatus," *Odes*, i. 38.

92. *I'll go to bed at noon.* The Fool's last speech, by some critics supposed to mean that he feels a premonition of death.

102. *Stand in assured loss*, will assuredly be lost. Cf. l. 107, *stand in hard cure*, will be hard to cure, is almost incurable; ii. 4. 261, iv. 1. 4, etc. In this common idiom *stand* is an emphatic substitute for the auxiliary.

104-108. *Oppressed . . . behind.* Omitted in the Ff.

105. *sinews*: used in the sense of nerves. Cf. *Venus and Adonis*, 903, " A second fear through all her sinews spread."

109–122. When we . . . lurk. This soliloquy is not in the Ff. Its genuineness has been doubted on the score of its style. In point of its rhythm and verse mechanism generally, it is inferior to the other rhymed passages in this play. But, on the other hand, it has much closer connection with the action of the play than an interpolation would be likely to have, and certain parts, *e.g.* " he childed as I father'd," are undoubtedly in the Shakespearean manner. The inferiority of the opening lines prejudices us against the passage, but there is nothing to disprove its genuineness.

117. *He childed as I father'd*, even as he had cruel children, so I had a cruel father.

118. *bewray*. Cf. ii. 1. 109, " Show thyself when false opinion, which now does thee wrong, thinks of thee justly and recalls thee to reconciliation."

121. *What will hap more*, whatever else happens.

SCENE 7

The Gloucester plot again supplements the main story. The villainy of Edmund is at last unmasked, but not until Gloucester, like Lear, has suffered by filial treachery. His mutilation on the stage has been the subject of much criticism. Johnson considered it " an act too horrid to be endured in dramatic exhibition "; and Coleridge declared that " in this one point the tragic in this play has been urged beyond the outermost mark and *ne plus ultra* of the dramatic." There is no denying the repulsiveness of the blinding of Gloucester. It is no extenuation that there are other instances, as several editors point out, of mutilation on the Elizabethan stage. Yet it may be urged that a bold and direct treatment of this second case of barbarity was necessary after the terrible scene on the heath, as a bare narration of it would not, under the circumstances, have conveyed an adequate impression.

11. *bound*, ready, prepared; as perhaps also in l. 8.

13. *my lord of Gloucester*, Edmund's new title (see iii. 5. 18–19); purposely contrasted with Oswald's use of the title.

17. *questrists*, searchers; not found again in Shakespeare.

18. *lords dependants*. Some editors read *lord's dependants*, *i.e.* Gloucester's dependants. The reading in the text means lords dependent directly upon Lear.

24. *pass upon,* pass sentence upon.   Cf. *Measure for Measure,* ii. 1. 19, " The jury, passing on the prisoner's life."

29. *corky,* shrivelled, withered with age.

39. *quicken,* come to life.

40. *favours,* features: " the features of your host." See Glossary.

32. *simple,* straightforward. This is the reading of the Qq; the Ff read *simple-answer'd.*

47. *set down,* written.

54. *I am tied to the stake.* Cf. *Macbeth,* v. 7. 1-2:

> " They have tied me to a stake : I cannot fly,
> But, bear-like, I must fight the course."

The *course* is a technical term in bear-baiting for each attack of the dogs; cf. " round " in boxing, " bout," etc.

56-66. Gloucester is turned to bay.

57. *Pluck out his . . . eyes.* One of the most striking of the many instances of dramatic irony in the play. Gloucester unwittingly mentions his own fate.

63. *stern.* The Qq have *dearn,* — an obsolete word meaning dark, drear, dire, — which occurs also in *Pericles,* iii. 15.

65. *All cruels else subscribed* (the Quarto reading), probably " all their other cruelties being forgiven." *Cruels* is an instance of the Elizabethan use of an adjective as a noun ; see Kellner, § 236. *Subscribed,* yielded, hence condoned, forgiven ; cf. i. 2. 24. The Ff read: *All cruels else subscribe,* probably meaning " All other cruel creatures, except you, forgive."

87-90. The climax of Gloucester's agony and of Regan's brutality.

89. *overture,* disclosure.

92. *prosper.* Cf. the transitive use in iv. 6. 30.

99-107. *I'll never . . . help him.* Omitted in the Ff.

101. *old,* usual, natural.

106. *flax and white of eggs,* a common application at that time for wounds.

ACT IV — SCENE 1

This scene is a direct sequel to the closing passage of the previous act. The help that Edgar gives to his father, who is in a sense the cause of the sufferings of both, is an exact counterpart to Cordelia's solicitude for Lear.

1. *known to be,* conscious of being.

6. *laughter, i.e.* a happy or better condition.

6–9. *Welcome . . . blasts.* Omitted in the Qq.

22. *Our means secure us,* etc. Our resources make us confident and careless, and our unalloyed defects prove our benefits. For this common E. E. sense of *secure,* cf. *Othello,* i. 3. 10, " I do not so secure me in the error," and for *com-modities,* cf. *2 Henry IV,* i. 2. 278, " I will turn diseases to commodity."

24. *abused,* deceived. Cf. iv. 7. 53, 77, and v. i. 11. This sense is retained in the negative *disabuse.*

54. *daub it further,* keep up the disguise.

62. Obidicut, probably suggested by *Hoberdicut,* one of Harsnet's fiends.

Hobbididance. See note on iii. 6. 32.

64. *mopping and mowing,* making grimaces; the two words are practically synonymous. Cf. *The Tempest,* iv. 1. 47, " Will be here with mop and mow." Malone quotes from Harsnet, " If she have a little helpe of the mother, epilepsie, or cramp, to teach her . . . make antike faces, grinne, mow and mop like an ape, then no doubt the young girle is owleblasted and possessed."

71. *slaves,* treats as a slave, makes subservient to his desire.

This passage is Gloucester's counterpart to Lear's utterance on pomp, iii. 4. 33–36.

SCENE 2

The clue to the dénouement is now given in the adulterous love of Goneril for Edmund, and in the conduct of Albany. When we last saw Albany (i. 4) he appeared in an unfavor-able light as a passive witness of his wife's schemes, or at best only able to hint his disapproval; and in this scene Goneril begins by treating him as a " milk-livered man." But the monstrous conduct of Goneril at last awakens him to think for himself and to take up firmly a line of his own.

2. *Not met us.* Cf. l. 53 and ii. 1. 77.

12. *cowish,* cowardly.

14–15. *Our wishes,* etc. The wishes we expressed on the way hither may be realized.

28. *My fool usurps my body.* The reading of the Ff. There are three distinct readings of this phrase in the Qq. Q1, un-corrected, has " My foot usurps my body "; Q1, corrected, has " A fool usurps my bed ; " while Q2 reads " My foot usurps my head."

29. Goneril refers to Albany's indifference to her.   This proverbial expression is given in the *Proverbs of John Heywood*, 1546, " It is . . . A poor dog that is not worth the whistling " (ed. Sharman, 1874, p. 76).

31–50. *I fear . . . deep.*   Omitted in the Ff.

31. *fear,* fear for.   Cf. *Richard III*, i. 1. 137, " his physicians fear him mightily."

32. *it.*   See note on i. 4. 236.

33. *border'd certain,* contained with certainty.

34. *sliver,* break off, strip off.   Cf. *Macbeth*, iv. 1. 28,

> " slips of yew
> Sliver'd in the moon's eclipse."

39. *savour,* have a relish for.

42. *head-lugg'd,* drawn by the head.

50. *Milk-liver'd.*   See note on ii. 2. 18.

53–59. *that not knows't . . . doe she so.*   Omitted in the Ff.

54. *villains.*   Probably an allusion to Lear ; possibly to Albany, France, or Gloucester.

58. *moral,* moralizing.   Cf. the use of *moral* as a verb in *As You Like It*, ii. 7. 29,

> " I did hear
> The motley fool thus moral on the time."

59–67. Albany's violent speeches are obscure.   Some scholars believe that he speaks of Goneril inconsistently, — first as a woman who has taken on a fiendish shape (" bemonstering " her " feature "), and then as a fiend in woman's shape. Others believe that throughout he addresses her as a fiend who has " self-covered " himself in the inappropriate form of woman.   The following notes are in harmony with the latter view.

60. *Proper deformity seems not in the fiend,* deformity seems not so horrid in a fiend, because proper to his immoral character, as it seems in a woman.

62–69. Omitted in the Ff.

63. *Be-monster not thy feature,* do not take on the outward form of a woman, unnatural to a devil.

Were't my fitness, were it fit for me, a man.

65. *apt*, ready.

68. *your manhood! mew!* The uncorrected sheets of the Q1 and Q2 read *your manhood now*, — a reading adopted by some editors; the corrected sheets read *your manhood mew*, — explained as " suppress, restrain your manhood." The reading in the text, *your manhood! mew!* is that given in the second edition of the Cambridge Shakespeare (1891), in accordance with a suggestion in Mr. Daniel's introduction to the facsimile reprint of Q 1 (1885). Here *mew* is an interjection of disgust and contempt. There are many contemporary instances of it.

73. *remorse*, pity, as generally in Shakespeare.

74. *bending*, turning, directing; cf. ii. 1. 48.

79. *nether*, earthly.

83. *One way*, in so far as Cornwall has been got out of the road — an idea to which she reverts in ll. 86–87, "another way, the news is not so tart."

85. *all the building in my fancy*, all my castles in the air. The fact that she is a widow and that Gloucester is with her may frustrate all my hopes and make life hateful to me.

91. *back*, *i.e.* going back.

SCENE 3

This scene is omitted in the Ff. It is accordingly not essential to the development of the plot. But it stands in dramatic contrast to the previous scene, while the description of Cordelia's grief on learning what has happened is one of the most beautiful of the gentler passages in the play.

21. *Were like, a better way*, were like sunshine and rain, but in a more beautiful manner. Several explanations and emendations of this difficult phrase have been given. Warburton reads " like a wetter May," and Malone, " like a better May; " but neither of these gives better sense than the original reading. Many editors omit the comma after " like."

33. *clamour moisten'd*, *i.e.* tears succeeded her cries of indignation at her sisters. This is Capell's emendation of the Quarto reading, *And clamour moistened her.*

34–37. A recurrence to the astrological theories expressed earlier in the play by Gloucester.

36. *self*, *i.e.* self-same. This adjectival use of " self," which is a survival from O. E., was still common in Shakespeare's time.

44. *elbows*, jostles, torments; literally, " thrusts with the elbow."

46. *foreign casualties*, hazards abroad.

53. *dear*, important. See note on i. 4. 294 and on iii. 1. 19.

SCENE 4

This scene likewise does not further the action of the drama; but it reintroduces Cordelia, who has not appeared since the very first scene.

4. *hor-docks*, the reading of the Qq; the Ff have *hardokes* and *hardocks*. The plant has not been identified. Many editions adopt the emendation *burdocks*.

cuckoo-flowers, a name given to several wild flowers which bloom when the cuckoo is heard; here probably the cowslip.

6. *century*. Generally defined as " a troop of a hundred men," as in *Coriolanus*, i. 7. 3. But *century* was an old variant of *sentry* — the *New English Dictionary* cites an example of this form as late as 1759 — and this is perhaps the meaning of the word here.

10. *helps*, cures; a common meaning in E. E. and later. Cf. Tennyson's *Locksley Hall*, l. 105:

> " But the jingling of the guinea helps the hurt that
>   Honour feels."

15. *anguish*: used commonly in E. E. of physical as well as of mental suffering. Cf. iv. 6. 6.

26. *important*, importunate. Cf. *Much Ado*, ii. 1. 73–75, " if the prince be too important, tell him there is measure in every thing."

SCENE 5

This scene likewise does not advance the plot; but it prepares us for the dénouement by showing the increasing jealousy of Goneril and Regan.

13. *nighted*, benighted, darkened.

18. The fidelity of Oswald to Goneril is the only thing that at all relieves the utter baseness and blackness of his character.

25. *œillades*, amorous glances. See Glossary.

29. *take this note*, take note of this.

SCENE 6

This important scene is divided roughly into three parts.
The first, which contains the famous description of Dover Cliff,
is a direct continuation of the opening scene of this act; the
second brings into comparison Lear and Gloucester in the
height of their suffering; and the third, unlike the others, is
devoted mainly to the unravelling of the plot.

10. *better spoken.* See note on i. 1. 275.

11-24. The following criticism of the description of Dover
Cliff was made by Johnson: " The description is certainly not
mean, but I am far from thinking it wrought to the utmost ex-
cellence of poetry. He that looks from a precipice finds himself
assailed by one great and dreadful image of irresistible destruction. But this overwhelming idea is dissipated and enfeebled
from the instant that the mind can restore itself to the observation of particulars, and diffuse its attention to distinct objects.
The enumeration of the choughs and crows, the samphire-man,
and the fishers counteracts the great effect of the prospect, as it
peoples the desert of intermediate vacuity, and stops the mind in
the rapidity of its descent through emptiness and horror." A
similar opinion is recorded by Boswell in his *Life of Johnson.*
" No, Sir; it should be all precipice — all vacuum. The crows
impede your fall. The diminished appearance of the boats, and
other circumstances, are all very good description, but do not
impress the mind at once with the horrible idea of immense
height. The impression is divided; you pass on, by compu-
tation, from one stage of the tremendous space to another."
This criticism amounts simply to a condemnation of the
" romantic " method of description. The " classical " manner
for which Johnson here pleads aims at a unity of impression
by means of generalized statements. Avoiding the mention of
particulars, so as not to give them undue importance or to take
away from the general effect, it leaves these particulars to be
filled in by the reader's imagination. The romantic manner,
on the other hand, follows an opposite course, and trusts to
particulars as a means of conveying the general impression.
There can be no question which manner is the more vivid in
its effect, and accordingly better suited for the drama. A
generalized description could present only a vague image of
altitude. It would never make us *feel* the giddy height.

15. *samphire,* sea-fennel, an herb which grows on cliffs and is used for pickling. The gathering of samphire was a regular trade in Shakespeare's time, and Dover Cliff appears to have been particularly famous for the herb. Cf. Drayton's *Polyolbion, the Eighteenth Song* (Spenser Society Publications, 1889, p. 300):

> " Rob Dovers neighboring cleeues of sampyre, to excite
> His dull and sickly taste, and stirre vp appetite."

The common Elizabethan spelling was *sampire* (so the Qq and Ff).

19. *cock*, i.e. cock-boat.

21. *unnumber'd*, innumerable. See note on i. 1. 262.

28. *another purse*. See iv. 1. 67.

33–34. Note the confusion of constructions.

39. *My snuff*, the useless remnant of my life. The metaphor is taken from the smoking wick of a candle.

42–43. The illusion of death may actually cause death. For *conceit*, see Glossary.

46. Edgar here assumes a different character, and pretends that he has come upon Gloucester at the bottom of the cliff.

47. *pass*, i.e. pass away. Cf. v. 3. 313.

53. *at each*, one on the top of the other.

57. *bourn*, boundary, i.e. to the sea.

58. *a-height*, i.e. on high, aloft.

shrill-gorged, shrill-throated.

71. *whelk'd*, rugged as with whelks.

72. *father*, a term of address to an old man, though used by Edgar to insinuate his relationship. See v. 3. 192.

73. *clearest*, most pure, as frequently in Shakespeare. Cf. *The Tempest*, iii. 3. 82, " a clear life."

81. *The safer sense*, i.e. sanity; *safer* = sounder, saner.

87–93. Lear's thought wanders from collecting recruits (" press-money ") to archery, then to mouse-catching, then to battle, then back again to archery and hawking, and then to sentry duty.

88. *crow-keeper*, one who keeps crows off fields. The comparison to a crow-keeper appears to have been common in describing an awkward archer; cf. Ascham, *Toxophilus* (ed. Arber, p. 145), " An other coureth downe, and layeth out his buttockes, as though he shoulde shoote at crowes."

88–89. *clothier's yard*, a " cloth-yard shaft," a common name for an arrow of the long-bow. Cf. the ballad of *Chevy Chase:*

" An arrow that a cloth-yarde was lang
   To the harde stele halyde he."

Cf. also *The Lay of the Last Minstrel*, iv. 15.

92. *brown bills*, halberds painted brown, used by foot-soldiers.

clout, the mark shot at in archery. Cf. *Love's Labour's Lost*, iv. 1. 136, " Indeed, a' must shoot nearer, or he'll never hit the clout."

98–99. *had white hairs*, etc., had the wisdom of age while yet a boy.

108. *trick*, characteristic, peculiarity.

111. *What was thy cause?* What were you accused of?

137. *piece*, equivalent to " masterpiece." Cf. *The Tempest*, i. 2. 56, " Thy mother was a piece of virtue "; and *Antony and Cleopatra*, v. 2. 99, " to imagine An Antony, were nature's piece 'gainst fancy."

140. *squiny*, squint, make eyes at. Lear does not yet recognize that Gloucester is blind. He is incapable in his madness of sympathizing with, or even appreciating, Gloucester's fate.

148. *are you there with me?* is that what you mean?

157–158. *handy-dandy*. A children's game in which the on-lookers are asked to say in which hand an object, that has frequently been changed from one hand to the other, finally remains; hence equivalent here to " choose which you will."

169–174. *Plate sin . . . lips*. Omitted in the Qq.

172. *able*, warrant, vouch for.

187. The " reason " in Lear's madness is but fitful. He has no sooner begun to moralize to Gloucester on the folly of this world than his thoughts again wander.

this', this is.

block, probably the shape of a hat; hence the succeeding thought, the hat being of felt.

199. *a man of salt*, *i.e.* a man of tears. Cf. *Hamlet*, i. 2. 154, " the salt of most unrighteous tears "; and *Coriolanus*, v. 6. 93, " for certain drops of salt."

212. *speed you*, *i.e.* God speed you.

214. *vulgar*, commonly known.

217. *the main descry*, etc., the appearance of the main body is hourly expected.

226. *art*, acquired faculty, experience.

feeling, heartfelt; a quasi-passive sense.

227. *pregnant*, ready, disposed. Cf. ii. 1. 78.

228. *biding*, *i.e.* biding-place.

230. *To boot, and boot.* " By the repetition Gloucester wishes to convey both meanings of ' to boot,' *in addition* (to my thanks) and (the bounty of heaven) *be your help* " (Herford).

231. *framed*, formed.

233. *thyself remember*, remember and confess thy sins.

240. Edgar adopts the Somersetshire dialect. It is commonly put into the mouths of rustics in the Elizabethan drama. *Chill* is a contraction of " ich will," *chud* of " ich would "; while the *v* in *vurther*, *volk*, etc. represents the southwestern pronunciation of *f*. *Che vor ye* stands for " I warn you," and *ise* for " I shall."

247. *costard*, a humorous term for the head, literally a large kind of apple. Cf. the modern " nut."

ballow, cudgel; a dialectal word.

251. *foins*, thrusts in fencing.

256. *British.* So the Qq. The Ff read " English." Cf. iii. 4. 189.

264. *Leave*, by your leave. A similar expression occurs in *Cymbeline*, iii. 2. 35, " Good wax, thy leave," and in *Twelfth Night*, ii. 5. 103, " By your leave, wax."

275. *servant*, a regular term for a lover.

278. *undistinguish'd space*, undefinable scope. See note on i. 1. 262.

will, desire.

281. *rake up*, cover over, bury.

284. *death-practised*, whose death was plotted. See note on i. 2. 198.

286. *ingenious*, sensitive, lively.

SCENE 7

This is another of the great scenes of the play. In point of bearing on the action of the drama, it is less important than i. 4 or ii. 4, the scenes with which it ranks in dramatic power. But the play contains no more affecting picture than that of Cordelia's care for Lear, his restoration to reason in her presence, and his recognition of her.

6. *suited*, clothed.

7. *memories*, memorials; abstract for concrete.

9. *Yet to be known shortens* . . . , to be known as yet would impair the plan I have made.

17. *child-changed*, changed by the conduct of his children.

24. *temperance*, calmness.

38. *Against*, at, before, over against; as commonly in E. E.

42. *all*, altogether; used adverbially. Cf. i. 1. 102.

47. *that*, so that.

53. *abused*, deceived. Cf. l. 77 and iv. 1. 24.

65. *mainly*, perfectly. See Glossary.

67. *nor . . . not*, one of the commonest forms in E. E. of the double negative. Cf. v. 3. 290.

70. " The ' so I am ' of Cordelia gushes from her heart like a torrent of tears, relieving it of a weight of love and of supposed ingratitude which had pressed upon it for years " (Hazlitt).

80. *even o'er*, account for, fill in fully, remember clearly. The metaphor is apparently from the language of accountants. Craig compares *Macbeth*, v. 8. 60–62:

> " We shall not spend a large expense of time
> Before we reckon with your several loves,
> And make us even with you."

85–97. *Holds it true . . . fought.* Omitted in the Ff, like the concluding lines of iii. 7.

91. It will be remembered that Kent had declared his intention to " shape his old course in a country new " (i. 1. 190).

96. *period*, end aimed at. Cf. *Henry VIII*, i. 2. 209,

> " There's his period,
> To sheathe his knife in us."

ACT V — SCENE 1

This scene is a preparation for the catastrophe. It shows how the evildoers are hastening to their destruction. Whatever Albany's sympathy for Lear, he has to oppose the French invasion; but his life is plotted against by Edmund, whose patriotism is subordinate to his ambition to assume the supreme power; and Goneril and Regan are now so bitterly divided by jealousy of Edmund that the issue of the battle is to them of secondary interest.

4. *constant pleasure*, fixed, final resolve. Cf. i. 1. 44.

13. *bosom'd*, in her confidence. Cf. iv. 5. 26.

as far as we call hers, as far as anything is hers; to the utmost.

16. *Fear*, doubt. Cf. iii. 1. 47, and contrast iii. 5. 4 and iv. 2. 31.

23–27. *Where I could not be honest*, etc. In these words Albany gives the explanation of his weakness at the beginning of the play. But he is not the weak character that Goneril thought him, or that he is so often said to be.

26. *bolds*, emboldens: " not in so far as France emboldens (*i.e.* supports) the king."

32. *ancient of war*, experienced soldiers, veterans.

36. *convenient*, befitting, expedient.

50. *o'erlook*, *i.e.* " look o'er." Cf. i. 2. 40.

54. *greet the time*, meet the occasion.

56. *jealous*, suspicious.

61. *carry out my side*, succeed in my plan, win my object. The metaphor is taken from games. Mason quotes from Massinger's *Great Duke of Florence* (iv. 2):

> " If I hold your cards, I shall pull down the side;
> I am not good at the game."

68. *Shall*, *i.e.* they shall. Cf. i. 1. 213.

69. *Stands on me*, requires me. See note, iii. 6. 102.

SCENE 2

Mr. Spedding suggested (*New Shakspere Society's Transactions*, 1877–1879, pt. i) that the acts of *King Lear* have been wrongly divided, and that the fourth act ends at the fourth line of this scene. According to his arrangement, the battle would take place between the fourth and fifth acts. He was prompted to this suggestion by the unsatisfactory description of the battle compared with other similar descriptions in Shakespeare. " In other cases a few skilful touches bring the whole battle before us — a few rapid shiftings from one part of the field to another, a few hurried greetings of friend or foe, a few short passages of struggle, pursuit, or escape, give us token of the conflict which is raging on all sides; and, when the hero falls, we feel that his army is defeated. A page or two does it; but it is done." But in this scene " the army so long looked for, and on which everything depends, passes over the stage, and all

our hopes and sympathies go with it. Four lines are spoken.
The scene does not change; but 'alarums' are heard, and
'afterwards a retreat,' and on the same field over which that
great army has this moment passed, fresh and full of hope,
reappears, with tidings that all is lost, the same man who last
left the stage to follow and fight in it." The suggested re-
arrangement is plausible, for it would remove the defects
alluded to without altering a word of the text. But there is
nothing to show that the scene is not as Shakespeare left it.
A fuller description of the battle would have tended to divert
the attention from the main interest of the story. Indeed the
dramatic purpose would have been as adequately fulfilled by
a bare narration of the result of the battle. Moreover, the
circumstances of the play demand the sympathy of the audience for the French army rather than for the British, and the
sturdy Elizabethan patriotism probably weighed with Shakespeare in making the description so meager.

11. *Ripeness*, readiness. Cf. *Hamlet*, v. 2. 234, " if it be
not now, yet it will come: the readiness is all."

SCENE 3

" The wheel is come full circle." All the chief characters,
who, contrary to Shakespeare's general custom, had been
brought on to the stage at the very beginning of the play to
participate in an event on which the whole play turns, re-
appear in this last scene to " taste the wages of their virtue
and the cup of their deservings." The dénouement, as in so
many of Shakespeare's plays, is rapidly achieved, and somewhat resembles, with its bustle and wealth of incident, the
closing scene of *Hamlet;* and, as in *Hamlet*, the guiltless fall
with the guilty.

2. *their greater pleasures*, the wills of these greater persons.

3. *censure*, pass sentence on.   See note on iii. 5. 3.

18. *packs*, confederacies. See note on iii. 1. 26.

23. *fire us hence like foxes*. An allusion to the practice of
smoking foxes out of their holes.

24. *good-years*. See Glossary.

35. *write happy*, call yourself happy. Cf. *All's Well*, ii. 3.
208, " I must tell thee, sirrah, I write man."

49. *To pluck . . . side*, to win the affection of the common
people.

50. *impress'd*, pressed into our service.

lances, *i.e.* lancers.

65. *immediacy*, close connection with nothing intervening, *i.e.* direct tenure of authority.

68. *addition*, title. Cf. i. 1. 138.

72. *That eye*, etc. " Alluding to the proverb : ' Love being jealous makes a good eye look asquint ' " (Steevens).

74. *stomach*. The stomach was supposed to be the seat of anger, as the liver was of courage (ii. 2. 18). Cf. *Titus Andronicus*, iii. 1. 234, " To ease their stomachs with their bitter tongues."

76. *the walls are thine*: apparently a metaphor signifying complete surrender. Wright thinks the words refer to Regan's castle, mentioned in l. 245. Theobald conjectured " they are all thine."

79. *The let-alone*, the prohibition. As events prove, Goneril has already taken means to frustrate Regan's wishes.

103. *virtue*, valor, as frequently in E. E. Cf. Latin *virtus*.

124. *cope*, commonly used transitively in E. E., as here.

129. *I.e.* It is my privilege, as I am a knight, to engage you, who are a traitor.

132. *fire-new*, brand-new; fresh from the fire or forge.

137. *descent*, " that to which one descends, the lowest part "; the only known instance of this use.

138. *toad-spotted*, treasonable as the toad is spotted.

143. *say*, proof. See Glossary.

144. *nicely*. See Glossary.

Edmund's character is not all bad. He could have refused to fight a nameless antagonist, but he manfully will not avail himself of this excuse. His subsequent statement, " Some good I mean to do, despite of mine own nature," is not out of keeping with his character, as it would have been with Goneril's or Regan's. Great as is his villainy, he had to some extent been prompted to it by the disabilities which he incurred by his birth and the taunts which he had to suffer even from his father.

147. *hell-hated*, hated like hell.

151. *Save him, save him!* Albany is anxious not to have Edmund killed on the spot, so that his guilt may be made known before his death.

practice, false play, treachery. Cf. i. 2. 198.

155. *this paper*, Goneril's love letter to Edmund; see iv. 6. 267.

160. *Ask me not what I know.* The Ff assign this speech to Edmund, the Qq give it to Goneril, and modern editors are divided in their choice. Those who follow the Ff ask why the question, " Know'st thou this paper? " should be addressed to Goneril, considering Albany has already said to her, " I perceive you know it." But this objection is not conclusive.

194. *success,* issue, result. Cf. i. 2. 157.

196. *flaw'd,* broken. Cf. ii. 4. 288.

204–221. *This would . . . slave.* Omitted in the Ff.

204. *period,* termination; note the different sense in iv. 7. 96.

205–207. *but another,* etc., but another story, amplifying what is already too much, would make what is much even more, and so pass the extreme limits.

234. *manners*: treated as a singular; but contrast i. 4. 184 and iv. 6. 264.

235. It is fitting that at this juncture attention should be drawn to Lear by Kent, who at the beginning of the play had professed his constant devotion to the king.

255. *fordid,* destroyed. Cf. l. 291.

262. *stone,* a crystal mirror.

263. *the promised end, i.e.* of the world. Mason compares *St. Mark*, xiii. 12 and 19. For *image of that horror*, cf. *Macbeth*, ii. 3. 82–83,

> "up, up, and see
> The great doom's image! "

285. Lear's thoughts again begin to wander. He cannot realize what Kent's devotion has been, and even the announcement of Regan's and Goneril's death has no effect.

288. *your first of difference,* beginning of your change.

290. *Nor no man else, i.e.* No, nor is any other man welcome.

301. *boot,* increase, enhancement.

305. *poor fool, i.e.* Cordelia; a common term of endearment. Some (*e.g.* Sir Joshua Reynolds) think that Lear refers to his Fool; but the Fool was not " hanged "; he has long since passed out of the play (iii. 6); and it is not likely that Lear would think of him when dying of grief at the death of Cordelia.

313. *pass.* Cf. iv. 6. 47.

322. *My master, i.e.* Lear. Kent's devotion is unbroken.

323–326. This concluding speech is given in the Qq to Albany, in the Ff to Edgar. It is assigned more fittingly to the latter.

APPENDIX A

THE SOURCES OF THE PLOT

The Lear story is here given as told by Raphael Holinshed, in his *Chronicles* (1577; second edition, 1587), by Higgins in *The Mirror for Magistrates* (1574), and by Spenser in the *Faërie Queene* (1590), and is followed by the passage in Sidney's *Arcadia* (1590), which is the undoubted original of the Gloucester story.

I. *Holinshed's Chronicles.* — *The Historie of Britain,* second edition,[1] Book ii, chapter 5, pp. 12–13.

Leir the sonne of Baldud was admitted ruler ouer the Britaines in the yeare of the world 3105, at what time Joas reigned in Juda. This Leir was a prince of right noble demeanor, gouerning his land and subiects in great wealth. He made the towne of Caerleir now called Leicester, which standeth vpon the riuer of Sore. It is written that he had by his wife three daughters without other issue, whose names were Gonorilla, Regan, and Cordeilla, which daughters he greatly loued, but specially Cordeilla the yoongest farre aboue the two elder. When this Leir therefore was come to great yeres, and began to waxe vnweldie through age, he thought to vnderstand the affections of his daughters towards him, and preferre hir whome he best loued, to the succession ouer the kingdome. Whervpon he first asked Gonorilla the eldest, how well she loued him: who calling hir gods to record, protested that she loued him more than hir owne life, which by right and reason should be most deere vnto hir. With which answer the father being well pleased, turned to the second, and demanded of hir how well she loued him: who answered (confirming hir saiengs with great othes) that she loued him more than toong could expresse, and farre aboue all other creatures of the world.

Then called he his yoongest daughter Cordeilla before him, and asked of hir what account she made of him, vnto whome she made this answer as followeth: "Knowing the great loue and fatherlie zeale that you haue alwaies borne towards me (for the which I

[1] The evidence of other plays shows that Shakespeare used the second edition; see *Shakspere's Holinshed, The Chronicle and the Historical Plays compared*, by W. G. Boswell-Stone.

maie not answere you otherwise than I thinke, and as my conscience leadeth me) I protest vnto you, that I haue loued you euer, and shall continuallie (while I liue) loue you as my naturall father. And if you would more vnderstand of the loue that I beare you, assertaine your selfe, that so much as you haue, so much you are worth, and so much I loue you, and no more." The father being nothing content with this answere, married his two eldest daughters, the one vnto Henninus the duke of Cornewall, and the other vnto Maglanus the duke of Albania, betwixt whome he willed and ordeined that his land should be deuided after his death, and the one halfe thereof immediatelie should be assigned to them in hand: but for the third daughter Cordeilla he reserued nothing.

Nevertheless it fortuned that one of the princes of Gallia (which now is called France) whose name was Aganippus, hearing of the beautie, womanhood, and good conditions of the said Cordeilla, desired to haue hir in mariage, and sent ouer to hir father, requiring that he might haue hir to wife: to whome answer was made, that he might haue his daughter, but as for anie dower he could haue none, for all was promised and assured to hir other sisters already. Aganippus notwithstanding this answer of deniall to receiue anie thing by way of dower with Cordeilla, tooke hir to wife, onlie moued thereto (I saie) for respect of hir person and amiable vertues. This Aganippus was one of the twelue kings that ruled Gallia in those daies, as in the British historie it is recorded. But to proceed.

After that Leir was fallen into age, the two dukes that had married his two eldest daughters, thinking it long yer the gouernment of the land did come to their hands, arose against him in armour, and reft from him the gouernance of the land, vpon conditions to be continued for terme of life: by the which he was put to his portion, that is, to liue after a rate assigned to him for the maintenance of his estate, which in processe of time was diminished as well by Maglanus as by Henninus. But the greatest griefe that Leir tooke, was to see the vnkindnesse of his daughters, which seemed to thinke that all was too much which their father had, the same being neuer so little: in so muche that going from the one to the other, he was brought to that miserie, that scarslie they would allow him one seruaunt to wait vpon him.

In the end, such was the vnkindnesse, or (as I maie saie) the vnnaturalnesse which he found in his two daughters, notwithstanding their faire and pleasant words vttered in time past, that being constreined of necessitie, he fled the land, & sailed into Gallia, there to seeke some comfort of his yongest daughter Cordeilla, whom before time he hated. The ladie Cordeilla hearing that he was arriued in poore estate, she first sent to him priuilie a certeine summe of monie to apparell himselfe withall, and to reteine a certeine number of seruants that might attend vpon him in honorable wise, as apperteined to the estate which he had borne: and then so accompanied, she appointed him to come to the court, which he did, and was so ioifullie, honorablie, and louinglie receiued, both by his sonne in law Aganippus, and also by his daughter Cordeilla, that his hart was greatlie comforted : for he was no lesse honored, than if he had beene king of the whole countrie himselfe.

Now when he had informed his sonne in law and his daughter in what sort he had beene vsed by his other daughters, Aganippus caused a mightie armie to be put in a readinesse, and likewise a great nauie of ships to be rigged, to passe ouer into Britaine with Leir his father in law, to see him againe restored to his kingdome. It was accorded, that Cordeilla should also go with him to take possession of the land, the which he promised to leaue vnto hir, as the rightfull inheritour after his decesse, notwithstanding any former grant made to hir sisters or to their husbands in anie maner of wise.

Herevpon, when this armie and nauie of ships were readie, Leir and his daughter Cordeilla with hir husband tooke the sea, and arriuing in Britaine, fought with their enimies, and discomfited them in battell, in the which Maglanus and Henninus were slaine ; and then was Leir restored to his kingdome, which he ruled after this by the space of two yeeres, and then died, fortie yeeres after he first began to reigne. His bodie was buried at Leicester in a vaut vnder the chanell of the riuer of Sore beneath the towne.

The Sixth Chapter. — Cordeilla the yoongest daughter of Leir was admitted Q. and supreme gouernesse of Britaine in the yeere of the world 3155, before the bylding of Rome 54 ; Uzia was then reigning in Juda, and Jeroboam ouer Israell. This Cordeilla after hir fathers decease ruled the land of Britaine right worthilie during the space of fiue yeeres, in which meane time hir husband died, and then about the end of those fiue yeeres, hir two nephewes Margan and Cunedag, sonnes to hir aforesaid sisters, disdaining to be vnder the gouernment of a woman, leuied warre against hir, and destroied a great part of the land, and finallie tooke hir prisoner, and laid hir fast in ward, wherewith she tooke suche griefe, being a woman of a manlie courage, and despairing to recouer libertie, there she slue hirselfe, when she had reigned (as before is mentioned) the tearme of fiue yeeres.

II. *The Mirror for Magistrates.* — From the story of *Queene Cordila*, written by John Higgins, edited by Haslewood, 1815, vol. i, pp. 124–132.

> 6. My grandsire *Bladud* hight, that found the bathes by skill,
> A fethered King that practis'd high to soare,
> Whereby hee felt the fall, God wot against his will,
> And neuer went, road, raygnd, nor spake, nor flew no more.
> After whose death my father *Leire* therefore
> Was chosen King, by right apparent heyre,
> Which after built the towne of *Leircestere.*

7. Hee had three daughters, first and eld'st hight *Gonerell*,
   Next after her his yonger *Ragan* was begot:
   The third and last was I the yongest, nam'd *Cordell*.
   Vs all our father *Leire* did loue to well, God wot.
   But minding her that lou'd him best to note,
    Because hee had no sonne t'enioy his land,
     Hee thought to guerdon most where fauour most hee fand.

8. What though I yongest were, yet men mee iudg'd more wise
   Than either *Gonerell* or *Ragan* more of age,
   And fairer farre: wherefore my sisters did despise
   My grace and giefts, and sought my wrecke to wage.
   But yet though vice on vertue dye with rage,
    It cannot keepe her vnderneath to drowne:
     For still she flittes aboue, and reaps renowne.

9. My father thought to wed vs vnto princely peeres,
   And vnto them and theirs deuide and part the land.
   For both my sisters first hee cal'd (as first their yeares
   Requir'd), their minds, and loue, and fauoure t'vnderstand.
   (Quoth hee) all doubts of duty to aband,
    I must assay your friendly faithes to proue:
     My daughters, tell mee how you doe mee loue.

10. Which when they aunswerd him they lou'd their father more
    Then they themselues did loue, or any worldly wight,
    He praised them, and sayd hee would therefore
    The louing kindnes they deseru'd in fine requite.
    So found my sisters fauour in his sight,
     By flattery faire they won their fathers heart;
      Which after turned hym and mee to smart.

11. But not content with this, hee asked mee likewise
    If I did not him loue and honour well.
    No cause (quoth I) there is I should your grace despise:
    For nature so doth binde and duty mee compell
    To loue you, as I ought my father, well.
     Yet shortely I may chaunce, if Fortune will,
      To finde in heart to beare another more good will.

12. Thus much I sayd of nuptiall loues that ment,
    Not minding once of hatred vile or ire,
    And partly taxing them, for which intent
    They set my fathers heart on wrathfull fire.
    "Shee neuer shall to any part aspire
     Of this my realme (quoth hee) among'st you twayne:
      But shall without all dowry aie remaine."

13. Then to *Maglaurus* Prince, with Albany hee gaue
    My sister *Gonerell*, the eldest of vs all :
    And eke my sister *Ragan* to *Hinniue* to haue,
    And for her dowry *Camber* and *Cornwall*.
    These after him should haue his Kingdome all.
        Betweene them both hee gaue it franke and free,
        But nought at all hee gaue of dowry mee.

14. At last it chaunst a Prince of *Fraunce* to heare my fame.
    My beauty braue, my wit was blaz'd abroad ech where.
    My noble vertues prais'd mee to my fathers blame,
    Who did for flattery mee lesse friendly fauour beare.
    Which when this worthy Prince (I say) did heare,
        Hee sent ambassage, lik'd mee more then life,
        And soone obtayned mee to bee his wife.

15. Prince *Aganippus* reau'd mee of my woe,
    And that for vertues sake, of dowryes all the best :
    So I contented was to Fraunce my father fro
    For to depart, and hoapt t'enioy some greater rest.
    Where liuing well belou'd, my ioyes encreast :
        I gate more fauour in that Prince his sight,
        Then euer Princesse of a Princely wight.

16. But while that I these ioyes so well enioy'd in *Fraunce*,
    My father *Leire* in *Britayne* waxt unweldy old.
    Whereon his daughters more themselues aloft t'aduance
    Desir'd the Realme to rule it as they wolde.
    Their former loue and friendship waxed cold,
        Their husbands rebels voyde of reason quite
        Rose vp, rebeld, bereft his crowne and right :

17. Caus'd him agree they might in parts equall
    Deuide the Realme, and promist him a gard
    Of sixty Knights on him attending still at call.
    But in six monthes such was his hap to hard,
    That *Gonerell* of his retinue barde
        The halfe of them, shee and her husband reft,
        And scarce alow'd the other halfe they left.

18. Eke as in *Albany* lay hee lamenting fates,
    When as my sister so sought all his vtter spoyle :
    The meaner vpstart courtiers thought themselues his mates,
    His daughter him disdayn'd and forced not his foyle.
    Then was hee fayne for succoure his to toyle
        With halfe his trayne to *Cornwall*, there to lie
        In greatest neede, his *Ragans* loue to try.

19. So when hee came to *Cornwall*, shee with ioy
 Receiued him, and Prince *Maglaurus* did the like.
 There hee abode a yeare, and liu'd without anoy:
 But then they tooke all his retinue from him quite
 Saue only ten, and shew'd him daily spite:
  Which he bewayl'd complayning durst not striue,
  Though in disdayne they last alow'd but fiue.

20. What more despite could deuelish beasts deuise,
 Then ioy their fathers woefull days to see?
 What vipers vile could so their King despise,
 Or so vnkinde, so curst, so cruell bee?
 From thence agayn hee went to *Albany*,
  Where they bereau'd his seruants all saue one,
  Bad him content him selfe with that, or none.

21. Eke at what time hee ask'd of them to haue his gard,
 To gard his noble grace where so hee went:
 They cal'd him doting foole, all his requests debard,
 Demaunding if with life hee were not well content:
 Then hee to late his rigour did repent
  Gaynst mee, my sisters' fawning loue that knew,
  Found flattery false, that seem'd so faire in vew.

22. To make it short, to *Fraunce* hee came at last to mee,
 And told mee how my sisters euell their father vsde.
 Then humbly I besought my noble King so free,
 That he would aide my father thus by his abusde:
 Who nought at all my humble hest refusde,
  But sent to euery coast of *Fraunce* for aide,
  Whereby King *Leire* might home bee well conueyde.

23. The souldiours gathered from ech quarter of the land
 Came at the length to know the noble Princes will:
 Who did commit them vnto captaynes euery band,
 And I likewise of loue and reuerent meere good will
 Desir'd my Lord, he would not take it ill
  If I departed for a space withall,
  To take a part, or ease my father's thrall.

24. Hee granted my request: Thence wee ariued here,
 And of our *Britaynes* came to aide likewise his right
 Full many subiects, good and stout that were:
 By martiall feats, and force, by subiects sword and might,
 The *British* Kings were fayne to yeeld our right:
  Which wonne, my father well this Realme did guide
  Three yeares in peace, and after that hee dyde.

III. *Spenser's Faërie Queene.* — Book ii, canto **x**, 27-32.

27. Next him king Leyr in happie peace long raynd,
     But had no issue male him to succeed,
     But three faire daughters, which were well uptraind
     In all that seemed fitt for kingly seed;
     Mongst whom his realme he equally decreed
     To have divided.   Tho when feeble age
     Nigh to his utmost date he saw proceed,
     He cald his daughters, and with speeches sage
 Inquyrd, which of them most did love her parentage.

28. The eldest, Gonorill, gan to protest,
     That she much more than her owne life him lov'd;
     And Regan greater love to him profest
     Then all the world, when ever it were proov'd;
     But Cordeill said she lov'd him as behoov'd:
     Whose simple answer, wanting colours fayre
     To paint it forth, him to displeasaunce moov'd,
     That in his crowne he counted her no hayre,
 But twixt the other twaine his kingdom whole did **shayre.**

29. So wedded th'one to Maglan King of Scottes,
     And thother to the king of Cambria,
     And twixt them shayrd his realme by equall **lottes;**
     But without dowre the wise Cordelia
     Was sent to Aggannip of Celtica.
     Their aged syre, thus eased of his crowne,
     A private life led in Albania
     With Gonorill, long had in great renowne,
 That nought him griev'd to beene from rule deposed **downe.**

30. But true it is that, when the oyle is spent,
     The light goes out, and weeke is throwne away;
     So when he had resignd his regiment,
     His daughter gan despise his drouping day,
     And wearie wax of his continuall stay.
     Tho to his daughter Regan he repayrd,
     Who him at first well used every way;
     But when of his departure she despayrd,
 Her bountie she abated, and his cheare **empayrd.**

31. The wretched man gan then avise too late,
     That love is not where most it is profest;
     Too truely tryde in his extremest state.
     At last resolv'd likewise to prove the rest,
     He to Cordelia him selfe addrest,

Who with entyre affection him receav'd,
As for her syre and king her seemed best;
And after all an army strong she leav'd,
To war on those which him had of his realme bereav'd.

32. So to his crowne she him restor'd againe,
In which he dyde, made ripe for death by eld,
And after wild it should to her remaine:
Who peacefully the same long time did weld,
And all mens harts in dew obedience held;
Till that her sisters children, woxen strong,
Through proud ambition against her rebeld,
And overcommen kept in prison long,
Till weary of that wretched life her selfe she hong.

IV. *Sidney's Arcadia.* — Book ii, chapter 10; edition of 1590,
fol. 142–144.

*The pitifull state, and storie of the Paphlagonian vnkinde King, and
his kind sonne, first related by the son, then by the blind father.*

It was in the kingdome of *Galacia*, the season being (as in the
depth of winter) very cold, and as then sodainely growne to so
extreame and foule a storme, that neuer any winter (I thinke)
brought foorth a fowler child : so that the Princes were euen com-
pelled by the haile, that the pride of the winde blew into their
faces, to seeke some shrowding place within a certaine hollow rocke
offering it vnto them, they made it their shield against the tempests
furie. And so staying there, till the violence therof was passed,
they heard the speach of a couple, who not perceiuing them (being
hidde within that rude canapy) helde a straunge and pitifull
disputation which made them steppe out; yet in such sort, as
they might see vnseene. There they perceaued an aged man,
and a young, scarcely come to the age of a man, both poorely
arayed, extreamely weather-beaten; the olde man blinde, the
young man leading him: and yet through all those miseries, in
both these seemed to appeare a kind of noblenesse, not sutable to
that affliction. But the first words they heard, were these of the
old man. Well *Leonatus* (said he) since I cannot perswade thee to
lead me to that which should end my griefe, & thy trouble, let me now
entreat thee to leaue me : feare not, my miserie cannot be greater
then it is, & nothing doth become me but miserie; feare not the
danger of my blind steps, I cannot fall worse then I am. And
doo not I pray thee, doo not obstinately continue to infect thee
with my wretchednes. But flie, flie from this region, onely worthy
of me. Deare father (answered he) doo not take away from me
the onely remnant of my happinesse : while I haue power to doo
you seruice, I am not wholly miserable. Ah my sonne (said he,

and with that he groned, as if sorrow straue to breake his hearte) how euill fits it me to haue such a sonne, and how much doth thy kindnesse vpbraide my wickednesse? These dolefull speeches, and some others to like purpose (well shewing they had not bene borne to the fortune they were in,) moued the Princes to goe out vnto them, and aske the younger what they were? Sirs (answered he, with a good grace, and made the more agreable by a certaine noble kinde of pitiousnes) I see well you are straungers, that know not our miserie so well here knowne, that no man dare know, but that we must be miserable. In deede our state is such, as though nothing is so needfull vnto vs as pittie, yet nothing is more daungerous vnto vs, then to make our selues so knowne as may stirre pittie. But your presence promiseth, that cruelty shall not ouer-runne hate. And if it did, in truth our state is soncke below the degree of feare.

This old man (whom I leade) was lately rightfull Prince of this countrie of *Paphlagonia*, by the hard-hearted vngratefulnes of a sonne of his, depriued, not onely of his kingdome (wherof no forraine forces were euer able to spoyle him) but of his sight, the riches which Nature graunts to the poorest creatures. Whereby, & by other his vnnaturall dealings, he hath bin driuen to such griefe, as euen now he would haue had me to haue led him to the toppe of this rocke, thence to cast himselfe headlong to death : and so would haue made me (who receiued my life of him) to be the worker of his destruction. But noble Gentlemen (said he) if either of you haue a father, and feele what duetifull affection is engraffed in a sonnes hart, let me intreate you to conuey this afflicted Prince to some place of rest & securitie. Amongst your worthie actes it shall be none of the least, that a King, of such might and fame, and so vniustly oppressed, is in any sort by you relieued.

But before they could make him answere, his father began to speake. Ah my sonne (said he) how euill an Historian are you, that leaue out the chiefe knotte of all the discourse? my wickednes, my wickednes. And if thou doest it to spare my eares, (the onely sense nowe left me proper for knowledge) assure thy selfe thou dost mistake me. And I take witnesse of that Sunne which you see (with that he cast vp his blinde eyes, as if he would hunt for light,) and wish my selfe in worse case then I do wish my selfe, which is as euill as may be, if I speake vntruly ; that nothing is so welcome to my thoughts, as the publishing of my shame. Therefore know you Gentlemen (to whom from my harte I wish that it may not proue ominous foretoken of misfortune to haue mette with such a miser as I am) that whatsoeuer my sonne (ô God, that trueth binds me to reproch him with the name of my sonne) hath said, is true. But besides those truthes, this also is true, that hauing had in lawful mariage, of a mother fitte to beare royall children, this sonne (such one as partly you see, and better shall knowe by my shorte declaration) and so enioyed the expectations in the world of him, till he was growen to iustifie their expectations (so as I needed enuie no father for the chiefe comfort of mortalitie, to leaue an other ones-selfe after me) I was caried by a bastarde sonne of mine (if at least I be bounde to beleeue the words of that base woman my concubine, his mother) first to mislike, then to hate, lastly to destroy, to doo my best to destroy, this sonne (I thinke you thinke) vndeseruing destruction. What waies he vsed to bring me to it, if I should tell you, I should tediously trouble you with as much poysonous hypocrisie, desperate fraude, smoothe malice, hidden ambition, & smiling enuie, as in anie liuing person could be harbored. But I list it not, no remembrance, (no, of naughtines) delights me, but mine own; & me thinks, the accusing his traines might in some manner excuse my fault, which certainly I loth to doo. But the conclusion is, that I gaue order to some seruants of mine, whom I thought as apte for such charities as my selfe, to leade him out into a forrest, & there to kill him.

But those theeues (better natured to my sonne then my selfe) spared his life, letting him goe, to learne to liue poorely: which he did, giuing himselfe to be a priuate souldier, in a countrie here by. But as he was redy to be greatly aduanced for some noble peeces of seruice which he did, he hearde newes of me: who (dronke in my affection to that vnlawfull and vnnaturall sonne of mine) suffered my self so to be gouerned by him, that all fauours and punishments passed by him, all offices, and places of importance, distributed to his fauorites; so that ere I was aware, I had left my self nothing but the name of a King: which he shortly wearie of too, with many indignities (if any thing may be called an indignity, which was laid vpon me) threw me out of my seat, and put out my eies; and then (proud in his tyrannie) let me goe, nether imprisoning, nor killing me: but rather delighting to make me feele my miserie; miserie indeed, if euer there were any; full of wretchednes, fuller of disgrace, and fullest of guiltines. And as he came to the crowne by so vniust meanes, as vniustlie he kept it, by force of stranger souldiers in *Cittadels*, the nestes of tyranny, & murderers of libertie; disarming all his own countrimen, that no man durst shew himself a wel-willer of mine: to say the trueth (I think) few of them being so (considering my cruell follie to my good sonne, and foolish kindnes to my vnkinde bastard:) but if there were any who fell to pitie of so great a fall, and had yet any sparkes of vnstained duety lefte in them towardes me, yet durst they not shewe it, scarcely with giuing me almes at their doores; which yet was the onelie sustenance of my distressed life, no bodie daring to shewe so much charitie, as to lende me a hande to guide my darke steppes: Till this sonne of mine (God knowes, woorthie of a more vertuous, and more fortunate father) forgetting my abhominable wrongs, not recking daunger, & neglecting the present good way he was in doing himselfe good, came hether to doo this kind office you see him performe towards me, to my vnspeakable griefe; not onely because his kindnes is a glasse euen to my blind eyes, of my naughtines, but that aboue all griefes, it greeues me he should desperatly aduenture the losse of his soul-deseruing life for mine, that yet owe more to fortune for my deserts, as if he would cary mudde in a chest of christall.   For well I know, he that now raigneth, how much soeuer (and with good reason) he despiseth me, of all men despised; yet he will not let slippe any aduantage to make away him, whose iust title (ennobled by courage and goodnes) may one day shake the seate of a neuer secure tyrannie.   And for this cause I craued of him to leade me to the toppe of this rocke, indeede I must confesse, with meaning to free him from so serpentine a companion as I am.   But he finding what I purposed, onely therein since he was borne, shewed himselfe disobedient vnto me.   And now Gentlemen, you haue the true storie, which I pray you publish to the world, that my mischieuous proceedings may be the glorie of his filiall pietie, the onely reward now left for so great a merite.   And if it may be, let me obtaine that of you, which my sonne denies me : for neuer was there more pity in sauing any, then in ending me ; both because therein my agonies shall ende, and so shall you preserue this excellent young man, who els wilfully folowes his owne ruine.

APPENDIX B

METRE [1]

1. BLANK VERSE

The normal verse consists of ten syllables alternately stressed and unstressed, beginning with an unstressed syllable, without rhyme (hence called "blank verse"), and with a sense pause at the end of the line, e.g.:

He raised' the house' with loud' and cow'ard cries' (ii. 4. 43).
Return' to her,' and fif'ty men' dismiss'd'? (ii. 4. 210).

As the line contains five feet, each of two syllables, and each stressed on the second syllable, it is commonly called an *iambic pentameter*.

2. NORMAL VARIATIONS

A succession of such lines, however, would be monotonous. Accordingly, there are several variations in the rhythm.

(a) *Stress Inversion.* — The normal order of *non-stress* and *stress* may be inverted; e.g. in the various feet:

(1) Why' have | my sisters husbands, if they say (i. 1. 101).
(2) But love, | dear' love, | and our aged father's right (iv. 4. 28).
(3) Which I must act: | brief'ness | and fortune, work! (ii. 1. 20).
(4) Let me beseech your grace | not' to | do so (ii. 2. 147).
(5) Though I condemn not, yet, under | par'don (i. 4. 365).

This inversion occurs commonly after a pause, and is thus found most frequently in the first, third, and fourth feet, *i.e.* after the pauses at the beginning or centre of the line. It is seldom found in the second foot, and it is very rare in the fifth foot. When it occurs in the fifth foot the effect is generally unrhythmical.

There are occasionally two inversions in the same line, e.g.:

(1, 4) Broth'er, | a word; descend: | broth'er, | I say! (ii. 1. 21).
(1, 4) Bold' in | the quarrel's right, | roused' to | the encounter
(ii. 1. 56).

[1] This appendix has been suggested largely by the "Outline of Shakespeare's Prosody" in Professor Herford's *Richard II*.

(1, 3) None' does | offend, | none,' I | say, none; I 'll able 'em
(iv. 6. 172).

Two inversions rarely come together, as in i. 4. 365.

(*b*) *Stress Variation.* — The stresses may vary in degree; a weak or intermediate stress (`) may be substituted for a strong stress (').

And dare, | upon` | the war | rant of` | my note (iii. 1. 18).

The weak stress is particularly common in the fifth foot, *e.g.:*

Which else were shame, that then neces | sity` (i. 4. 232).

There are, in fact, comparatively few lines with the normal five strong stresses. But there are certain limits to the variations: *e.g.* there are never more than two weak-stressed feet in a line, and two weak-stressed feet rarely come together (see, however, iii. 4. 15). Frequently the absence of a strong stress in a foot is made up for by (1) two weak stresses, as:

Prith'ee | go` in` | thyself'; seek thine own ease (iii. 4. 23) ;

or (2) an additional stress in a neighboring foot, either before or after, as:

Both' wel' | come and` | protection. Take up thy master
(iii. 6. 99).
The les | ser is` | scarce' felt.' | Thou 'ldst shun a bear (iii. 4. 9).

Two strong stresses are fairly common in the fifth foot, *e.g.:*

Although | the last | not least, | to whose | young' love'.

(Cf. i. 1. 148, iii. 2. 42, iv. 6. 187.)

(*c*) *Addition of Unstressed Syllables.* — An unstressed syllable is frequently added. It may be introduced in any foot, which then corresponds to an anapæst instead of an iambus.

(1) I am al | most mad myself : I had a son (iii. 4. 171).
(2) And when | I have stol'n | upon these sons-in-law (iv. 6. 190).
(3) Thou 'ldst meet the bear | i' the mouth. | When the mind 's free (iii. 4. 11).
(4) Whereto our health is bound ; | we are not | ourselves
(ii. 4. 108).
(5) You sulphurous and thought-exe | cuting fires (iii. 2. 4).

Occasionally there are two such extra syllables in the same line, *e.g.:*

(2, 4) When maj | esty stoops | to fol | ly. Reverse | thy doom
(i. 1. 151).

But see 4 (*b*) (1) (2). These additional syllables within the line occur commonly at the pause or *cæsura*.

Extra-metrical. — This additional unstressed syllable is most commonly found at the end of the line, where it is extra-metrical, *e.g.*:

> I tax not you, you elements, with unkind | ness;
> I never gave you kingdom, call'd you chil | dren (iii. 2. 16–17).

It forms what is known as a *double* or *feminine ending*. It is comparatively rare in Shakespeare's early plays, but it becomes more and more common, until in *The Tempest* it occurs once in every three lines. Of the 2238 lines of blank verse in *King Lear*, 567 have double endings.[1]

Two extra unstressed syllables are occasionally found at the end of a line, *e.g.*:

> My heart into my mouth : I love your maj | esty (i. 1. 94).
> That he suspects none : on whose foolish hon | esty (i. 2. 197).

But no sharp division can be made between a line such as this and a six-stressed line or Alexandrine (3 (*a*)) ; and it is sometimes best to consider the first of the two extra syllables as slurred (4 (*b*) (1) (2)).

Examples of these extra syllables are common in lines containing proper names, *e.g.*:

> And you, our no less loving son of Al | bany (i. 1. 43).

But most lines containing proper names contain an extra *stressed* syllable, *e.g.* i. 1. 46. Such lines are especially common in the English Histories. "They appear to be often on principle extra-metrical, and in any case comply very loosely with the metre."

(*d*) *Omission of Unstressed Syllables.* — On the other hand, an unstressed syllable is sometimes, though rarely, omitted, *e.g.*:

> — Ay, | and lay | ing au | tumn's dust. | Good sir (iv. 6. 201).
> As may | compact | it more. | — Get | you gone (i. 4. 362).

Such omissions generally occur after a marked pause, and hence (1) are found commonly, like stress inversion, in the first, third, and fourth feet ; and (2) are frequently caused by a change of speaker, *e.g.*:

> *Edg.* Hark, do | you hear | the sea ?
> *Glou.*   — No' | truly (iv. 6. 4).

[1] See Fleay's *Shakespeare Manual*, p. 136.

(e) *Pauses.* — The normal verse has a sense pause at the end of the line, and a slighter pause (cæsura) within it. These are clearly marked in early blank verse (*e.g. Gorboduc*), where the pause within the line falls commonly after the second foot. The varied position of this pause, and the omission of the pause at the end of the line, constitute, in Shakespeare's later plays, his commonest departure from the normal type. The lines in which the sense is, in Milton's words, "variously drawn out from one verse into another," are called *run-on* or *unstopped* lines; while the non-coincidence of the full sense with the end of the line forms what is known as *enjambement* or *overflow.* Like the double or feminine ending, the run-on line was gradually used more and more by Shakespeare. In *Love's Labour's Lost,* a typical early play, it occurs about once in every eighteen lines, while in *The Tempest, Cymbeline,* and *The Winter's Tale* it occurs on an average of twice in every five lines.

(f) *Light and Weak Endings.* — The most pronounced form of the run-on line is that with a *light* or *weak* ending. Such endings have the distinctive quality of being monosyllabic. Thus:

> Let it fall rather, though the fork invade
> The region of my heart (i. 1. 146).

is merely an instance of a run-on line. But there is a *light* ending in

> You have begot me, bred me, loved me! I
> Return those duties (i. 1. 98–99).

and in

> How sharper than a serpent's tooth it is
> To have a thankless child (i. 4. 310–311).

The difference between *light* and *weak* endings is that "the voice can to a small extent dwell" on the former; while the latter so "precipitate the reader forward" that he is "forced to run them, in pronunciation no less than in sense, into the closest connection with the opening words of the succeeding line." Hence *light* endings consist of the auxiliaries, personal pronouns, etc., and *weak* endings of prepositions, conjunctions, etc. They are characteristic of Shakespeare's later plays; some of his earlier plays, *e.g.* the *Comedy of Errors* and the *Two Gentlemen of Verona,* do not contain a single instance of them. Of the two, the *light* ending was the earlier in use, and it is always the commoner; but its relative importance gradually diminished. Thus, in *Macbeth,* for 21 *light* endings there are only 2 *weak* endings, but in *The Winter's Tale* the numbers are respectively 57 and 43.[1] There does not appear to be any instance in *King Lear* of a *weak* ending; the following example is taken from *Henry VIII*, iii. 2. 173:

> To the good of your most sacred person and
> The profit of the state.

It should be noted that the closing of a line with a preposition or other similar word is not alone sufficient to constitute a *weak* ending; *e.g.* iv. 7. 16. Lines closing in *so* followed by *as* (*e.g.* v. 3. 36) generally form *light* endings.

3. OCCASIONAL VARIATIONS

(*a*) *Addition of Stressed Syllables.* — Lines are occasionally found with six stressed syllables (*i.e.* with an additional foot), *e.g.*:

> To speak and purpose not: since what I well intend (i. 1. 228).

The pause in the six-stressed line (commonly called an *Alexandrine*) is found most frequently after the third foot. It occurs after the first in ii. 2. 153, and after the fourth in iv. 3. 44. It is generally very marked; hence it often occurs when there is a change of speaker, *e.g.*:

> *France.* Could never plant in me.
> *Cor.*   I yet beseech your majesty (i. 1. 226).

(*b*) *Omission of Stressed Syllables.* — Lines with only four stressed syllables are much rarer. The omission of the stress likewise may generally be accounted for by a marked pause. Hence it also occurs most commonly at a break in the dialogue, *e.g.*:

> *Lear.* Come.
> *Edm.*   Come hither, captain; hark (v. 3. 26).

Indeed a marked pause is the source of most metrical irregularities.

(*c*) *Short or Broken Lines.* — There are many short lines containing only *one* to *four* feet. They occur most frequently at the beginning or end of a speech; but there are several examples of them in *King Lear* in the middle of a speech, where they mark the completion or change of a subject or idea. These short lines, however, generally consist of questions, commands, exclamations, addresses, etc.: *e.g.* i. 4. 239, i. 1. 278, iv. 5. 36, i. 4. 284. Some of

---

[1] See Professor Ingram's paper in the *Transactions of the New Shakspere Society*, 1874, pt. ii.

the shorter lines may be regarded as extra-metrical. It will be noted that the short line is especially frequent in the more passionate speeches: *e.g.* i. 4. 299, ii. 4. 286, and iv. 6. 112–129.

The broken speech ending is a characteristic of the later plays.

4. APPARENT VARIATIONS

Many apparent irregularities are due to difference of pronunciation in Shakespeare's time.

(*a*) *Accentual.* — The accent has changed in many words: *e.g.* Shakespeare always has *aspéct* (ii. 2. 112), *impórtune* (iii. 4. 166) and *sepúlchre* — the verb — (ii. 4. 134). *Retinue* has the accent on the second syllable in i. 4. 221, and *observants* has it on the first in ii. 2. 109 — the only occasions in Shakespeare in which these words occur in verse. *Consort*, as a noun in the sense of company, is accented on the last syllable (ii. 1. 99).

Certain words had not a fixed pronunciation. It is often only by the position of the word in the verse that we can decide on which syllable the accent falls. Thus the noun *sepulchre* has usually the accent on the first syllable, but in *Richard II*, i. 3. 196, it is pronounced, like the verb, with the accent on the second syllable. Similarly *revénue* in i. 1. 139 and ii. 1. 102, but *révenue* in *Richard II*, i. 4. 46; *éxtreme* (iv. 6. 26), but *extrémest* (v. 3. 136). Note also *síncere* in ii. 2. 111. In general an adjective preceding a noun of one syllable, or a noun accented on the first syllable, is not accented on the last. A striking example of this accentual change is found in *Henry VIII*, v. i. 132:

> Might *córrupt* minds procure knaves as *corrúpt*.

The same change invariably takes place in such two-syllabled adjectives as *complete, exact, obscure, extreme, sincere,* etc.[1] The pronunciation which now survives is generally that which represents most closely the Latin quantity. The *English* accentuation of these Romance words tended in Shakespeare's time to make the stress fall on the first syllable; but the influence of Latin has frequently in Modern English restored the accent to its original place.

(*b*) *Syllabic.* — (1) A vowel may be lost before a consonant at the beginning of a word: *e.g.* '*scape,* '*gainst,* '*bove; and*'*s* for *and his,* '*t* for *it,* '*s* for *his* (i. 4. 114), for *us* (iii. 4. 110), and for *is* (iv. 6. 163). Cf. *this*' for *this is* (iv. 6. 187).

The same omission takes place within a word (syncope):

[1] See Schmidt's *Shakespeare Lexicon,* vol. ii, Appendix.

a. In the inflexion, as in the past tense and past participle, in the second person singular, as *mean'st* (ii. 2. 114), in the possessive, as *Phœbus'* (ii. 2. 114), and in the superlative ('*st* for *est*). These shortened forms become more and more common in Shakespeare.

b. In the second last syllable of words of three syllables accented on the first: *e.g. courtẹsy* [1] (ii. 4. 182) and *majẹsty* (i. 1. 151), though *ma-jẹs-ty* (v. 3. 299). This contracted pronunciation has become fixed in such words as *business, medicine*. It is most commonly caused by a "vowel-like" (see (3) below).

(2) Two vowels coming together may coalesce, whether in the same word or in adjacent words: *e.g. influ͡ence* (ii. 2. 113), *radi͡ant* (ii. 2. 113), *materi͡al* (iv. 2. 35), *vi͡olent* (iv. 7. 28), *immedi͡acy* (v. 3. 65), *soci͡ety* (v. 3. 210), *th͡e expense* (ii. 1. 102), *th͡e untented* (i. 4. 322). *Royal* and *loyal* are generally dissyllabic.

There is no definite pronunciation of the terminations *-ion, -ious, -eous,* etc. Thus we find *conditi-on* (iv. 7. 57), but *benedicti͡on* (iv. 7. 58), and *gorge-ous* (ii. 4. 271) but *gorge͡ous* (ii. 4. 272). The contracted pronunciation — that now in vogue — is the more common in Shakespeare's verse, though the dissyllabic pronunciation was recognized throughout the seventeenth century.[2]

(3) The liquids *l, m, n,* and *r* have the function of either a consonant or a vowel, and are therefore called "vowel-likes."

a. By the consonant (non-syllabic) function they may cause the loss of a syllable, either immediately before or after: *e.g. amọrous* (i. 1. 48), *murdẹrous* (ii. 1. 64), *stubbọrn* (ii. 2. 134), *pelịcan* (iii. 4. 77), *memọries* (iv. 7. 7), *tempẹrance* (iv. 7. 24), *victọry* (v. 1. 41), *countẹnance* (v. 1. 63), *prisọners* (v. 3. 75), *intẹrest* (v. 3. 85), *privịlege* (v. 3. 129), *absọlute* (v. 3. 300). Also in words of four syllables: *e.g. unfortụnate* (iv. 6. 68), *despẹrately* (v. 3. 292), and *particụlar* (v. 1. 30), though *partic-u-lars* (i. 4. 286).

b. By the vowel (syllabic) function they may form a new syllable: *e.g. entrance*, sometimes written *enterance, through*, sometimes written *thorough, hel-m* (iv. 7. 36), but *helm* (iv. 2. 57), *light-n-ing* (iv. 7. 35), but *light-ning* (ii. 4. 167).

The vowel-like *r* frequently resolves a preceding long vowel or diphthong into two syllables: *e.g.* such words as *hour, hire, fire* are sometimes dissyllabic.

(4) Sometimes a consonant, usually *th* or *v*, coming between two vowels is omitted, the vowels coalescing; in these cases the second vowel is followed by *r* or *n*. Thus *even* (adv.) is generally

---

[1] The mark (.) under a vowel means that it is mute.
[2] See Sweet's *History of English Sounds*, § 915.

a monosyllable; so also *ever*, *never*, *over*, often written *e'er*, *ne'er*, *o'er*. The *th* is often omitted in *whether* (sometimes written *where*), *rather*, etc.

5. RHYME

According to Mr. Fleay's calculation, there are seventy-four rhymed lines in *King Lear*. Shakespeare's use of rhyme gradually diminished, but he retained throughout his career the couplet at the end of a scene. There are several instances of it in *King Lear*, *e.g.* i. 2, iv. 7, v. 1, and v. 3. Rhyme also marks the close of a speech and the exit of an actor, *e.g.* i. 1. 257–264. In iv. 6. 284–285 it is used to mark a change of subject. It has also the closely connected purpose of giving point to the expression (*e.g.* i. 1. 276–277, i. 4. 338–339); and hence it readily lends itself, by reason of this epigrammatic force, to clinching the argument and making an effective ending. The only rhymed passage of any length occurs at the end of iii. 6. It illustrates the use of rhyme in passages of moralizing or of "*plaintive* emotion." Rhyme is not used in passages of passionate emotion, — the tendency is rather to pass into prose, — nor for narrative, nor for the development of the action of the drama.

GLOSSARY

advise (ii. 1. 29), reflect, consider; used reflexively. Similarly *advice* = consideration, judgment. O.Fr. *aviser*, *avis*, Late Lat. *ad-visum*. Originally " the way in which a matter is looked at, opinion, judgment " (Murray).

aidant (iv. 4. 17), helpful. O.Fr. *aidant*, pres. part. of *aider*.

alarum'd (ii. 1. 55), aroused, called to arms. *Alarum* is another form of *alarm*. O.Fr. *alarme*, Italian *allarme* = *all' arme!* " To arms! " Thus originally an interjection, but used later as a name for the summons to arms. The derivative sense of " fright," which is confined to the form *alarm*, is not found in Shakespeare.

allow (ii. 4. 194), approve of, sanction. O.Fr. *alouer*, representing both Lat. *allaudare*, to praise, and *allocare*, to place, assign. Hence the two senses of " approving " and " granting," which are so close as to blend. The former sense is more common in M.E. and E.E., the latter in Mod. E. Cf. **allowance** (i. 4. 228), approval.

an (i. 4. 112; ii. 2. 48, 106; ii. 4. 65), if. Spelled *And* in the Qq and F1, and generally in E.E. Its derivation is uncertain, but it is probably the same word as the coördinate.

attaint (v. 3. 83), impeachment. O.Fr. *ateinte*, from p.p. of *ateindre*, " to attain," hence " to strike, condemn." Lat. *attingere*, " to touch upon."

It is a distinct word from *taint*, " stain," which comes from Fr. *teindre*, Lat. *tingere* or *tinguere*.

attend (ii. 1. 127; ii. 4. 36), await. O.Fr. *atendre*, L. *ad* + *tendre*. Primarily " to stretch to." Hence the meanings " to direct the mind to," " to look after," " wait upon," and " to wait for."

avaunt (iii. 6. 68), begone! Fr. *avant*, forward! Lat. *ab ante*.

bandy (i. 4. 92; ii. 4. 178). The origin is obscure. Fr. *bander*, to strike a ball to and fro, as in tennis; perhaps from *bande*, a side.

benison (i. 1. 269; iv. 6. 229), blessing. M.E. *beneysun*, O.Fr. *beneison*, Lat. *benedictionem;* hence a doublet of " benediction."

boot (iv. 6. 230; v. 3. 301). O.E. *bót*, advantage, good, profit; related in derivation to " better," " best." It occurs commonly in the phrase *to boot*, " to the good," " in addition," as in iv. 6. 230. The verb is represented in M.E. by *bōten*.

caitiff (iii. 2. 55), wretch. Norm. Fr. *caitif*, " captive," " miserable," Lat. *captivum*. Its Norman origin is shown by the retention of the Latin *c* before *a*. French dialects generally represented this *c* by *ch*: cf. *castle* and Fr. *château*, *caitiff* and Fr. *chétif*. There was an early English variant *chaitif*, which came from a central **Fr.**

form. The word is occasionally used in E.E. in the original sense, "captive."

can (iv. 4. 8). O.E. *cunnan*, "The O. Teut. sense was 'to know, know how, be mentally or intellectually able,' whence 'to be able generally, be physically able, have the power'" (Murray).

champains (i. 1. 65), or *champaigns*, plains. M.E. *champayne*, O.Fr. *champaigne*, Lat. *campania*; ultimately from Lat. *campus*, a level field. The word was taken into English in the central French form *champaigne*, not in the Norman French form *campaigne* (Murray); contrast *caitiff*.

cockney (ii. 4. 123); a pampered, affected woman; see note. M.E. *cokeney*, apparently *coken*, "of cocks" + *ey*, "egg"; thus literally "cock's egg." The word was either a child's name for an egg, or a name for a small or misshapen egg. It was then applied as a humorous or derisive name for an unduly pampered child, a milksop. From this it was applied to a townsman, as being effeminate in comparison with a countryman. Finally it has got its modern special reference to a native of London (Murray).

comforting (iii. 5. 21), aiding, assisting; a common legal sense. O.Fr. *conforter*, Lat. *confortare*, to strengthen, *con* intensive + *fortis*, strong. In legal phraseology it is commonly used along with the synonymous word "aiding," *e.g.* "aiding and comforting," "giving aid and comfort."

commend (ii. 4. 28; iii. 1. 19), deliver, commit. Through O.Fr. from Lat. *commendare*, *com* + *mandare*, to commit to one's care. The secondary sense of "praising" arose from the idea that what is committed is worthy of acceptance. The sense of "committing" survives in such phrases as "commend to memory"; but it was much commoner in E.E. than the sense of "praising."

compeers (v. 3. 69), equals, is a compeer with. O.Fr. *comper*, *com* + *per*, a peer (in Mod. Fr. *pair*), Lat. *parem*.

conceit (iv. 6. 42), imagination, illusion. Probably formed from *conceive* on the analogy of *deceit*, *deceive*, there being apparently no corresponding O.Fr. word. It never occurs in Shakespeare in the modern sense of "high opinion of oneself."

convey (i. 2. 109), carry out, do secretly. M.E. *conveien*, O.Fr. *conveier*, Late Lat. *conviare*, *con* + *via*. Originally "to accompany on the way," "to convoy"; but used later of inanimate things = "to transport, carry," and especially with a sense of secrecy. Cf. i. 4. 300.

cozen'd (v. 3. 154), cheated, beguiled. The derivation is uncertain. It has commonly been connected with Fr. *cousiner*, defined by Cotgrave, 1611, as "to clayme kindred for advantage, or particular ends; as he who, to save charges in travelling, goes from house to house as *cosin* to the honor of everyone." But there is no idea of "pretext of relationship" in *cozen* in E.E., in which the meaning is simply to "cheat." Cf. **cozener**, iv. 6. 167.

curious (i. 4. 35), complicated, intricate. O.Fr. *curius*, Lat. *curiosus*, full of care, scrupulous. Cf. **curiosity**, "scruples," i. 2. 4, "nicety of suspicion," i. 4. 75, and "careful investigation," i. 1. 6.

darkling (i. 4. 207), in the dark. M.E. *darkeling*, *dark* + *ling*, an old adverbial formative. Cf. *flatling* or *flatlong*, *headling* or *headlong*, *sidelong*.

debosh'd (i. 4. 237), an early variant of "debauched." Taken, about 1600, from Fr. *débaucher*, to draw away from duty; hence to lead astray, corrupt. "Obsolete in English before the middle of the seventeenth century; retained longer in Scotch; revived by Scott, and now frequent in literary English with somewhat vaguer sense than *debauched*" (Murray). *Deboshed* is the only form in Shakespeare.

deer (iii. 4. 144). Not used in its modern special sense, but applied to animals generally, usually to quadrupeds as distinct from birds and fishes. O.E. *déor*. Not connected with Gr. θήρ, a wild beast.

demand (iii. 2. 65; v. 3. 62), ask; the commoner meaning of the word in Shakespeare. Cf. the substantive, i. 5. 3. Fr. *demander*, Lat. *de* + *mandare*.

digest (i. 1. 130), divide, dispose of. Lat. *digerere*, to carry asunder, divide, *dis* + *gerere*. Schmidt's explanation that it is used figuratively in the sense of "enjoy" is untenable.

earnest (i. 4. 104), money paid beforehand as a pledge. The derivation is uncertain. Cf. O. Fr. *erres*, Mod. Fr. *arrhes*, from Lat. *arrha*. The Scottish form *arles* is apparently from the same root.

engraffed (i. 1. 301), engrafted. *Graff* was the original form, and was in common use in E.E. The current form *graft* probably arose from the use of *graft* (*graffed*) as the p. part. of the old form. O.Fr. *grafe*, *greffe* (Mod. Fr. *greffe*), a slip of a tree, originally a pointed instrument. Late Lat. *gra-*

phium, a writing style. Gr. γράφειν, to write. The Qq have the form *ingrafted*.

enormous (ii. 2. 176), abnormal, monstrous. Lat. *enormis*, *e* + *norma*, pattern, rule. This is the only instance of the word in Shakespeare's plays. The usual sense now — "huge" — is derivative.

entertain (iii. 6. 83), take into service; a common meaning in E.E. Cf. *Two Gentlemen of Verona*, ii. 4. 110, "entertain him for your servant." Fr. *entretenir*, Lat. *inter* + *tenere*.

esperance (iv. 1. 4), hope. O.Fr. *esperance*, Late Lat. *sperantia*, *sperare*, to hope.

essay (i. 2. 47), trial, test. O.Fr. *essai* or *assai*, Lat. *exagium*, "weighing," hence "examination," *exigere*, "to weigh, consider," *ex* + *ago*. The commoner form in Shakespeare is *assay*; *essay* occurs only here and in *Sonnets*, cx. 8. Cf. *say*.

exhibition (i. 2. 25), allowance. O.Fr. *exhibicion*, Late Lat. *exhibitionem*, maintenance, *exhibere*, to maintain, support, in legal sense. (Cf. *exhibitio et tegumentum* = food and raiment.) Its original meaning was "maintenance, support"; hence, as here, "allowance, pension." This sense survives only in its specialized use as a kind of scholarship given by an English college, etc. It has the sense of "present" in *Othello*, iv. 3. 75: "I would not do such a thing for a jointring . . . nor any petty exhibition." The meaning "display," etc., is comparatively late.

favours (iii. 7. 40), features. M.E. *favour*, Nor. Fr. *favor*, Lat. *favorem*, kindliness. The meaning "face," "features," arose from the common transition from the feeling or disposition to that which expresses it. The meaning " face " is more common than the specialized meaning " features of the face "; but cf. *1 Henry IV*, iii. 2. 136, " and stain my favours in a bloody mask." Cf. the colloquial use of the verb in the sense of " to resemble."

feature (iv. 2. 63), outward form, appearance. O.Fr. *faiture*, Lat. *factura*, from *facere*, to make. In E.E. it preserved its original general sense of " make, form, shape." It is not used in Shakespeare in the specialized modern sense of the parts of the face.

fell (v. 3. 24), strictly a hide, skin with the hair on; but often used of the human skin, as in the phrase *flesh and fell*, which means the whole body. O.E. *fel*, cognate with Lat. *pellis*.

flaws (ii. 4. 288), shivers, splinters; akin to *flake* and *flag* (stone). Cf. *flaw'd*, broken, cracked (v. 3. 196).

fond (i. 2. 51; i. 4. 323; iv. 7. 60), foolish. M.E. *fonned*, p.p. of *fon*, primarily " to lose savour," hence " to be foolish "; probably the source of M.E. *fon*, " foolish," " a fool," as well as of the later word *fun*. From meaning " foolish, silly," it came to mean " foolishly tender," then " affectionate," the change arising from the association of warm feeling with mental weakness. The inverse process has taken place in the M.E. *silly*, which comes ultimately from O.E. *sǽl*, " happiness."

forfended (v. 1. 11), forbidden. M.E. *forfenden*, ward off, *for* + *fenden*, a shortened form of *defenden*, from Lat. *defendere*. As *for* is an English prefix — of similar force to the Latin prefix *de* — *forfenden* is thus a hybrid.

fret (i. 4. 307), wear, eat away. O.E. strong verb *fretan*, consume, from O.Teut. *fra* + *etan*, to eat. The verb is weak in E.E., but a strong p.p. survives in *fretten*, the Quarto reading of *The Merchant of Venice*, iv. 1. 77.

frontlet (i. 4. 208). See note. O.F. *frontelet*, dim. of *frontel*, ultimately from Lat. *frons*, the forehead.

fumiter (iv. 4. 3), fumitory. O.Fr. *fumeterre*, Med. Lat. *fumus terrae*, " smoke of the earth "; so called because " it springeth . . . out of the earth in great quantity." Hence " *rank* fumiter."

gallow (iii. 2. 44), terrify. An obsolete form of *gally*. O.E. *agælwan*, to alarm. Cf. *galli-crow*, used in Wessex for " scarecrow."

gasted (ii. 1. 57), frightened. O.E. *gǽstan*. The verb *gast* is the same as the verb *agast*, of which the only part in use is the p.p. *agast*, now erroneously spelled *aghast*.

germens (iii. 2. 8), germs, the seeds of life. Lat. *germen*. Cf. *Macbeth*, iv. 1. 59, " though the treasure Of nature's germens tumble all together."

good-years (v. 3. 24). An indefinite name for an evil power or agency. The word was first used as a meaningless expletive, as in the phrase " What the good year ! " But apparently from the equivalence of this phrase with " What the devil ! plague ! " etc., it came to be used in imprecations and curses for an undefined evil power. The phrase " What the good-year," which was probably adopted from the Dutch *wat goedjaar*, occurs in *The Merry Wives*, i. 4. 129 (spelled *good-jer*), *Much Ado*, i. 3. 1, and *2 Henry IV*, ii. 4. 64 and 191. The present is the only instance in Shakespeare in which it is used in its secondary force. The word is commonly defined, since Sir Thomas Hanmer's edition of Shakespeare, 1744, as the name of a disease. It is said to be a corruption of the Fr. *goujeres*, a hypothetical derivative of *gouje*, a camp-follower. But this derivation and definition are erroneous (Bradley).

holp (iii. 7. 62). Of the strong inflexions of *help*, the normal M.E. past tense was *halp;* the pl. was *holpen*, later *holp* or *holpe*, which c. 1500 was extended also to the sing., and continued in frequent use till the seventeenth century (Murray).

hurricanoes (iii. 2. 2), waterspouts. Span. *huracan*. The modern form *hurricane* was established only in the latter half of the seventeenth century. It is not found in Shakespeare. The form *hurricano* occurs also in *Troilus and Cressida*, v. 2. 172, where also it has the sense of waterspout.

inheriting (ii. 2. 20), possessing. M.E. *inheriten, enheriten*, O.Fr. *en-heriter*, Lat. *hereditare*, to inherit. Often used in E.E. in the loose sense of " come into possession of." Cf. the Biblical phrase, " shall inherit the earth."

interess'd (i. 1. 87), have an interest (or right) in. *Interess* (noun and verb) is the early form of *interest*, and is common in E.E. From M.E. and Anglo-Fr. *interesse* (subst.), Lat. *interesse*, to concern, be of importance.

intrinse (ii. 2. 81), intricate, involved. Perhaps an abbreviation of *intrinsicate;* see *Antony and Cleopatra*, v. 2. 307. Cf. *reverbs*, i. 1. 156.

justicer (iii. 6. 23, 59). O.Fr. *justicier*, Late Lat. *justitiarius;* thus identical in derivation with " justiciar " or " justiciary." It is used by Shakespeare in the sense of " justiciar " or " administrator of justice "; but it has often the less specialized meaning of " one who maintains justice, upholds the right," as in iv. 2. 79. In iii. 6. 23 the Ff and Qq read *justice;* Theobald's emendation *justicer* is supported by line 59.

knapped (ii. 4. 125), knocked, struck. Of onomatopoetic formation, the original meaning being "to strike with a hard, sharp sound."

knave (i. 1. 21; i. 4. 46, 103), boy, servant. M.E. *knaue*, O.E. *cnafa, cnapa*, a boy. Cf. Ger. *knabe*. From meaning a male child, it came to mean a boy employed as a servant, in both of which senses it is used in *King Lear*. Shakespeare uses it also in its modern sense of " rascal," " villain."

liege (i. 1. 36), sovereign. M.E. *lige, lege, liege*, O.Fr. *lige, liege*, O.H.G. *ledic*, free, unrestrained. Hence properly used, as in the title *liege-lord*, of the feudal suzerain. Skeat quotes from Barbour's *Bruce*, " Bot and I lif in lege pouste " = but if I survive in *free and indisputed* sovereignty. But by supposed connection with Lat. *ligatus, ligare*, to bind, the word was applied to the vassals of the liege-lord. Hence the modern use in the sense of citizens, as in the phrase " the safety of the lieges."

mainly (iv. 7. 65), perfectly. Cf. *main* = chief, principal. O.Fr. *maine, magne*, great, Lat. *magnus*. Commonly in Shakespeare with the sense " forcibly," " mightily."

marry (iii. 2. 40; iv. 2. 68), an exclamation derived from the oath " by the Virgin *Mary*."

maugre (v. 3. 131), in spite of, O.Fr. *maulgre* (Mod. Fr. *malgré*), literally " ill will." Ultimately from Lat. *malus*, bad, and *gratum*, a pleasant thing.

meiny (ii. 4. 35), household, M.E. *meinee*, *mainee*, a household, O.Fr. *maisnee*, Low Lat. *mansionata*, a household, Lat. *mansio*, a dwelling. The word is spelled *many* in Spenser, *Faërie Queene*, v. 11. 3, 2. It is the source of *menial*.

mere (iv. 1. 22), unalloyed, pure. O.Fr. *mier*, Lat. *merus*, unmixed, especially of wine.

mess (i. 1. 119), dish of food. O.Fr. *mes*, a dish, literally that which is placed on the table; Low Lat. *missum*, *mittere*, to place; Lat. *mittere*, to send. Cf. Mod. Fr. *mets*.

minikin (iii. 6. 45), dainty, pretty. Cf. Dutch *minnekyn*, a cupid, darling, a diminutive of *minne*, love, cognate with O.H.G. *minna*, love. Allied to *minion* and Fr. *mignon*.

miscreant (i. 1. 163), wretch. Originally an " unbeliever," and perhaps used here in this sense. O.Fr. *mescreant*, Lat. *minus + credentem*. Cf. **recreant**, below.

modest (ii. 4. 25; iv. 7. 5), moderate. Fr. *modeste*, Lat. *modestus*, moderate, measurable, from *modus*, a measure. Shakespeare uses the word both in this original sense and in its derivative and current sense, " decent " or " diffident."

moiety (i. 1. 7), part, portion: strictly a half. Anglo-Fr. *moyte* (Mod. Fr. *moitié*), a half, Lat. *medietatem*, from *medius*, middle. Shakespeare uses it in both senses, " half " and " part."

motley (i. 4. 160), M.E. *mottelee*, O.Fr. *mattelé*, " curdled."

Hence " spotted," " variegated." Strictly an adjective, but used by Shakespeare as a substantive : (1) as the dress of the Fool, as here ; and (2) as the Fool himself, *e.g.* " And made myself a motley to the view," *Sonnets*, cx. 2.

naughty (iii. 4. 116; iii. 7. 36), bad, wicked, as frequently in E.E. M.E. *naught*, O.E. *nawhit*, *na*, no + *whit*, thing; hence " worthless," " good for nothing," " wicked." The sense " mischievous " is modern. Cf. *naught* = wicked, ii. 4. 136.

nicely (ii. 2. 110; v. 3. 144), punctiliously, with nicety. O.Fr. *nice*, simple, Lat. *nescius*, ignorant. The original meaning in English was " foolish," as in Chaucer; but in E.E. it had acquired the meaning of " fastidious " as applied to persons, and " petty," " trifling " as applied to things. " The remarkable changes in sense may have been due to confusion with E. *nesh*, which sometimes meant ' delicate ' as well as ' soft ' " (Skeat). Shakespeare does not use the word in the modern sense " pleasant."

œillades (iv. 5. 25), glances, amorous or inviting. The Qq read *aliads*, the Ff *eliads* (1st) and *iliads* (2d, 3d, and 4th). " It cannot be decided whether Shakespeare wrote the French word or some anglicized form of it." The word occurs also in *Merry Wives*, i. 3. 68.

offend (i. 1. 310), hurt, harm. M.E. *offenden*, Fr. *offendre*, Lat. *offendere*, to strike or dash against. *Offend* is strictly the opposite of *defend*, this sense surviving in the phrase " on the offensive," etc. The strong sense of " hurt," " harm " is comparatively rare in Shakespeare, who uses the word chiefly in its modern signification; but cf. *2 Henry IV*, ii. 4. 126, " She is pistol-proof, sir; you shall hardly offend her."

or ere (ii. 4. 289), before. The two words are identical in meaning, both being derived from the O.E. *ǽr*, before. But it is probable that *ere* was considered a contraction for *ever* = e'er. Shakespeare has both forms, *or ere* and *or ever* (*Hamlet*, i. 2. 183).

owes (i. 1. 205), possesses; **owest** (i. 4. 133). M.E. *owen*, *awen*, O.E. *agan*, *ah*, " possess." The current sense of " obligation " arises from the idea of possessing what belongs to another. The word is used in this modern sense in iii. 4. 108.

pelting (ii. 3. 18), paltry — which has partly the same source. The Northern word *paltrie* or *peltrie*, a substantive meaning " trash," was probably the source of E.E. *paultring*, *peltering*, " petty," and *pelter*, " a mean person." By association with these, *pelt*, " skin," acquired the suggestion of " trash," and from it appears to have been formed, during the sixteenth century, the word *pelting*, on the analogy of *peltrie*, *peltering* (Herford). Note the modern *pelting*, a distinct word, in iii. 4. 29.

perdu (iv. 7. 35). Not from Fr. *enfant perdu*, a soldier of a forlorn hope, but from *sentinelle perdue*, a sentry placed in a very advanced and dangerous position. Thus " to *watch* — poor perdu ! "

perdy (ii. 4. 86), an exclamation. From Fr. *par Dieu*.

plaited (i. 1. 283), folded. M.E. *plaiten*, O.Fr. *pleit*, *plet*, a fold (Mod. Fr. *pli*); Lat. *plicatus*, *plicare*, to fold. The Qq read

pleated, the Ff *plighted*, which are both doublets of *plaited*. The form *plight*, which is found in Spenser, — *e.g.* " with many a folded plight," *Faërie Queene*, ii. 3. 26, 5, — comes from M.E. *pliten*, the *gh* being an intrusion. It is quite distinct from **plight** (i. 1. 103), pledge, which comes from O.E. *pliht*, risk, danger, cognate with Ger. *pflicht*, duty.

pother (iii. 2. 50), turmoil. From the same source as *potter* and *poke;* not connected with " bother." The Ff read *pudder*, another form of the same word.

power (iii. 1. 30; iv. 2. 16; iv. 5. 1; v. 1. 51), army: a common meaning in E.E. M.E. *pouer*, O.Fr. *povoir*, Late Lat. *potere* = *posse*, to be able. Thus derivatively a substantival use of the infinitive mood. Cf. Fr. *pouvoir*.

presently (i. 4. 159; ii. 4. 34, 118), immediately, at once; the usual sense in E.E.

puissant (v. 3. 216), strong, great. F. *puissant*, Low Lat. *possens*, a pres. part. due to confusion between the correct form *potens* and the inf. *posse*. A doublet of *potent*.

quit (iii. 7. 87), requite. M.E. *quiten*, O.Fr. *quiter*, Lat. *quietare*, to set at rest. *Quit* is derivatively a shorter form of *quiet*.

recreant (i. 1. 169), coward. Strictly, one who has changed his faith. O.Fr. *recreant*, Lat. *re* + *credentem*. Cf. **miscreant** above.

renege (ii. 2. 84), deny. M.E. *reneye*, Low Lat. *renegare*, whence " renegade," etc. The *g* is pronounced hard. The spelling of the Qq is *reneag*.

reverbs (i. 1. 156), reverberates. Perhaps " a coined word, by contraction " (Skeat). Cf. *intrinse*, ii. 2. 81,

saw (ii. 2. 167), saying, proverb. M.E. *sawe*, *saʒe*, O.E. *sagu*, a saying, allied to *secgan*, to say. Cf. *As You Like It*, ii. 7. 156, " Full of wise saws."

say (v. 3. 143), proof, taste ; a common aphetic form of *assay* or *essay* (q.v.). Cf. the verbal use in *Pericles*, i. 1. 59–60, " Of all say'd yet, mayst thou prove prosperous. Of all say'd yet, I wish thee happiness ! "

sennet (i. 1, stage direction), a set of notes on a trumpet announcing the entry or exit of a procession. The word does not appear in the text of Shakespeare. The forms *synnet*, *sonnet*, *cynet*, and *signet* also occur.

several (i. 1. 45), respective, as commonly in E.E. O.Fr. *several*, Low Lat. *separale*; a doublet of " separate."

sith (i. 1. 183; ii. 4. 242), since. M.E. *sithen*. O.E. *siððan*, from *sið ðam*, after that. A doublet of *since*, which is from M.E. *sithens*, i.e. *sithen* + the adverbial termination -*s* or -*es*, as in *whiles*. Note that *sith* usually has the sense of " as," " seeing that," though it has a temporal force in *Hamlet*, ii. 2. 12.

sizes (ii. 4. 178), allowances. Short for *assize*, a fixed quantity. M.E. *assise*, O.Fr. *assis*, " an assembly of judges," " a sitting," " an impost," " quantity adjudged," ultimately from Lat. *sedere*, to sit. Hence the Cambridge term *sizar*, a scholar to whom certain " allowances " are made.

spill (iii. 2. 8), destroy. M.E. *spillen*, O.E. *spillan*, *spildan*, to destroy. Cf. *Hamlet*, iv. 5. 20:

So full of artless jealousy is guilt,
It spills itself in fearing to be spilt.

stelled (iii. 7. 61), starry, stellate. Lat. *stellatus*, *stella*, a star. Schmidt and Craig take

it to mean " fixed "; cf. *Sonnets*, xxiv. 1, " Mine eye hath played the painter and hath stell'd Thy beauty's form," and *Lucrece*, 1444, " To find a face where all distress is stell'd."

suggestion (ii. 1. 75), underhand action, the usual meaning of the word in Shakespeare. Cf. *suggest*, to prompt, incite criminally. M.E. *suggesten*, from p.p. of Lat. *suggerere*, literally " to carry or lay under," *sub* + *gerere*. *Suggest* and *suggestion* are commonly used in a bad sense in E.E.

tell (ii. 4. 55), count. M.E. *tellen*, O.E. *tellan*, to count, narrate.

tithing (iii. 4. 140), district. Originally a district containing ten families. O.E. *teoða*, a tenth.

treachers (i. 2. 133), traitors. M.E. *trecchour*, *trychor*, O.Fr. *trecher*, to cheat; ultimately of Teutonic origin; cognate with *trick*. This is the only instance of the word in Shakespeare, but it was common in E.E.

trowest (i. 4. 135), believest. M.E. *trowen*, O.E. *treówian*, to have trust in, *treówa*, trust.

tucket (ii. 1, stage direction), a flourish on a trumpet or cornet. Cf. *Henry V*, iv. 2. 35 :

Then let the trumpets sound
The tucket sonance and the note
to mount.

It. *toccata*, from *toccare*, to touch.

vaunt-couriers (iii. 2. 5), forerunners. Fr. *avant-coureur* (see *avaunt*). Cf. the contraction in *van*, *vanguard* (Fr. *avant-garde*).

villain (iii. 7. 87; iv. 6. 257), servant. O.Fr. *vilein*, Low Lat. *villanus*, a farm-servant; *villa*, a farmhouse. The word has here its original sense, but the current degraded sense "scoundrel" is the more common in Shakespeare (*e.g.* i. 2. 180).

whiles (ii. 3. 5 ; iv. 2. 58), strictly the genitive of *while*, time, used adverbially. Cf. *twice*, from *twi-es*. This old genitive survives in *whilst*.

worships (i. 4. 288), dignities, credit. M.E. *worschip*, *wurðscipe*, O.E. *weorðscipe*, *wyrðscipe*, honor ; a contraction of *worthship*, the *th* being lost in the fourteenth century.

INDEX OF WORDS

(The references are to the Notes *ad loc.* Other words will be found in the Glossary.)

handy-dandy, iv. 6. 156–157.
Hecate, i. 1. 112.
home, iii. 3. 13.
Hopdance, iii. 6. 32.
Hysterica passio, ii. 4. 57.

immediacy, v. 3. 65.
incense, ii. 4. 309.
ingenious, iv. 6. 287.

Jug, i. 4. 245.

kibes, i. 5. 9.

Lady the brach, i. 4. 125.
lag of, i. 2. 6.
lances, v. 3. 50.
like, i. 1. 203; i. 1. 304; iv. 2. 19.
loathly, ii. 1. 51.

main, iii. 1. 6.
milk, i. 1. 86.
monsters it, i. 1. 223.
mother, ii. 4. 56.

names my very deed of love, i. 1. 73.
nether, iv. 2. 79.
notion, i. 4. 248.
nuncle, i. 4. 117.
nursery, i. 1. 126.

Obidicut, iv. 1. 62.
observants, ii. 2. 109.
office, ii. 4. 107.
old, iii. 4. 125.
on 's, i. 4. 114; i. 5. 20.
on 't, i. 4. 168.
out, i. 1. 33.
owes, i. 1. 205.
owest, i. 4. 133.

packings, iii. 1. 26.
packs, v. 3. 18.
pelican daughters, iii. 4. 77.
pight, ii. 1. 67.
Pillicock, iii. 4. 78.
poise, ii. 1. 122.

practices, i. 2. 198; ii. 1. 75, 109; v. 3. 151.
practised, iii. 2. 57.
prefer, i. 1. 277.
pretence, i. 2. 95; i. 4. 75.
proper, i. 1. 18.
property, i. 1. 116.
Pur! iii. 6. 47.
put on, i. 4. 227.

queasy, ii. 1. 19.
questrists, iii. 7. 17.

regards, i. 1. 242.
resolve, ii. 4. 25.
ripeness, v. 2. 11.
roundest, i. 4. 58.
rubb'd, ii. 2. 161.

sallets, iii. 4. 138.
sectary astronomical, i. 2. 164–165.
set, i. 4. 136.
set my rest, to, i. 1. 125.
shealed, i. 4. 219.
showest, i. 4. 131.
sliver, iv. 2. 34.
snuffs, iii. 1. 26.
some year, i. 1. 20.
soothe, iii. 4. 182.
sop o' the moonshine, ii. 2. 34–35.
spherical predominance, i. 2. 133–134.
square of sense, i. 1. 76.
squiny, iv. 6. 140.
subscribed, i. 2. 24.
subscription, iii. 2. 18.
succeed, i. 2. 157.
success, v. 3. 194.
sumpter, ii. 4. 219.
superserviceable, ii. 2. 19.

taking, ii. 4. 166.
tender, i. 4. 230.
terrible, i. 2. 32.
thought-executing, iii. 2. 4.
three-suited, ii. 2. 16–17.
thwart, i. 4. 305.

GENERAL INDEX

Abbott, *Shakespearian Grammar*, i. 1. 213; i. 2. 93; i. 4. 26, 114, 236, 255, 271; i. 5. 36; ii. 1. 77; iii. 1. 23–24; iii. 2. 13.

abstract used for concrete, iv. 7. 7.

adjective, adverbial use of the, i. 4. 360; iv. 6. 3.

adjective, substantival use of, ii. 1. 61; iii. 7. 65.

Æsop's Fables, allusion to, i. 4. 176–177.

antecedent, omission of the, ii. 1. 125.

as, omission of, i. 1. 213.

auxiliary, omission of the, ii. 1. 77; iv. 2. 2.

be in E.E., uses of, i. 5. 36.

Bedlam beggars, ii. 3. *init.*

Capell, i. 4. 18.

Chapman, i. 1. 119.

Coleridge, i. 1. 109, 110, 175; i. 5. 50; ii. 1. 69, 103; ii. 4. 267; iii. 4. *init.*

comparative and superlative, double, i. 1. 80.

constructions, confusion of, iv. 6. 33–34.

contractions, euphonic, i. 4. 114.

Craig, W. J., i. 1. 119; i. 2. 161–162; i. 4. 283.

Declaration of Popish Impostures, Harsnet's, ii. 4. 54–55; iii. 4. 54–55, 120; iii. 6. 32.

Dekker's *Bell-man of London*, ii. 3. *init.*

-ed in past participles, i. 1. 262.

ellipsis, examples of, i. 1. 213.

ethic dative, example of, i. 2. 106.

Ex nihilo nihil fit, i. 1. 92.

fish on Fridays, i. 4. 18.

Furness, iii. 2. 27–34.

gerundial infinitive, ii. 4. 112.

Guillim's *Heraldry*, ii. 1. 87.

Gunpowder Plot, i. 2. 111–127.

Hanmer, ii. 2. 168–169.

Harvey's (Gabriel), *Pierce's Supererogation*, ii. 2. 34–35.

Hazlitt, i. 1. 147, 279; iii. 4. 72; iii. 6. 65.

hendiadys, examples of, i. 2. 48, 191–192; i. 4. 364.

here, substantival use of, i. 1. 264.

Herford, i. 5. 25; iii. 4. 126.

Horace's *Odes*, iii. 6. 85.

Johnson, i. 1. 201; i. 2. 113–114; i. 4. 181–184; i. 5. 43; ii. 2. 19; ii. 2. 168–169; iv. 6. 11–24.

Jonson's, Ben, *English Grammar*, ii. 2. 69–70; *Bartholomew Fair*, iii. 4. 103; *Silent Woman*, ii. 2. 16–17.

Kellner, i. 1. 275; ii. 2. 107; iii. 2. 13; iii. 7. 65.

Lipsbury pinfold, ii. 2. 9.

liver, as the seat of courage, ii. 2. 18.

Lyly's *Euphues*, ii. 2. 168–169.